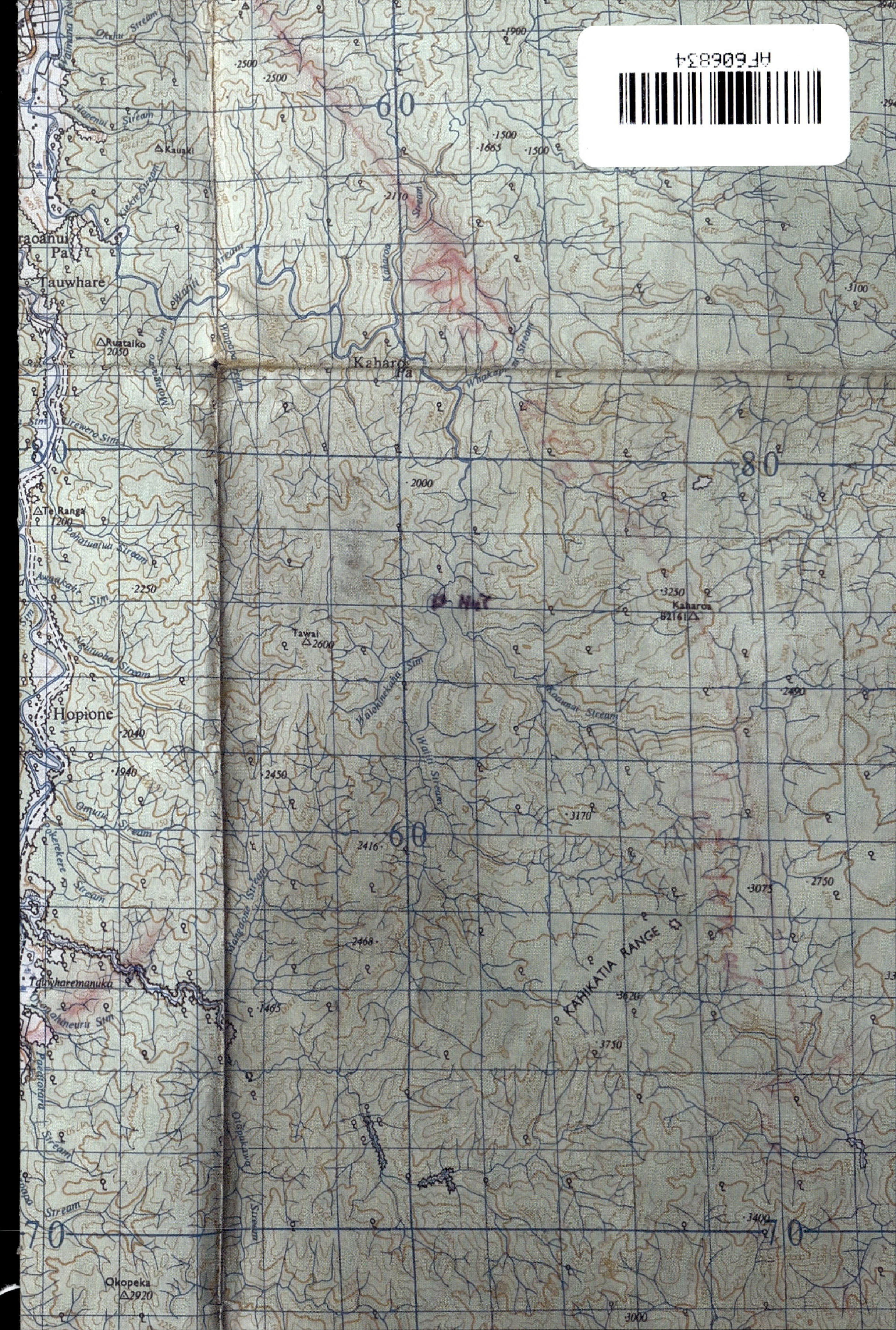

Tauwhare
Kaharo Pa
Ruataiko 2050
Kauaki
Te Ranga 1200
Hopione
Tawai 2600
Kaharoa B2161
KAHIKATIA RANGE
Tauwharemanuka
Okopeka 2920
Whakapapa Stream
Kaharoa Stream
Koaunui Stream
Waiiti Stream
Mangaone Stream
Omutu Stream
Hapenui Stream
Ngunguhu Stream
Pahautuatua Stream

SAM THE TRAP MAN

CRACKING YARNS AND TALL TALES FROM THE BUSH

SAM GIBSON

ALLEN&UNWIN
AUCKLAND • SYDNEY • MELBOURNE • LONDON

First published in 2024

Allen & Unwin
Level 2, 10 College Hill, Freemans Bay
Auckland 1011, New Zealand
+64 (9) 377 3800
auckland@allenandunwin.com
www.allenandunwin.co.nz

83 Alexander Street
Crows Nest NSW 2065, Australia
+61 (2) 8425 0100

A catalogue record for this book is available from the National Library of New Zealand.

ISBN 978 1 99100 669 1

Cover image Brennan Thomas
Design by Megan van Staden
Set in typeface Tiempos
Printed and bound in China by 1010 Printing Ltd
10 9 8 7 6 5 4 3 2 1

For all those that didn't quite fit in and found a home in the nooks and crannies of the back country. For all the dyslexic farmers, the hard case bushmen and women and the quirky characters that find the outdoors to be their greatest classroom. This one's for you.

Mostly though, I write this one for my kids, Rehua and Te Kōtuku. May you both have lifetimes of adventures defined by the various wonders of the world that capture your interest and spark your imaginations.

CONTENTS

A BOY FROM THE BUSH

When I was a kid there was this colossal set of antlers hanging above the deck at my grandfather's house. I remember playing under them and constantly worrying they would fall on me. I didn't know it at the time, but Poppa was a bushman, the type of hunter who sucked moisture out of moss when creeks ran dry, the type of man who sought to give deer a sporting chance by switching to a bow long before it became trendy, the type of fisher who knew instinctively what pool a giant trout was hiding in and exactly how to catch it. He was always one to scrimp on the unimportant things in life but invest in quality where it mattered.

To me he was just Poppa, who, along with Nanna, took me into the hills as a boy to chase ducks, pheasants and pigeons. He was the man who taught me the ways of fish, the balance and moods of the ocean.

My father, too, took me on many tramping adventures as a child in tents, canoes, rafts and huts. A man who overcame the limitations of injury to trek to Everest's base camp with my mother, my dad was the one who really got me into the bush. He used to bring me along on the Duke of Edinburgh camps he would run for his high-school students, where I'd be thrown into the bottom of white-water rafts and told to 'stay there and hold on' as we hurtled our way down treacherous stretches of rapids. Other times we would walk to huts in the bush, scouting them for an upcoming school camp. It was always Dad and me on an adventure together, with his amazing ability to tell stories about the creatures and trees around us capturing my imagination and making me fall in love with the bush.

Then there's the one who brought me into the world, my incredibly nurturing and confident mother, who gave me a unique start to a unique life. There aren't many people who can say they were born on a mattress in the attic of a stone-walled, thatched-roofed apple barn in the middle of Devonshire,

ABOVE I have always been more at home in back country huts than in a feather bed in town. © Cam Henderson, *Hunters Journal*

England. But that's my lot as the eldest son of a couple of adventure-loving New Zealanders whose overseas adventures were interrupted by the arrival of a gangly wee boy who would later grow into a pūkeko-legged, bearded bushman more at home in wool and wet than the creature comforts of town.

My two sisters and I grew up in a creaky three-bedroom Lockwood home in Gisborne that my dad built. As kids the timber knots in the wooden walls of the house looked like eyes; we used to lie on our beds turning the grains of the timber into animals and fish in our imaginations. The Hamanatua Stream wrapped around two sides of the property and the other two had a good buffer of scrub before we saw any neighbours. At the time we were pretty broke but Mum and Dad did a good job of shielding us from their financial worries. They had arrived back from their overseas adventures in 1989 with two backpacks, two bikes and an unexpected child to their name. My sisters, Briar and Greer, followed not long after. What my parents lacked in finances though they made up for in stories, determination and fun.

Mum grew a vegetable garden, made her own bread, and soaked broad beans, chickpeas and lentils in big metal bowls on the kitchen counter. She cooked for the family out of big sacks of wholefoods she kept in the pantry.

Like a scene out of a 1980s hippy homesteading movie, we had chickens and it was my job to dodge the imaginary panthers as I wound my way down the carved bushy pathway to their coop each evening to feed them and collect the eggs. We were vegetarian except when we went to Nanna and Poppa's for dinner. It was more of a 'meat costs too much' thing than an ethical thing.

There were times when we all had to pack up and go to live with my grandparents because the 'interest rates had got too high', whatever that meant. Being at Nanna and Poppa's meant all kinds of adventures as there were more adults to play with, to build us toys and to take us out to the rivers, beach or bush.

Dad worked as a kindergarten teacher, a milkman and later a high-school teacher while Mum taught vegetarian cooking classes at the local high school in the evenings. She was a qualified nurse but chose to stay home and help us grow, returning to nursing only when we were all well into primary school. Her return to work didn't seem to stop the neighbourhood kids being sent round to our place to be treated, though. Mum had a huge apothecary collection of plant-based and herbal medicines in a Tupperware container under the bathroom sink. The landline phone's handset was often wedged between her ear and shoulder, the long, coiled cord dangling above the

ABOVE Poppa Graham Vette with the great big 17-point stag that sat on the wall above where I played as a kid.

kitchen floor as she tried to balance cooking the evening meal and helping some mum with a sick kid or a young woman going into labour.

That was pretty much our childhood — building huts in the Hamanatua Stream, hanging out at the beach and each weekend loading up Dad's rusted-out old station wagon for a tiki tour to some unknown place.

The other great thing about being a kid in our family was that we had two sets of grandparents nearby. Dad's folks lived at the beach and specialised in backyard cricket, sweet jugs of Raro and a mixture of spaghetti and baked beans on toast. Poppa was mischief in a good way and Nanna didn't mind as long as it was all in good fun.

> As time went on I got to go duck- and pheasant-shooting too, loading the dogs into the boot of Poppa's V6 Holden Berlina, shotguns across the back seat and cigarette smoke billowing from the window. It's easy to see how the smell of gun oil, tobacco and wet dogs fills me with nostalgia even now.

Mum's folks, on the other hand, were a never-ending supply of indulgence when it came to taking me fishing at the wharf, building bonfires at the beach to cook sausages, and adventures to one of their two baches in Whanarua Bay on the East Cape and Onepoto in Te Urewera. What started out as catching sprats at the wharf soon merged into fully-fledged ocean-fishing adventures chasing tarakihi, tāmure and maomao. As time went on I got to go duck- and pheasant-shooting too, loading the dogs into the boot of Poppa's V6 Holden Berlina, shotguns across the back seat and cigarette smoke billowing from the window. It's easy to see how the smell of gun oil, tobacco and wet dogs fills me with nostalgia even now.

As life would have it, I would go on to be a professional bushman. Somehow I have always managed to make a living as a trapper, hunter, dog culler, kiwi wrangler, takahē catcher, whio netter and part-time yarn teller. I cut my teeth in the bush in the remote, misty valleys of Te Urewera, did a few seasons track-cutting in the Ruahine Range and later got shipped down to Fiordland for three of the most incredible years of my life.

Changes at the Department of Conservation meant I was soon heading north again to carve out a career looking after the forests, rivers and streams I was raised in. I would meet a wonderful woman who understood my hankering for our wild places and had a lust for adventure herself. We would raise our kids in the bush, the only way we knew how. As I sit here at my desk looking out over the forest steaming in the early-morning light, I am proud as punch that our little ones feel as comfortable finding their own food in the ngahere as they do eating from a lunch box.

It'd be fair to say that we live a hunting and fishing lifestyle, but to us it's not just about extracting resources from the land. With it comes the responsibility to rebuild our landscapes to a state of abundance, for when the bush thrives, we thrive as people.

I guess there was never any question that I was going to love the bush, coming as I do from a long line of hunters, fishers, trampers, healers and teachers. Maybe I'm a mixture of them all. A poor reflection of each I'm sure, but as a whole hopefully I capture some of the better parts: the storytelling from my father, the love of healing plants from my mother, and the hunting, fishing and twinkle of fun-loving mischief from my grandparents. In any case this book is a collection of yarns about some of my adventures. Tales of animals, birds, fish, plants and people — and the quest for a stag to rival my grandfather's.

1. MY START IN TE UREWERA

As I sat there munching on a kareao vine, it crossed my mind that this was a whole lot more interesting than school. Wet and hungry, I'd found myself in the heart of Te Urewera, Waimana Valley to be precise, a place where the river was still the main road, where men on horseback deterred outsiders from entering the valley (sometimes by brandishing rifles) and where wealth was measured in horses rather than cash.

I'd been sent here by people who cared about me. It wasn't that I was doing badly at school; I was twelve years old, too early to be really mischief but old enough to be distracted, and I was getting caught up in the bogan, drug-fuelled surf scene that was rife in the coastal village of Haumoana in the early 2000s. My parents and teachers were getting a little worried, so a plan was hatched. The headmaster and my dad knew I needed a change of scene if I was to get through the next few years unscathed and I wasn't going to get that in Haumoana.

My boss for the day was an old-timer called Keith. Keith wore black tracksuit pants, a black woollen T-shirt and no shoes. The machete in his hand was discarded for eating and sleeping but the rest of the time it stayed grasped loosely in his gnarled, arthritis-riddled fingers. Keith was softly spoken and the fact that he never smiled meant the first time I found out he had no teeth was when I cooked him steak for breakfast. He spent a good hour gumming it to death before it finally softened enough to swallow. Keith was tall and gangly, his eyes grey and glazed over like one of the old tuna (eels) in the creeks that found food by scent rather than vision.

Keith was a real bushman. A veteran of the Korean War, he once told me if you ever wanted to shoot down a helicopter, you could do it with one bullet straight through the rotor head. He started his day at 4 a.m. with a head torch, as that was when the bush was still and calm, the time it was most spiritually alive and Keith could speak with the tīpuna.

While working for Keith you didn't take food or water with you on the hill as there would be no lunch breaks. According to Keith, when we look after the ngahere as trappers, the ngahere looks after us. This relationship with the bush just seems to make sense in Te Urewera. When we were thirsty a stream would appear, when we were hungry there was fruit on the ground or tasty kareao shoots to tide us over. Somehow there was always meat, too: deer shot in the creeks or the time Keith managed to get a slow pig with his machete. We were playing our role in the ecosystem by trapping introduced predators and in return the bush around us was abundant and bountiful. Well, that's how Keith saw it anyway and, as I learned while stumbling along behind him as a young fella, I was inclined to agree.

Waimana Valley at the time was what the Department of Conservation called a 'mainland island'. Its focus was on breeding kōkako and learning more about this species. Kōkako are very sensitive birds which are easily predated on by rats, stoats and possums. Ever since the time Kōkako brought Māui a drink from the stream when he was parched and exhausted from slowing down the sun, kōkako have been rewarded with the tastiest fruits from the bush.

These days their reward is more of a curse than a blessing as many of our fruiting species are being quickly eaten by possums, rats and deer. Kōkako, when they aren't being eaten by predators, are slowly going hungry. But Te Urewera has long been a sparkling glimmer of hope among the forests of the North Island. As a teenager, I was regularly sent out to help with establishing rat and stoat traps around the last remaining kōkako in Te Urewera. This deal, struck between my concerned parents, my open-minded principal, my godfather Darren, who worked for DOC, and me is what got me through my teenage years.

I'd started going bush as a twelve-year-old during school holidays or on the weekend with Darren, mostly because I enjoyed it. As I grew older and the party scene started to sink its barbed hooks into me, my relationship with the bush grew into something absolutely vital to keeping me afloat.

Each morning we would wake up — or in my case, be woken up — and just in front of the hut veranda would be a kōkako doing its thing, singing from the top of its lungs. Kōkako are the tree monkeys of the Aotearoa bush. During the day they bounce around from tree to tree eating only the most lolly-like fruit. They are a slender bird, full of energy and fun. But in the morning when the billowing clouds of mist roll through the sleepy Te Urewera landscape, the kōkako settle down on their branches to create song. These fun-loving creatures have a deep, mournful side to them, a sad song full of lament, one of the most beautiful sounds one can bear witness to. Before singing, the kōkako sits, settles itself and quietly gulps mouthfuls of air. It puffs itself up like a balloon to what seems like triple its normal size. Out pounds this deep, rich, church-organ-like sound as the kōkako releases each gasp of breath from its lungs. It's incredible to witness, and I'm grateful to have heard and seen it at such a formative age.

> When we look after the ngahere as trappers, the ngahere looks after us. This relationship with the bush just seems to make sense in Te Urewera. When we were thirsty a stream would appear, when we were hungry there was fruit on the ground or tasty kareao shoots to tide us over.

In Te Urewera there were permanent deer cullers plugging away, living in the bush pretty much full time with their indicator dogs. Periodically we would drop them boxes of supplies from the helicopter which they would stash under the bunks in each hut with their name clearly plastered across them. To break into another man's box of food was one of the most severe crimes possible in the bush and something I have ashamedly done only when absolutely necessary.

There were possumers, too, who were incentivised not by skins or fur but by money; they were paid $15,000 a block to get the possum numbers under control. They would get helicoptered in to remote huts loaded up with all manner of luxuries and DOC would foot the bill. A comfortable trapper was a productive trapper. The skins and fur were a bonus to the trappers, not to be wasted, but equally not where the bulk of the money was to be made. After about a month of trapping we would fly in an auditor to check the block. They would set lines of 100 leg-hold traps in random areas. If the traps caught fewer than five possums the $15,000 would be paid; five or more and the trapper would have to stay in the bush for another month to complete the job.

Then came us, the rat and stoat crew. A ragtag mix of contractors, staff and volunteers. There was Lindsay, the boss with a smile like the Cheshire cat.

Lindsay had cut his teeth on possum skins back in the heyday, saving enough to buy himself a helicopter and a plot of land. Next he used the helicopter to make a go of the venison boom. His mate would fly and he would shoot; they had a good crack at it until they crashed their helicopter in the Whakatāne River. Thankfully they weren't badly hurt and they'd made enough cash to finance another chopper. So, they kept going. Soon Lindsay had set himself up with a hand-built two-storey log cabin with a riverstone floor, set on a hill in Ōpōtiki. A nice wee trophy fallow deer herd with which he supplied the budding trophy-hunting industry grazed in the valley below the house and a small avocado orchard promised a prosperous future. Ruru snatched pepetuna under porchlight at night and Lindsay was constantly shooing weka from his back door. There wasn't much about running operations in the bush that Lindsay didn't know and there weren't many bush yarns he couldn't tell, so that made him head man in anyone's book.

Then there was Pete. Pete strayed from the usual backcountry uniform of black woollen T-shirt, knife belt, short shorts and Buller boots. He wore DOC-issue bib overalls in a colour that wasn't sure if it was brown or green, old John Bull steel caps, and that's about it. In winter he would wear a shirt underneath but in summer he wore not much at all. But one thing was unquestionably within reach at all times: his pack of smokes sat in the front pocket of those paint-stained and faded overalls. Pete was 'Mr Quick-brew-and-we're-off', famous for measuring a day in cups of tea and smoko breaks. When Pete brewed the billy, the tea was proper teeth-rottingly sweet. Each enamel mug was loaded to the gunnels with sugar and the tea only came black; there was no place for milk in the bush. Pete was what you'd call a generalist, capable in just about all elements of bush life. He knew his way around a chainsaw, a helicopter, a rifle and the traplines. He had a soft side and handled kiwi, kōkako and whio with a gentleness that belied his nature. To top it all off, he could fix just about anything.

Then there were the workers. Dan Baigent and Hemi Barsdell were two super-fit, super-competitive young bushmen in their thirties. These were the two men I was trying to emulate, the two I watched and learned from. Darren would point out how they would race off in the morning to be the first to the heli-load of traps. They would jostle each other out of the way to make sure they carried more, worked harder and outdid the other. It was all in good fun but far out, these two led by example and it took a lot of work on my part to keep up with them. It wasn't enough just to work hard. As a young person it

TOP My mentor Darren Peters, a man who saw the potential in a gangly young 12-year-old and started taking him bush in Te Urewera. © Nick Graham

BOTTOM LEFT We would often keep our boots dry by carrying traps across the Waimana River in our bare feet in the mornings. © Darren Peters

BOTTOM RIGHT Te Urewera gave me somewhere I could just be me, somewhere away from life's distractions. © Darren Peters

was my job to choose the traplines with the steep hills, sneak the heaviest packs away from the older guys and make sure I thrashed myself harder than anyone. This is how I had to prove myself as a bushman. It was the culture we had in Te Urewera.

After a day on the hill I'd be beat, often falling asleep before dinnertime. My legs ached, my body was cut up and sore from pushing through dense scrub, but I was proud as punch to be part of this work.

Still, by the time I turned fifteen I was also dead proud of my ability to party with reckless abandon two or three nights a week, every week. The older surfers had taken me under their wing for my outrageous fashion sense, my ability to hold philosophical conversations and my willingness to fetch beers, roll joints and knit woollen Rasta beanies, a skill taught to me as a quirk of a Steiner school education.

I wasn't even a great surfer. In fact, I was pretty terrible. Dad, despite having a dicky ankle from a motorcycle accident in his teens, had a reputation for charging the heavy overhead river-mouth breaks of the Hawke's Bay. On the other hand, I was a nervous and cowardly surfer who preferred the gentle waist-high peelers of point breaks like Te Awanga and Napier Reef. I was never going to make it as a gung-ho surfer in the bogan shortboard scene of the time. But far out, I was keen to prove myself as a partier.

I was getting sucked into the downward spiral of booze, drugs, fights, girls and figuring out ways to pay for it all. I picked apples at the weekend, did a bit of work on farms and mowed lawns around the neighbourhood, but let's just say the funds gathered through honest endeavours weren't meeting my financial expectations.

Dad would take me on surf trips to Taranaki, Gisborne and even Tonga. We had some great times but in classic teenage fashion I treated him like crap. He was just too close to me; being a teacher at school and coach of the surf team as well as my dad, it just felt like he was everywhere around me. Any trouble in the classroom meant I got trouble at home, and if he told off my mates at school I got crap for it from them as well.

Teachers at their wits' end with my behaviour would just pack me up and send me to Dad's classroom, which I thought was more than a little unfair. Dad even suspended me one time when he was acting principal for going to the bottle shop at lunchtime with my fake I.D. to buy beer for a Friday-night party. But it wasn't just school; Dad was in the surf scene too. He picked the Scholastics surf team, organised all the school contests and pretty much ran the whole deal if you were a young surfer in Hawke's Bay at the time. He did an amazing job, and it was his way of giving back to the community and finding a way for us to do things together, but I was constantly searching for a way to get out from under his shadow. I desperately needed something of my own to distract me, something more meaningful than reinventing a skinny-jeaned version of *Lords of Dogtown*.

I was so disruptive at school that in order to get some sort of buy-in from me, the principal cut me a deal. He would give me a week off in the middle of each term to go bush if I agreed to keep up with my schoolwork and commit to passing all my subjects.

> As a young person it was my job to choose the traplines with the steep hills, sneak the heaviest packs away from the older guys and make sure I thrashed myself harder than anyone. This is how I had to prove myself as a bushman. It was the culture we had in Te Urewera.

That week in the middle of each school term and the two-week school holidays in the bush were slowly becoming more important to me than partying, more meaningful than surfing. I was just a teenager searching for my place in the world and the bush was somewhere I could succeed. It was the ability to work towards something more important than myself, something bigger, that drew me in. The fact that our trapping was enabling kōkako to breed successfully meant that every other part of the ecosystem flourished too — a result I could clearly see each time I returned. Kākā, kiwi, whio, titipounamu, kākāriki, pōpokotea and many more creatures were also benefiting from our work.

Because of our possum, deer and rat control, the bush seemed to see us, to recognise our effort. Haumia-tiketike ensured Tāne's manu were fat and in good condition to breed. Fruit covered the trees and many fell to the forest floor for us to eat. The deer were in low enough numbers that the kareao vines had fresh tips protruding in all directions, abundant pikopiko grew deep in the base of mouku and huruhuru whenua, and even kōwaowao clung from the trees and rocks in swathes for us to eat. When work allowed we would nip out for the odd hunt or fish; we were often unsuccessful as numbers were low but we shot enough to keep our freezers full and the crew fed.

This introduction to the bush would shape the rest of my life. I would follow in these trappers' footsteps; Lindsay, Dan and Hemi would all become my bosses at different stages of my career. Darren would always remain my mentor and Keith's introduction to our place in te taiao allowed me to step away from what could have been a completely different trajectory in life.

The bush and these people opened my eyes to how alcohol and drugs cloud the brain like the mist of the Te Urewera valleys; they stop us being able to see clearly. When we can't clearly read what's coming at us, our natural instinct is to be defensive, and a defensive disposition results in anger and violence like a dog in a trap. This lesson has stuck with me my entire life.

And that's exactly how I was acting as a teenager, defensive and angry. I reckon it had a lot to do with the fog I was creating in my brain through all the partying. But by eighteen I had convinced myself that to be a better bushman I needed to be clear-minded. I needed to be able to read what the birds, the trees and the rivers were telling me. To be a bushman I needed to be open to the spiritual side of the bush, to the little tappings and knowings we get in the quiet, damp stillness of the scrub.

By eighteen I'd decided to go straight edge. No alcohol, no drugs and no muck in my system. I even gave up coffee. I would still party with my mates, I would still surf, but as the haze of substance abuse lifted from my brain I remember just getting so much happiness and joy from the world in little weird, hippy ways, like sunrises and sunsets, and sitting out the back in the ocean on my surfboard watching how birds ride the air currents in the same way we surf the waves. My mates noticed a difference in me and supported me not to drink and I was just a way better human to be around. Instead of treating my girlfriends like crap, I started to be able to hold down relationships, be a lot more honest and in some cases even kind and generous.

I didn't care that other bushmen drank, smoked weed or later on used amphetamines to go faster on their traplines. I know some pretty incredible outdoorsmen and -women that can handle their drink and smoke while functioning well in the scrub, but for me it just doesn't work like that.

These days I might have the odd drink, mostly a rum, whiskey or beer when it's socially necessary or on the odd quiet evening if I want to still my brain. But the bush has definitely shaped my outlook. My model of a bushman is what I was taught by Keith in Te Urewera, a model of clarity and clean running, about being in balance with the bush and open enough to pick up on the world around me.

2. MY FIRST DEER

As he upended a can of pineapple into the mince that had been simmering away in the communal pot in which I'd just had my evening wash, I became dubious about the state of hygiene around our camp. Kaiapoi Mills was a different breed: short, stocky, torn clothes and a scraggle of unkempt hair gracing his slowly balding head. A bit of a bush weka, more comfortable sleeping under a tarpaulin than in a comfy bed in town.

It was the university holidays; I was in my early twenties and studying for a conservation degree in Tauranga through the Toi Ohomai Institute of Technology and, needing something to fill in my time and my pockets, I had signed up for a track-cutting job going down in the Ruahine. To say I was excited about the prospect of spending summer in the bush would be an understatement. I'd been up to my eyeballs in books all year and when I wasn't studying I was reading Crumpy's tales about the forest-service era of cutting tracks with slashers, tickling trout in creeks and shooting more than your fair share of deer after work. It all sounded like a bit of me; having grown up sweating for a crust, I wasn't scared of hard graft if it meant an adventure was on offer.

I threw my kit on top of the mattress in the back of my beat-up Mitsubishi Mirage station wagon we called the 'God Botherer' due to all the religious stickers plastered across its rear end. I had picked her up cheap from a mate's grandparents the year before, a one-old-lady-owner scenario.

I set off at a top speed of 80 kilometres per hour downhill, then struggled my way up the other side of the valleys while being overtaken by logging trucks. Finally I scraped my way up the drive of the Ongaonga Department of Conservation field base with a car bonnet so hot you could have cooked an egg on it.

I was looking for a man by the name of Kaiapoi Mills, and was surprised when I was greeted by a little Pākehā fella. The story goes that his real name was Ken Mills, but he was called Kaiapoi because he'd got so drunk one night he couldn't give his name, and the blokes looking out for him saw a 'Kaiapoi Mills' label on his singlet. (The singlet was made by Kaiapoi Woollen Mills, near Christchurch.) The name stuck.

Anyway, Kaiapoi instructed me to pour us both a milky, sugar-loaded cuppa, the type guaranteed to rot your teeth on a rainy day, and we sat down for a yarn.

He'd heard I was interested in the track-cutting job, and explained that interview processes went a little different round here.

Kaiapoi: 'You do a bit of hunting, young fella?'

Me, lying through my teeth: 'Yep, I chase the odd red in the Kaimais. Grew up worrying pigs and deer all through Te Urewera and the East Cape. Looking forward to having a crack at this Ruahine country though.' (Kaiapoi didn't need to know that although I had kicked around on other people's hunts, I was yet to shoot my first deer and, to be honest, I really had no idea what I was doing when it came to hunting. I was sure I'd learn on the job.)

Kaiapoi: 'Do you have your rifle with you?'

A question I could answer honestly: 'It's stashed under the mattress in my wagon.'

And with that we walked outside to the Botherer and I showed Kaiapoi my pride and joy: a newly acquired Lee-Enfield .303, a hundred-year-old rifle I'd spent hours working oil into and rust out of. It was a thing of beauty with a solid wooden stock cut down from its original long-tom timber into what was considered a sporterised rifle. Its iron sights were busted so I had installed a scope someone had been given free as part of a package deal with a new rifle; it was cheap, nasty and glinted bright silver in the afternoon light. What the rifle gained in full woodgrain aesthetics it lacked in accuracy. The barrel had worn out long ago and it shot like an alcoholic with the shakes. Thankfully it came with a nine-shot mag, and I had stacked away over 200 rounds of ex-military ammunition as old as the rifle itself. As they say, if there's lead in the air there's hope, and that was definitely my approach to hunting with this rifle.

Fuelled up on deer-culling literature from Barry Crump and Connor McKenzie, in my mind I was ready to hit the hills and embody everything a deer-slaying track cutter was made of. What Kaiapoi saw when he looked at me was a long-haired, long-legged young fella, totally ill-equipped for life as a hunter but keen to learn and strong enough to carry his own kit as well as ease the load on old Kaiapoi's aching knees.

I must have cut muster because Kaiapoi offered me the job on the spot. He later explained that although my rifle was an antique I obviously took pride in it and cared for it, and that showed him everything he needed to know about a man. A man who looks after a rifle looks after his tools and that was good enough grounds to hire someone as far as he was concerned.

> Although I had kicked around on other people's hunts, I was yet to shoot my first deer and, to be honest, I really had no idea what I was doing when it came to hunting. I was sure I'd learn on the job.

So off I drove in the Botherer to find a quiet spot to park up for the weekend, having been instructed to return Monday to load the helicopter for work.

I was soon to learn that the life of a track cutter was exceptionally hard graft. We were required to work a ten-hour day, no more and no less, two of us swinging from the end of our scrub bars while Kaiapoi ambled along behind us with his arms outstretched, making sure we were cutting the tracks wide enough for the comfort of the recreational tramper.

Then it was back to the hut for a feed and off to pursue whatever adventure tickled our fancy that day. For me it involved charging up and down rivers as fast as I could and calling it hunting. My gangly pūkeko legs made short work of the tight backcountry boulders and the weight of the Lee-Enfield slung over my shoulder kept me grounded. I carried just about enough ammunition to start a small revolt, the herds of the deer-culling era described in the books fresh in my imagination.

On one evening's high-paced 'stalk' I actually managed to bump into a deer. He was quite a decent-sized stag with a fresh knobble of velvet protruding from his squat, square head. If I remember correctly, it was just prior to Christmas and we'd parked up at a DOC hut called Kawhātau Base. This hut was a place of legend and was inaccessible to the public. We had the rare luxury of hot water hooked up to a diesel generator, a claw-foot bath and non-regulation inner-sprung mattresses. The place was incredible. More importantly the local deer herd hadn't been tampered with much, so my mate and I actually had a chance at spooking one.

After finishing our day's track-cutting right on the dot of 6 p.m., I'd pick up the .303 and head for the river flats. Tree lucerne covered much of the available flat area while high cliffs bordered both sides of the stream. One evening, while wading my way through the knee-deep water for about the hundredth river crossing, dead set on covering as much ground as possible before dark, a stag jumped up from the scraggle of shrubs in front of me.

Oddly he just stood and looked at me. Maybe he hadn't seen people before or maybe he knew his escape routes up the cliff were limited. This was my chance, my opportunity to become a hunter. The pressure hit home like a lightning bolt and my arms turned to jelly. The end of my rifle, raised to my shoulder, started doing circles. At 30 metres I pointed at the stag's shoulder and squeezed the trigger.

BANG!

The stag did not drop. He just kind of looked at me then ambled off down the river flats.

Baffled that I had missed at such a close range, I shouldered the rifle again. BANG!

The stag kind of stumbled but managed to keep his footing. Looking pretty crook now, he wobbled into the river where I put five more bullets into him before he finally fell.

Embarrassed and a little worried that this hunting caper was a whole lot more difficult than I'd expected, I scanned the scrub around me for potential witnesses to my poor shooting. I hoped my mate at the hut hadn't heard the barrage of shots, seeing as I only had one deer to show for it. My mind and my gut were both tied up in knots. On the one hand I was proud that I had shot my first deer. On the other hand, this wasn't at all what I had expected from deer hunting. I'd put seven bullets in the stag and he'd refused to go down. Granted the shots were freehand without a shooting rest, but at such a close range could I really have been that poor a shot?

Having grown up as a trapper, I by no means wanted to inflict unnecessary suffering on my quarry. In fact, I was pretty devastated. It had been drummed into me that my role as a hunter was to uphold the mana of the lives I took. I hunted to feed my family and trapped to protect our vulnerable native species. Each life I took needed to have a purpose. But today the balance was out of kilter. This deer had had a pretty rough end, barraged to death by .303 in the river.

As my steaming rifle barrel cooled, I sat with the stag on the river's

TOP Fat velvet stags often looked down at us from grass-clad slips.

MIDDLE The pools of the Ruahine was where I washed after a hard day's track cutting and soothed aching muscles.

BOTTOM My first deer. I had no idea what I was doing but as with many self-taught hunters I just figured it out.

edge, questioning my future as a hunter. Maybe I wasn't cut out to be the bushman I had imagined?

To make matters worse, it suddenly dawned on me that I'd never gutted or carried a deer in my life and I didn't know how to do either. I'd been so focused on shooting a deer that I hadn't even thought about what came next. As a kid I'd been paid ten cents a bird to gut and pluck the ducks my grandfather shot when we went hunting, but somehow I figured this might be a little different. As the cool air of evening told me dark was just around the corner, I set to work figuring it out with my blunt knife in hand.

Before too long I'd sort of dressed out the stag. I'd lost the eye fillets to misguided strokes while gutting (to be honest I had no idea what an eye fillet was at the time anyway). Then I rolled the stag over to a bank so I could get underneath to backpack him, the way I had read about in the books. With a heave I ended up overbalancing and fell face first, nearly drowning in the river with a deer on my back holding me under. A panicked twist popped my shoulders free from the carcass and we both floated a little way downstream before I came up for air.

Looking round to see if anyone had witnessed my stupidity, I clambered out of the creek sodden and bedraggled, dragging said stag behind me. Bugger this, I thought. Not only am I a crap shot with a rifle but I can't even carry out my own deer. What an epic failure of a bushman I'm turning out to be.

So, counting my losses and the minutes until dark, I hacked out the back steaks and severed the spine above the back legs — poo tube still intact — and carried the meat back to camp. The carcass I left for Papatūānuku.

I arrived well after dark to my mate's beaming smile — he was stoked for me. He still hadn't shot a deer that summer and as a trainee ranger with a brand-new synthetic stock .270 he'd considered himself to have a better chance than me. Oddly, rampaging up river systems had paid off for me that day. I had meat hanging in the shed and a hot bath to wash off the blood; not a bad way to secure my place as the more successful hunter of us two.

A couple of weeks later, having heard about my hunting escapades and playing it off to his mates as shooting a spiker (a yearling stag) rather than a stag with potential, Kaiapoi took me to the local hunting store to buy a second-hand Ruger .243 and a brand-new Leupold 3-9x40 scope, a purchase which came to the princely sum of just over a thousand dollars. The Ruger was a proper trappers' gun. It was short, loud, light for a wood and blued (to stop the rust). Just what I needed really, but it cost me an entire fortnight's wages.

We also asked the gunsmith to have a look at my .303. He reckoned the barrel was well past its use-by date and the fact that I was shooting *Full Metal Jacket* military ammo meant that at close range the bullets didn't have a chance to expand on impact. They would have shot straight through my stag with an exit wound the same size as the entry point, which explained why the deer didn't go down first shot. Learning this did a lot to help me regain my confidence.

With a new rifle and a couple of boxes of modern ammunition I was all set to take on the Ruahine reds.

Life as a track cutter was excellent. Mondays were spent sharpening blades, packing tools and doing food shops for Tuesday's helicopter trip. Each Tuesday we'd arrive bright and early to whichever road end we were flying from for the compulsory banter session with our pilot Jimmy Blue Eyes and Blue, his ground crew.

I didn't know it then, but Jimmy Blue Eyes was one of the best helicopter pilots I would ever have the pleasure of flying with. He was the kind of guy that if he saw you walking up a braided river on a scorching summer's day, he'd more than likely drop down and offer you a ride. He was about the only pilot I knew who dropped his helicopter down in the middle of the road outside the local store to run in to get a pie, a drink and the compulsory smokes for Blue.

Blue was about as hard case a ground crew as you can ever imagine. He smoked like a train — in fact I don't think I ever saw him without a fag glued to his lips. He spoke with one, laughed with one, hell I bet he even kissed his missus with a lit ciggy in his mouth. But worse than that, he smoked while he fuelled up the chopper, he smoked leaning against the AV gas tank, he smoked when the chopper came in to land and he smoked as he filled up your jerry cans. Crikey I have no idea how that fella didn't blow us all up with his blatant disregard for flammable substances, but it definitely kept me as far away as possible from the chopper while it was fuelling.

On Tuesdays Jimmy would sling-load our gear in to the bush. He'd drop it in a big pile at the hut clearing then whizz back out to collect us. He'd always make sure to take the scenic route, showing us all the likely slips where we could expect to see a deer and telling us the best access points to different parts of the river. There's not much old Jimmy Blue Eyes didn't know about the Ruahine and he sure didn't mind sharing it with us greenhorns.

By lunchtime on helicopter day we had camp sorted. Chilly bins stashed in the all-day shade on one side of the hut clearing, fuel on the other. Mountain radio set up for comms or the portable repeater a certain unnamed foreman had poached from a forgotten corner of a DOC shed many years earlier. The gas stove was placed on the table, and the communal pot which we washed and ate from was turned upside down over the elements. Bunks were designated not chosen: Kaiapoi on a bottom bunk because of his bad knees, greenhorns on top and a bunk left over to sit on.

> As my steaming rifle barrel cooled, I sat with the stag on the river's edge, questioning my future as a hunter. Maybe I wasn't cut out to be the bushman I had imagined?

The remainder of Tuesday was spent cutting track. Kaiapoi was up front with the chainsaw cutting any branch thicker than a thumb, us on the scrub bars behind kicking up rocks and dust as we went. The system worked well. Kaiapoi cut a really wide track, my mate walked behind him clearing the cut branches and pretending to do a little scrub-bar work, then I'd cut the bulk of the undergrowth as I threw my scrub cutter from side to side.

Every two hours we stopped for water and to sharpen our blades. We climbed slowly through all the mountain tracks of the Ruahine in this way. After stashing our gear in the bush at night, us greenhorns would run back to the hut to eagerly pick up our rifles and fishing rods for an evening adventure while Kaiapoi hobbled his way down with his worn-out knees.

I would quietly slip off to a frigid river to wash the day's dust away; after realising the wash pot was the same as the cooking pot I'd decided the river was a better option. I often spent my evening swims with the whio that inhabited these mountain streams. They got pretty friendly once they got to know you.

After my wash I headed upstream to search for slips. The land has a way of breathing out in the evenings. Something about the land cooling and the ocean being warm. This makes evenings the perfect time to hunt upstream as the wind is favourable.

One afternoon Kaiapoi sent me up a particular side creek to a slip where he knew deer would often feed out in the open. He was always real generous like that. He would share his honey holes with you when most older guys just left you to figure it out by yourself. Maybe it was because of his knees, maybe it was because he liked to see us young fellas having adventures. Either way he always did his best to point us in the right direction for a deer or a fish.

So, I was climbing up this steep, scree-covered side creek, pushing through leatherwood and tussock when the scrub opened out into a beautiful plateau of grass. There were several gravel shoots feeding into this plateau, each dappled with lush green grass and shingle slopes. Getting around without making any noise was difficult in the tight scrub as the scree had a way of shifting noisily underfoot.

I managed to spook a hind and yearling feeding high up in the right-hand shoot as I climbed and quickly sought the shelter of the valley's steep sides and solid rockfaces. I kept climbing until once again the shoots opened into a second grass-covered plateau where a stunning eight-point velvet stag was feeding.

> I would quietly slip off to a frigid river to wash the day's dust away; after realising the wash pot was the same as the cooking pot I'd decided the river was a better option.

At 200 metres I just sat and watched for a bit as he fed. Periodically the stag would lift his head with its perfectly formed velvet and look my way. This was a stunning animal and one I would be proud to take, but for the life of me I couldn't find a decent gun rest — and having learned from my first shooting experience, I was now only taking shots I could make rather than freehanding and hoping for the best. As I fluffed around, another two stags emerged from the bush to join their mate feeding on the slip. There were no trees to give me something steady to brace against, no big boulders to lean on, and I hadn't brought a pack with me.

Should I stay put and take a risky shot or move forward in search of a rest and risk spooking the deer on the noisy ground?

I opted to move closer, and to do that I needed to climb higher up the gully. Problem was the terrain became even steeper and more unstable. I had to tuck my way inside a narrow slit of rock to gain access to the next plateau so with my rifle on my back I scaled my way up the rockface. Emerging back into sight and sneaking onto the clearing I rounded a corner to find . . . no stags!

I was pissed off. I'd been as quiet as I could, but somehow they'd disappeared. That evening in the hut Kaiapoi revealed he'd been watching the drama unfold through his binoculars as he sat on a sunny log on the valley floor. He reckoned as I disappeared into the rocky crevice a fourth stag had emerged from the leatherwood and chased the others off into the scrub. Turns out he was the biggest of the lot, a proper trophy. I guess that day just wasn't my day.

And that's how we spent our summer. Ten days at a time in the bush, cutting tracks and hunting, then four days off visiting my then-girlfriend, Sacha, in town. We would knock off on a Wednesday evening and be back at work first thing Monday. Each Wednesday I would usually head straight to town, catch up with Sacha, who was living at her mum's place in Flaxmere, have a spa, eat some fresh vegetables and fruit and sleep in a comfortable bed. I'd hang out with Sacha in the evenings and while she was working at a café in town during the day I would head to my parents' place to do my washing and take it easy. Come Monday it was time to head back to Ongaonga and get ready for the helicopter once more.

3. **HOW TO DIG A DUNNY**

Have you ever dug a long drop? I'll have you know there's an art to digging an adequate poo hole. When a tramper angrily rung up or wrote in to DOC about a certain splashback experience not too far from their favourite hut in the Ruahine Range it was our job to fix it. So in we'd fly. Metal bar, spades, Waratahs, a reel of number 8 wire and, most importantly, a pot with a strong handle.

Now I've seen a lot of backcountry long drops in my time: some that cave in with sand, some that fill up with water so everything floats to the surface, and some that get so much use anyone standing downwind wonders who's been cooking spicy beans. I've met bad bastards who fill long drops with cans and bottles; I've had unexpected possums shoot up between my legs when popping a squat; I've even shot a deer from the dunny. But before I had to dig the all-important hole myself, I didn't pay much attention to the artform of long-drop creation.

The first thing we assess when digging a good hole is the soil type. Any form of gravel, clay or compact soil is usually pretty straightforward. You have to watch out for solid rock these days as dynamite comes with too big a health and safety risk, but the worst soil you can dig in is sand or soft, dry dirt. It just falls in.

Location of the new hole is also key. You want somewhere shady because a hot stink-house is never a pleasant experience. Much like a greenhouse in the sun, the moisture in the hole will heat and rise up, coating the entire interior of your crap capsule in warm, perspiring toilet water. The walls, the seat and the roof will drip and most discouragingly the bog roll will be warm and damp. A long drop located where the sun can cook it is not advisable. Instead, we look for a cool, shady spot surrounded by trees, the place you'd naturally stash your chilly bin or a meat safe on a multi-day trip.

The first step is to remove the outhouse building from the existing hole.

This can be leant on its side or against some bushes and manoeuvred into place above the new hole later. Next, cover the old hole with branches and ponga fronds. As there's usually a pretty well-worn track to the long drop, you want to make the pile really big so folks won't try to step on it or think it's firewood. It's a known fact that a layer of soil over the hole's contents is only so useful and many a lowly DOC ranger has miscalculated the strength of a hole covering and sunk a boot right through. It always surprises me how long a leather boot will hang on to the stank of a long drop, and no amount of river walking seems to help.

Then, we dig. Digging a long drop is a two-person job. A team of mates can smash out a good long drop even in rocky terrain in just a couple of hours. First of all, it's a case of marking out the square hole and setting to work digging as deep as we can with a spade and a metal bar to soften the dirt. At some point the narrowness of the hole makes it too difficult to flick dirt out with a spade and the pot can be used to gather up the loosened dirt to be passed up to the mate taking a rest at the top of the hole. A good hole needs to be at least head height —in my case being six foot four inches I like to dig a seven-foot hole. No one wants to be called back in a couple of months because the tourists have really set to in the pooping department and the hole has filled up.

No one wants to be called back in a couple of months because the tourists have really set to in the pooping department and the hole has filled up.

Once the outhouse has been placed over the hole, it's time to anchor it to the ground. You'd be surprised how many dunnies have been toppled by a gust of wind (from outside rather than in). Two strong metal Waratahs are hammered into the ground on either side of the building and a length of wire is run from one Waratah, across the roof and tightened against the Waratah on the other side. The last thing we'd want is for someone to end up arse over tit in a gust of wind while attending to a pressing matter.

The best long drop I ever dug was with a track-cutting mate called Clayton. He and I blasted country music on a small portable speaker and blunted our spades on rocks until the skin slipped from our hands and our wrists and elbows ached then went numb from hitting rock at full force. We raced each other foot by foot, each dragging the other up and out of the hole every five minutes for a break. After about an hour we were splayed out in the shallow river absolutely wrecked, with dirt in our eyes, our hair stuck to our faces with sweat, and grime clogging up the bloody pads of our hands where old calluses had been ripped from the flesh to make way for new scars. I don't know why but at that point in our lives we considered ourselves too tough for leather gloves and too proud for health and safety. It was nothing a soak in the river and a few weeks of hardening the skin on our hands through arduous work wouldn't fix.

It wasn't all hard men digging dunnies though. We broke a lot of kit that year on the hill too. I was teamed up with a proper cuddler of a DOC worker for the season; let's just call him Carl. Now, we might have all worked for the department, but Carl was a real DOC disciple. Coming up through the trainee-ranger course in Nelson had shaped his brain into a square, in order to fit the book and the rules. When Kaiapoi would fart or burp or crack a crude joke, instead of a good-humoured chuckle Carl would meet these backcountry antics with a disapproving glare.

When I was trying to coax trout out of a pool with a worm and hook, Carl would be back at camp cleaning the hut roof or some other unnecessary task. When I was off in the evening searching for deer, Carl would be eyeballs deep in *Forest & Bird* or *Wilderness* magazines, brushing up on as much bird-cuddling literature as possible. It would be fair to say that we were cut from very different cloths — he was a high-tech polar fleece and I was a scratchy, hair-covered Swanndri.

While I preferred stumbling my way to a pragmatic solution, Carl liked to pull out an ill-fitting S.O.P. (Standard Operating Procedure). There was an S.O.P. for everything in the department. Food shopping, building a hut bench, even brushing your teeth.

I definitely didn't know more than Carl, but I did have a bit of a chip on my shoulder that he had been placed further up the food chain than me just because he'd done a DOC course. As far as I was concerned, he didn't amount to much as a bushman and left a lot to be desired when it came to banter and seeking mischief. Carl was a track cutter because he had been overlooked for summer placements cuddling birds someplace else and the Ruahine was conveniently close to his girlfriend. I was a track cutter because I wanted to shoot deer, catch fish, see a bit of the Ruahine and hang out with hilarious old foremen like Kaiapoi Mills.

4. CUDDLING BIRDS

Us trappers, we cheekily looked down on what we called 'the cuddlers' in our DOC team. While we were out there killing critters and saving species they were 'cuddling' them: poking, prodding and monitoring. Not that there's anything wrong with that, it just made for good banter between the teams.

Once upon a time DOC staff did a bit of everything. They were proper rangers, generalists who knew how to cut tracks, build huts, cull deer, trap critters and change a kiwi's transmitter. It was all in a day's work. I reckon it's better to have a team that can turn their hands to anything than a team of specialists. That way, when something comes up in the bush, chances are someone in your team can deal with it then and there and get the job done.

I reckon it's better to have a team that can turn their hands to anything than a team of specialists. That way, when something comes up in the bush, chances are someone in your team can deal with it then and there and get the job done.

That's how things were when I first started kicking around in the scrub as a twelve-year-old. When I came online as a fully-fledged salaried DOC ranger ten years later in the South Island, things had changed a wee bit. DOC had restructured us into three teams: Visitor Assets (the crew that looked after huts and tracks); Threats (trappers and hunters aka the cold hard killers); and Biodiversity Assets, who we affectionately called 'cuddlers' due to their desire for photo opportunities with threatened native species after us killers had done all the work to protect them. I can admit now that the cuddlers actually did important work, but as far as we were concerned at the

ABOVE I had no idea how time spent on days off catching takahē and cuddling whio was going to shape my career. It just seemed like a fairly normal thing to do at the time. At no point did I realise my day-off adventures would be considered unusual to most people living in Aotearoa. © Nicole Haerewa

time, they were taking all the credit and glory from the folks on the ground who made sure the critters didn't die in the first place.

My old boss from Te Urewera, Lindsay Wilson the Cheshire cat, had also headed south and he knew me well — I wasn't one to turn down an adventure, even with the cuddlers. He had worked his way up the ladder and was now head of the biodiversity team in Fiordland. While other lowly killers took weekends off to spend with their families or rot in the pub, Lindsay would line me up with amazing opportunities to accompany the cuddlers on some high-quality excursions.

Some days I'd be sent flying into the Murchison Mountains with telemetry gear hanging out the side of the helicopter, trying to locate takahē from the beep beep of a transmitter in a headset. Each pair of takahē had their own territory among the steep, craggy tops of Fiordland's most rugged mountain range. We would locate the birds using a repeater attached to their legs, determine whether they were alive or not, then fly down for closer investigation.

Although they look like a lazy, fat roast on legs, takahē can actually run really quickly.

As a rule of thumb, the helicopter pilot would drop us uphill from the takahē. Although they look like a lazy, fat roast on legs, takahē can actually run really quickly. From the top of the hill it was my job, along with the top takahē cuddler, to run down the mountainside making a whole lot of noise, flushing the takahē out before us so we could grab them. Although the birds were big, typically we had the advantage. With our gangly Road Runner legs we had our speed up well before the takahē saw us leaping over tussock, avoiding ankle-shattering rocks, keeping our eyes peeled for the ideal grab.

The grab we were looking for was an outstretched hand clasping both thick, red, scaly legs, avoiding at all costs a grab of the football-shaped body. As with many of our flightless birds here in Aotearoa, the takahē's body is decidedly weak. Being flightless, these birds have no need for a solid chest frame to support flight muscles. Instead, they've evolved to have a light frame, agility and a lack of structural integrity.

Once successfully tackled we would gently cradle the takahē in order to assess its condition and how it was placed to breed for the next season. This way the cuddlers could keep an eye on which birds were productive and which birds were barren. Poor breeders are pretty commonplace in modern takahē society.

Sadly, sometimes the beep of the telemetry gear would reveal a fatality. Takahē have a weird habit of getting caught in landslides or avalanches as well as drowning themselves in lakes. Us trappers do a pretty good job of keeping on top of the stoat numbers in the Murchies so thankfully that's not a huge issue as long as we keep trapping. Unlike most birds, the adult pair keep their teenage chicks around to help raise the next clutch. To me that's a really amazing adaptation.

On other cuddling trips I would be sent out with the whio catchers, led by a great fella by the name of Max Smart (after the 1960s television show *Get Smart*). This was great fun. We would wander down remote streams with a whio dog who would point out whio in the river. We would sometimes do a census to see which birds were where, reading their bands and checking that the pairs of whio had stayed in monogamous relationships since we had last checked in on them.

If something wasn't right we would set up a net across the stream and gently herd the ducks into it. This way we could catch and handle them, checking their bands and condition before letting them go once more. I loved catching whio; what I'd thought of as a kind of easy-going, jovial creature was actually a vicious little bird with a lot of scrap in it. Whio are notorious for fighting other species of duck and do not tolerate intruders in their territories, be they whio or otherwise. Usually if we had to catch a duck we would leave with scratches on our hands rather than the other way round. At the time I had no idea how much of my life would end up spent dedicated to protecting these comical little warriors of the white water. But we'll get to that later.

5. CANADIAN CANOES AND EASY DEER

An often-forgotten hut, Back Valley Biv is nestled in a valley more suited to day-hunting than long overnight stays; a productive land of swamp, brown-tannined rivers and open beech forest. For a couple of years this was my place of solitude. A respite from people, politics and work. The four corrugated-iron walls, the small pot-belly stove and the two single bunks became my sense of home during my years working in Fiordland.

On my days off, in the early morning while it was still dark, I'd strap my yellow plastic Canadian canoe to the roof of my trusty Toyota Corolla station wagon, drive for a few minutes while the village slept, then slip the canoe into the steaming, freezing waters of the Lower Waiau River and stroke my way across Lake Manapōuri, the lights of the village twinkling behind me.

A quick stop at the electricity company scientist's hīnaki to 'borrow' their catch of tuna for the day and I'd be on my way, eels sliding around in the bottom of the plastic boat and destined for the smoker. While I was down there, around 2015, the electricity company was running some sort of programme testing whether tuna could get past the dam or not. It was probably important science, but I was sure they wouldn't miss a couple of fat eels from their survey results. Night-time sure had its advantages. No boats, no tourists, no sandflies and no prying eyes. Just the still lapping of the lake on the shore and the subtle, rhythmical dip of my paddle as it broke the water's surface.

Stowed in the front of my canoe was a pack full of creature comforts: fresh fruit, vegetables, a magazine and a book. All things in short supply on our long ten-day work trips. But at Back Valley Biv I lived a life of luxury. Strapped to the side of the canoe was my trusty Ruger .243 — a short bush rifle, deafeningly loud but accurate and deadly enough with its 3-9x40 Leupold scope mounted on top.

The rifle was one of the few possessions I had brought with me to

ABOVE Thoro wac something nostalgic about the smooth way a Canadian canoe navigated the waters of Fiordland. After helicopters and jet boats, moving slowly felt good on my days off.

Fiordland, piled into the back of my station wagon, along with a pack of clothes, a banana box of books and some bedding all piled on top of a torn, old foam mattress. I hadn't really known what to expect. I just knew that Darren, my godfather and mentor in the bush, had given me the hard word that I would only get so far with DOC running round the comfortable forests of Te Urewera, and that Fiordland was the land of opportunity.

It had been a big call leaving a job I loved, a girlfriend I cared about and the comforts of things I knew to drive 22 hours south to a place I had been to only once before, as a bush instructor on a university course the previous summer. But there I was, a young coasty in Fiordland with no shortage of adventures at my fingertips.

The first day in the office had been interesting. Lindsay was busy telling me he'd sorted me with a job and a flat when just at that moment a pretty English girl with blonde ringlets stepped into the hallway. 'And a good lead on a girlfriend,' he added with a twinkle in his eye and that Cheshire cat smile. But that's a story for another time.

Back to Back Valley Biv. After skimming across the lake in the still morning quiet I would drag my canoe up into the scrub at the edge of the lake, unload my pack and rifle, hang the eels from a tree then flip the hard yellow shell over, the bright hull obvious to anyone passing by. Thankfully this wasn't the East Coast and things were less inclined to go walkabout or I would have lost my canoe many times over and been stranded there on the other side of the lake.

I would turn on my head torch, punch my way up the bank onto the track and then mosey along to Back Valley Biv. Usually it wouldn't be long until a deer stepped into my path and usually the .243 would do its job. I'd have the animal hanging in a tree before sun-up. The winter cold of Fiordland would keep the meat fresh and I'd stuff the cavity of the carcass with fern fronds to deter the flies over the next few days.

The beauty of Back Valley Biv is the very low foot traffic. Most people day-hunted the area from a boat and few wanted to spend a night in such a poky, closet-like hut. But for me it was paradise. I would sit outside on the hut's one lonely chair reading my book in the sun, boil a billy for a wash at midday, drip dry in complete privacy, make a meal that included salad and fresh vegetables, and not have to walk anywhere. After a week climbing mountains stinking like stoat bait, this was absolute luxury.

In the mornings I would wake early as my body clock was set to

TOP After a quick morning shoot with the Ruger .243 I would stash the animal in the icy shade of a tree. In winter it would stay cold all day. Sometimes I would find it half frozen by the time I returned for it in the evening.

BOTTOM One of the many beautiful waterfalls I stumbled across. © Fez, courtesy of Game Gear

sparrows' fart. I'd nip out in nothing but my Swanndri, bare feet crunching on the frosty ground, and at first light I'd do a circuit of the local clearings. More often than not I'd have an animal swinging from the lean-to that was the hut's woodshed by breakfast, sweep my feet clean of dirt and leaves then climb back in my sleeping bag for a snooze. We were paid pretty lousily at the time so venison was both table fare and currency. We traded back steaks for riches right across Southland and Otago. From memory that's how I acquired my Canadian canoe.

One time I was carrying a deer out from the hut to my canoe, rifle slung over my neck, when a beauty of a young stag ambled across the track in front of me. Something got hooked up with my rifle and try as I might I couldn't throw the deer I was carrying from my shoulders to take a shot. Despite the futility of my situation I tried raising my rifle with the deer still attached. I couldn't get the butt to rest properly against my shoulder and the scope was bouncing around. The stag just kept walking stiffly across the track, totally oblivious to my presence, and carried on his way. The ngahere has a way of providing what we need and that day I was taught not to be too greedy.

I reckon I caught up with that same stag on another trip into Back Valley during the roar the following year. I was day-hunting from the canoe as I had a short window between work trips. I had stalked my way towards one of my favourite grassy swamps just a short distance from where I'd seen the stag the year earlier. There was stag sign everywhere and as I crept along the scrubby swamp edge I heard thrashing in the scrub ahead.

Knowing better than to roar at an already located stag, I crept in. He was giving some raupō a pretty hard time and a few coprosma bushes were also copping it. This was a thoroughly pissed-off stag and, as is often the way with these fellas when they're preoccupied, he didn't seem to give two hoots about my presence. I just snuck in and sat downwind of him, hiding behind a tree with my rifle on my knees waiting to get a better look.

After what seemed an eternity he raised his head in a way I had been waiting for a stag to do my entire hunting career. He lifted his head and strung about his antlers was a great tangle of raupō leaves, moss and twigs. A very picturesque image — I just wish I'd had my camera with me to capture it. He was still just a youngster, boasting a nice rack of eight-point antlers. Not enough to get excited about in Fiordland, so he went back to thrashing in the bushes while I gave him a smile and carried on to find a tasty hind or yearling.

ABOVE We would often stumble across deer in the early hours of the morning in the Iris Burn Valley. There was no shortage of grassy slips and clearings. © Strike Photography

6. ROCKY POINT HUT: SWAMPS AND BLACK MOULD

During my second winter in Fiordland the good folks in the DOC office decided we needed to install a bait-station network up the sheer vertical sides of the Iris Burn valley. My mate Paddy had found bats in there the summer before with a crew of university students and my boss Lindsay was dead set on not losing them to rat or possum predation. He tasked me and another mate Phil with the job of protecting them.

Problem was it was winter and winter in the Iris Burn valley is unrelenting. There's a saying in Fiordland, 'When you can see the hills, it's about to rain and when you can't, it's raining'. Well that was definitely true of the Iris Burn except you could never see the hills and when it wasn't raining it was snowing.

They had us camped up in a working man's hut called Rocky Point. Instead of building it on high dry rocks overlooking the river, as the name suggested, they had generously built it on top of a swamp. The walls were thick with black mould and water seeped up through the floorboards each time you took a step. Condensation dripped from the ceiling and if you left your sleeping bag on the mattress in the morning you could guarantee it would be a soggy mess by the time you returned. There was an old coal range in the kitchen without any coal and the wood in the bush as you could imagine was perpetually wet.

It was what we'd come to expect from the Department of Conservation in terms of lodging. An icy-cold hut in the darkest, dampest part of the valley they could find. They didn't want to cut down any trees and flat land was essential for a hut so why not build it in the only available flat clearing — a bloody bog. Arguably the worst part of our accommodations was the long drop. A hole dug in a swamp will quickly fill with water. This resulted in the need to awkwardly suspend yourself about a foot from the toilet seat on your hands to avoid getting a spurt of water up your rectum from the splashback.

Rocky Point Hut had its advantages though. If you sat on the roof it did cop about an hour of sunshine at midday. I innovatively built us a washing line with a length of wire and two kānuka poles nailed to the side of the hut to dry out our sleeping bags and socks on the odd sunny day. But the department wasn't putting up with this level of comfort. On the next hut inspection they tore it down, claiming it was an eyesore and a potential helicopter hazard. They also removed Miss January from our wall, claiming she was unprofessional. (I figured anyone looking as good as she did had probably been paid for the photoshoot so in my books that made her a professional, but arguing with the higher-ups about semantics was never a winning cause.) They were however content to leave behind the stack of mildewed vintage seventies' peep mags as compensation. I'm thankful to say they remained unread in their dark damp corner of the hut for the duration of our stay at Rocky Point.

Arguably the worst part of our accommodations was the long drop. A hole dug in a swamp will quickly fill with water. This resulted in the need to awkwardly suspend yourself about a foot from the toilet seat on your hands to avoid getting a spurt of water up your rectum from the splashback.

What I'm trying to say is that Phil and I felt a little taken for granted carting 30-kilogram sacks of poison up near-vertical bluff faces that winter. We both cared about protecting the bats in the Iris Burn but we couldn't help but wonder if this was an operation drawn up on a computer by some office dweller then handed out to us to figure out its failings on the ground. The top of the bait lines were at the top of steep bluffs and the way they had drawn the map had us scaling near-vertical slippery waterfalls to achieve the correct density of stations. A little tweaking was needed on our part if we were keen to survive the winter.

It was okay for me. My six-foot-four (1.93-metre) frame was made for carting heavy loads up steep hills but as for my good mate Phil . . .

Oh hang on, have I not introduced Phil yet? My apologies, that's a bit bloody rude of me.

Well, Phil's a proper good bugger. A wiry chap: quiet, considered and calm until you throw a couple of vodka Red Bulls into him on Fiordland's only dancefloor, The Moose. Then the otherwise reserved chap brings out the cowboy dance moves with a vengeance. With a Hilux, a chainsaw and a pile of old Swanndris you could forgive yourself for thinking he was a young Māori chap straight from the pages of a Barry Crump novel.

However Phil was actually the progeny of a fiery, short-wheel-based Scot and a beautiful Filipino woman, each with a love of the outdoors and tramping. Each Christmas young Phil took to the hills with his parents where they spent the festive season in any number of backcountry huts. I had heard of this legendary family a few years earlier, but it took coming to Fiordland to finally catch up with Phil.

He was the kind of guy that if you asked if he wanted to go for a hunt he would just chuckle quietly at you and say, 'Can't give away my spots.' On his days off Phil had an uncanny ability to sleep. He would just go to bed on the Friday night and sleep until Sunday, rising a few times to find a feed and head straight back to bed. Sometimes he would take a week's leave just to sleep and think.

He was a bit of an enigma to me at first but the more time I spent with him, the better we got along. It's hard not to when you're stuck in a hut in the bush together for months on end, but after a while Phil became my closest mate.

We balanced each other out. While I talked a big game and was good at yarning with the bosses, Phil was a details man who could deliver on the practicalities of organising a trip without a hitch. When it came to doing helicopter sling-loads I'd get the funding signed off from the bosses, order the traps and do the paperwork, and Phil would make sure the helicopter side of the operation was managed according to the S.O.P.

But back to Rocky Point Hut. In the mornings we would fry up a huge pan of leftover spuds from the previous evening's meal, as well as sausages, bacon and at least four eggs each. They reckon the hungry must be fed so we packed ourselves full of as much sustenance as possible at the start of the day to avoid the need to break for lunch. Stopping for lunch is an absolute no-no in Fiordland. In summer the sandflies hammer you as soon as you pause for more than 30 seconds and in winter it's so cold that if you stop it's hard to get your body moving again. We lived on muesli bars and drinks from the stream between our morning and evening meals. The sludge of wet, cinnamon-flavoured green poison coating our ungloved hands was an added disincentive to eat.

That winter we were joined by two contractors at Rocky Point — a

TOP I have always loved the way that mist clings to the valley floors in the morning.

BOTTOM Heavy packs and steep hills were an everyday occurrence as a trapper in Fiordland's Murchison Mountains.

dreadlocked fella called Hemi from the East Coast like myself and a tiny wee Pākehā fella called Jim. The reason we had company was simple: Phil and I lacked the necessary qualifications to use cyanide and while we waited for the piece of paper to arrive in the mail from a course we had attended in Invercargill, we had to put up with these frontcountry scoundrels in our hut.

Hemi didn't seem like too bad a chap until he ate the whole trip's food in the first couple of days. While Phil and I were lugging 30-kilogram sacks up steep cliff faces Hemi was tasked with ambling along behind us putting a couple of tiny wee cyanide capsules into the front of each bait station, so the possums didn't eat all the rat poison. It seemed like a simple enough job and Phil and I were doing the heavy lifting. But Hemi somehow managed to build up a hunger that rivalled England's historical need for colonies. Each night he would polish off a mountain of chops, spuds, mince and vegetables then reach for the pot of spuds we were saving for breakfast. Within just a few days we were reduced to two-minute noodles and whatever we could hunt, fish and forage from the bush around us. This could not continue.

We tried flying in sacks of rice to curb Hemi's hunger but he ate his way through those as well. When Hemi made a move for the last packet of biscuits one evening and Phil mentioned with only a little hint of humour that there was a whole room in the hut piled high with cinnamon-flavoured pellets to which he was welcome to help himself, it was then that I knew we had to move Hemi on.

Hemi was soon replaced by the timid Jim. Jim was a softly spoken, petite Southland chap who looked like he would blow over in the first gust of wind. How he'd gravitated to a life in the bush was anybody's guess but he had just come in from a job checking possum traps on a quad bike as part of a TBfree operation on farmland. Phil and I took a nervous look at him and wondered if we had traded in one useless mate for another.

In the first week Jim managed to fall down a bluff when the rotten log he was climbing up gave way. He managed to limp back to the hut where we found him that evening. He was a little shaken up and wondered if he might need to be medevacked. I asked him if anything was broken. When it was clear that nothing was, I suggested he take a hut day the next day to come right.

On his hut day our mate managed to have such a thorough rest that there was no dinner waiting for us when we returned from our day on the hill, head torches bobbing down the track in the pouring rain. The billy wasn't even warm. There was no smoke coming from the fire and the one thing our mate had got stuck into was the several packets of potato chips we saved for special occasions.

Yep, Jim was lying there passed out on his bunk, where he'd been for most of the day. That evening we were regaled by all the wondrous stories he'd read in one of the hut's old, stained novels as we sat freezing our butts off, warmed only by the pile of wood Jim had not cut.

At least he didn't eat as much as Hemi, and when he eventually did manage to crawl from his sleeping bag he gave as full a day on the hill as his small frame would allow. In the end though, we got to the tail of the ten-day trip and Jim hadn't finished his side of the work. Sacha was flying down from the North Island to visit and there was no way I was going to be sticking around to supervise Jim when I could be in town with her.

We cut our sorry mate a shed-load of wood, piled kindling high against the wall and made sure he had a radio with plenty of charged batteries in case anything happened. There was still plenty of food as our new mate, unlike our old mate, ate like a bird, which was in keeping with his work ethic. Phil and I were scarpering to the nearest road end for a much-needed weekend and we would catch up with Jim in four days' time if he was still about.

Four days later, Phil and I returned to the office to hear that Jim was no longer on the job. After a quick chat with the boss, Phil and I headed back to the bush to await our next mate or our controlled substances licence, whichever came first. Thankfully a big brown envelope arrived at the office that week, which signalled the end of our frontcountry mates. The department now considered us safe enough to dispense a couple of cyanide pellets in with the pindone on our bait-station lines. Hopefully now we'd be left in peace until summer.

With summer came the opening of the tourist season. Snow was replaced by sandflies and instead of the cold, penetrating wet of winter we now had a warm, muggy wet that seemed to make any scratch or cut fester in a matter of minutes.

Having overcome the challenges of ill-selected workmates, we now found our entertainment in talking with tourists. The days were long, with daylight arriving at 4 a.m. and fading again at 11 p.m. We were allowed to work a maximum of ten hours a day according to DOC health and safety policies, so that left us a lot of time for hunting and socialising.

Typically in the morning we'd be up at sparrows' fart. After stuffing

TOP When I first arrived in Fiordland the hills looked impossibly steep and tall, but after a while you come to realise that any hill is climbable with the right mindset.

BOTTOM Some of the huts in Fiordland have plenty of character. Unfortunately they also lack a lot of comfort. Interestingly we came to love the snow. At least it was good insulation.

our faces with a good fry-up for the morning meal we'd disappear with rifles in hand to any number of nearby clearings, hoping to find an easy deer before the tourists hit the tracks. There's nothing a tourist fears more than unidentified rifle fire.

After a morning hunt when we usually shot a deer, we would stash our rifles under fallen logs, keeping them dry in a housing of black rubbish bags. The deer we hung in a shady tree for later collection. We made sure bolts and ammunition came with us, stashed in the top pockets of our packs, and we'd go about our work filling bait stations and climbing hills.

> Hemi somehow managed to build up a hunger that rivalled England's historical need for colonies. Each night he would polish off a mountain of chops, spuds, mince and vegetables then reach for the pot of spuds we were saving for breakfast.

Our bait lines had a habit of crossing the main Kepler Track and more often than not we would bump into tourists. I'd be lying if I said on occasion we didn't purposely wait until an unsuspecting group of trampers were wandering past before suddenly erupting from the undergrowth in an explosion of leaves and branches, giving them a little excitement in their day. Maybe we'd been alone in the bush too long but we found an odd satisfaction in scaring the tourists.

Since the days were long we tried to meet back at the hut for a proper cooked lunch at about noon. Here we could chew the fat and take a break from the inhospitable drone of sandflies. We made it our responsibility to invite any passing tourists in for a cuppa and to share our food with them. We figured it added to the user experience and it gave us no end of entertainment, especially watching Phil trying to chat up the finer-looking wahine.

We invited one lovely young woman into the hut who turned us down on milk in her tea and then proceeded to lecture us on the injustices the Department of Conservation was inflicting on the poor rats and possums in the environment around us and how could us bushmen hunt the lovely wee deer running around the hills? After awkwardly explaining that this was pretty much our life's work we unsuccessfully tried to hit the eject button several times and eventually succumbed to patiently watching her cup of tea ever so slowly be drained in minuscule sips as we sat through a barrage of descriptions of the suffering we were inflicting on animals. It got so bad I started to ask myself the hard questions and had almost resigned myself to becoming vegan. She eventually left, almost needing a crowbar to pry her from her seat.

Our next visitor was a lovely wee Asian woman who spoke not a word of English. We found her hobbling along the track at 6 p.m., not looking at all comfortable. She had on town clothes and was carrying supermarket bags under each arm. The fatal mistake though was her choice of footwear: to climb the Kepler Mountains she'd decided to wear some very fashionable high-heeled Nike wedge sneakers that were more at home on a catwalk than in the remote backcountry. How anyone could walk in those things full stop had me baffled, let alone climb a mountain, and she was three painful days into her hike.

So, gesturing hospitably, we brought her inside, made her a cup of tea and sat her down on the most comfortable seat we had. We made her take off her six-inch heels and what we saw underneath was shocking. Just about every part of her foot had been rubbed raw and bloody; when she saw it she started to cry. She'd been walking all day to travel the same distance we'd cover in three hours and the next hut was still at least a three-hour walk away. She had grit, I'll give her that, but she wasn't keen on finishing her trip and when the helicopter arrived to fly her out she did look quite grateful.

It's amazing the things you see on the Great Walks tracks. Misinformed people turning up with no food, expecting the huts to be catered. Not bringing any bedding, not realising that the huts only provide an uncomfortable DOC mattress. But most common of all are all the folks who are just unaware of how unforgiving the backcountry of Aotearoa can actually be. But to Phil and I, this was our home.

7. COMING UNSTUCK

One time in Fiordland I was unlucky enough to fall off a bluff. I'd been dropped off by a helicopter at the top of a ridge and tasked with descending to the valley floor through some pretty steep country.

Along the way my task was to monitor the beech trees to see what type of mast year we were in for and therefore what impact we could expect the predators to have on our native biodiversity. A mast year is when the trees produce a bumper crop of seed and nuts, which stimulates plagues of mice and rats which in turn fuel an increase in stoat numbers. Not good news if you're a native bird.

On my descent somehow I ended up in a bluff system, and every route I explored had the same outcome: sheer, vertical rocks.

The old adage 'deer don't go stupid places but people do' was playing in my head on repeat. How had I managed to end up somewhere where there were no deer tracks whatsoever? That was a sure sign I was in some horrible country.

As I was exploring a possible route, the earth I was standing on gave way and sent me hurtling in free fall down a bluff.

In mid-flight I had enough time to think about my choices leading up to this point, and resigned myself to the fact that things were going pretty pear-shaped.

Then I struck the ground. Well, not ground. I struck rock, feet first.

Luckily this rock was covered in a thick layer of moss that absorbed most of the impact and sent me skidding down the hill to the valley floor below.

I looked myself over for any bent or protruding bones but somehow I had come off alright. I just couldn't walk on my ankle.

I decided to use the adrenaline coursing through my body before it

ABOVE I have a lot to thank the soft mosses for. They wash my hands, act as a soft toilet paper and can even offer up a drink if you're thirsty. In this adventure though I was just grateful that they cushioned my fall. © Strike Photography

ran out, so I picked up my rifle and, using it as a crutch, hobbled my way to where I could find the track. From here it was a three-kilometre hobble to the nearest hut, which I made in two and a half hours.

Taking a load off at the hut, I was cold and sweaty, maybe a little in shock. I searched around for something warm and found an old mildew-smelling Swanndri hanging on a hook.

I then removed my boot . . . worst decision ever. My ankle puffed up like a rugby ball. It started to throb and became quite painful.

I slept that night wrapped in my Swanndri before calling in on the radio in the morning. They wanted to medevac me out but in a state of misplaced pride and terror that I would end up in the local paper as a human unfit of the title 'bushman', I picked up my pack and the boot that would no longer fit on my foot and again, using my rifle as a crutch, I limped my way down the track towards the nearest road end.

Next thing I knew there was a helicopter flying overhead and this time I was the one being flown out with a busted hoof.

Three months off work but it could have been much worse without the amazing moss that cushioned my fall.

8. **BLOOD EVERYWHERE**

Let me tell you about the time I woke up on a freezing winter's night with a crotch covered in blood.

In the depths of the Murchison Mountains lies a valley called the McKenzie Burn. An old run-down deer cullers' hut sits on a grassy terrace at the junction between river and lake. Built of corrugated iron, Te Au Hut has an open fire, four bunks, a bench and a small lean-to for firewood. The windows don't close fully and the hut is constantly filled with sandflies by day and mosquitos at night. Its single room fills with smoke whenever you light a fire as the fireplace is built on the wrong side of the hut for the prevailing wind.

Te Au Hut is the kind of hut where on arrival you open the door and the smell of damp black mould billows out, making your nostrils flair.

The hut book reads of days gone by, when cullers and trappers spent 52 days in relentless rain. When sleepy sickness (depression) ruined people's careers. When airdrops of food didn't come often enough because clear days to fly in Fiordland are few and far between. This would be Phil and my home for the winter.

Te Au Hut is the kind of hut where on arrival you open the door and the smell of damp black mould billows out, making your nostrils flair. Condensation runs down the wall at night to be quickly absorbed by your sleeping bag. Maybe that's why the bunks had been pushed into the middle of the room?

We'd been dropped by helicopter on the saddle between Woodrow Burn and McKenzie Burn. It had just snowed on the tops and the snow had

TOP My hat goes off to the amazing bush pilots of Aotearoa. Nothing beats seeing the Hughes 500 at the end of a long trip.

BOTTOM The lengths we go to to protect these amazing birds. © Nicole Haerewa

settled into a persistent, wet sleet, cold enough to freeze your fingers but wet enough to work its way through your clothes. Our task for the next few weeks was to lay out stoat traps to protect the local takahē population.

I'd spent the previous few days with our helicopter pilot, sling-loading fadges of wooden boxes from our base in Te Anau to a snowy dump spot high in the rocky peaks. From this craggy outcrop we'd again sling-load the traps down to strategic GPS points along the track. The plan was, if I'd done my maths right, that us trappers would be laying down our last traps as we stumbled across the next bundle. I'd learned this method as a twelve-year-old from Lindsay in Te Urewera. As we worked, our pilot carefully slotted bundles of traps through the canopy on a long sling line and placed them gently on the track below for us to find in due course.

Phil and I had been dropped on our snowy perch to pick up our first load of trap boxes. They'd been soaked by the rain and later frozen solid by the cold, almost doubling their original weight. It was going to be a slow and knee-buckling descent to the valley floor, with each of us carrying a 40-kilogram pack down slippery granite tracks.

Every hundred metres or so we would stop and drop a trap box, baiting it with the stoat's favourite tucker — a chicken egg and chunk of frozen venison.

As we walked, we noticed a pack of juvenile kea following us. They were keen to investigate the new toys we'd left them as they bounced and squawked along behind us. Some trappers feed kea the old rotten eggs from their traplines. I used to have a pet kea that would share my lunch on Resolution Island. The bird was a bit of a nuisance though, returning the favour by tearing all the polystyrene insulation out from underneath the hut.

Trap boxes have evolved significantly in response to the kea's antics. In the early days we used wire mesh on the ends of our traps, but the kea easily bit through the mesh to get to the egg and meat inside. We tried double-thick wire mesh, but the kea bit through those too. We eventually settled on a stainless-steel punch-cut end, a little expensive but indestructible. Finding that they couldn't get into the trap boxes from the end, it didn't take long for the inquisitive kea to attack the lid. We were using stainless-steel square-head screws at the time, which the kea decided to dig out. They would gnaw chunks out of the wooden trap box surrounding the screw and then work the head of the screw around until the box popped open, exposing their prize. We retaliated by using heavier, extra-long hex screws and this still has them fooled.

Upon discovering that they couldn't get into the trap box, the kea decided to lie on their back like Tāne himself pushing Rangi and Papa apart, and push the trap over, which meant the egg rolled to the end of the trap and broke against the stainless steel. The egg would then drip out through the gaps and be licked up by an excited kea. A short length of reinforcing steel nailed to the side of the trap and hammered into the ground sorted out this behaviour.

As we walked, we noticed a pack of juvenile kea following us. They were keen to investigate the new toys we'd left them as they bounced and squawked along behind us.

It takes a lot of extra work to fool a kea. How did we figure all this out? Cameras! Hours and hours of hilarious camera footage where we saw the kea using sticks, rocks and anything else they could get their beaks on. For now, I think we have the upper hand. There's a reason kea are considered the smartest birds in the world.

The tracks in Fiordland are another hazard when you're trapping. As we pick our way down rocky tracks where the topsoil has been worn away by generations of deer, deer cullers and trappers, it's easy to be thankful when it snows. At least in the snow and sleet the ground is solid and you can use the exposed rock for grip as you jam the edge of your boot into crevices, so that you can sidle across steep rockfaces. The consequences of stuffing up some of these manoeuvres with a heavy pack on isn't worth thinking about. Not long prior, a mate had to scrape a tourist off the rocks below a tricky section of track in the neighbouring mountains on the Milford Track. Fortunately, the public aren't given access to the Murchison Mountains and it's not just because this is the last wild remnant of a once widespread takahē population. The terrain is massively challenging and it's easy to come to grief if you don't know it well.

On the valley floor we spot signs of takahē, their large footprints much heavier than a kiwi and turds that resemble those of a paradise duck, full of undigested plant fibre. Takahē are incredibly adaptable birds; they spend much of the warmer months on the tussock tops pulling blades from hardy grasses and eating the palatable ends. In winter they move down the slopes into the forest in search of other food. Much like the deer cullers, trappers

TOP I have always found it interesting that takahē retreat down from the tops in the depths of winter to forage for forest herbs among the trees. © Nicole Haerewa

BOTTOM Te Au Hut: one of the darkest and dingiest huts ever to be considered adequate for lodging in Fiordland. There was not much right about this hut and its only saving grace was the big box of old mildewed Western novels in the cupboard.

learn about the species they are trapping and about the ones they are trying to protect.

By lunchtime we were exhausted, the cold having soaked into our bones. The sleet on the valley floor had long since worked its way through our inadequate DOC-issue raincoats and our fingers weren't listening very well. It was too cold to stop so we fished out some squashed sandwiches from our packs and kept trudging. These valley floors turn to swamps in winter, and many sections of track are knee-deep in water; the more modern huts are built on stilts.

In some respects, I was glad to be based out of Te Au Hut. Our other option was Woodrow Hut some twelve kilometres away, which floods so often that there is a series of lines on the wall where someone sitting on their bunk has marked the rising water level. At some point it has almost reached the mattress. Nothing quite compares to the feeling of stepping out the front door into waist-deep swamp water, and you can imagine the splashback in the long drop.

By lunchtime we were exhausted, the cold having soaked into our bones. The sleet on the valley floor had long since worked its way through our inadequate DOC-issue raincoats and our fingers weren't listening very well.

As we continued laying traps back to Te Au, we came across a six-point stag on the track — was he sleeping? On closer inspection we discover he's dead. No bullet holes and he looked in good condition. Phil suggested the animal may have died from depression in such a cold, horrible place.

Just before dark, the sleet eased to rain and we stumbled up to our humble abode. Sanctuary from the wet at last. We set about bleaching the black mould from the mattresses, the cooker, the billy and even the plates. We then went about collecting the driest wood we could find as there was none left in the lean-to. With head torches on, we set about trying to light a fire, but a torrent of water was pouring straight down the chimney and our first few attempts were snuffed out. Even the old cowboy novels from the cupboard were too damp to burn. In the end we gave up. We just sat in our sleeping bags, exhausted, eating our hot food from a billy that 30 minutes ago was home to at least three different species of mould. Finally, we warmed up and fell asleep.

I woke at 3 a.m., startled and embarrassed. Turns out I'd pissed myself. Surely not? I hadn't done that since I was a kid; I must have been tired. What was Phil going to say? But there was a warm, wet feeling coming from my crotch. I subtly turned on my head torch to investigate, hoping not to alert Phil to my shame. I looked into my sleeping bag and it's wet alright, soaked in fact. The wetness was red and to my horror I saw blood everywhere. Panicking, I woke up Phil.

My mind was racing. Something big was going on; surely that much blood must mean an emergency 'down there'? It wasn't even worth thinking about the long-term repercussions of a severe injury to my manhood. If we called the DOC radio no one would answer, it was 3 a.m. We might have been able to get a message via the fisherman's radio to the coastguard, but would a rescue helicopter fly in this storm?

Phil just looked at me through sleepy eyes and laughed. 'Mate, did you put the stoat bait on the top bunk last night?'

Sure enough, the venison that was frozen when we'd arrived at camp had defrosted overnight. The bags we pack them in aren't waterproof at the best of times and deer blood had seeped out, dripping from the top bunk onto my sleeping bag, leaving me in a bloody mess.

Squirming with embarrassment, I replied, 'Sorry mate,' and scurried back inside my soggy sleeping bag. I'd take the next couple of weeks sleeping in deer blood over whatever medical emergency my imagination had thought was going on. I still had my manhood intact.

A FISH IS A FISH WITHOUT FISHING

I am a man that must fish
As I am a fisherman
A fish is a fish without fishing
Yet a man without fishing's no man

To separate man from fisher
Is a greater feat than I
For fisher's been man and man fisher
Since the very start of time

ABOVE Working alone in the bush is where I feel most at home. © Strike Photography

9. BEING SHOT AT

That shiver down your spine, that rush of adrenaline, the quiet whistle as a bullet screams past your ear. Then the obligatory pat-down for blood and the disbelief — firstly that you're alive and secondly that some numpty just pulled the trigger thinking you're a deer.

Have I been shot at during my time in the bush?

Hell yes, I've been shot at! Multiple times.

Thankfully the same pricks who were shooting at me didn't take the time to place their shots well.

The first time I was shot at, I was filling up bait stations in the Iris Burn valley. We were living in the bush at the time, in the mouldy little camp of Rocky Point Hut. Each morning we prised ourselves from damp sleeping bags, donned equally damp clothes and headed out into the much damper bush to distribute poison. Our hut smelled of cinnamon from the toxicant stored in the one dry corner of the hut. (I'm pretty sure that goes against every rule of modern health and safety, but at the time we ate around toxins, slept around toxins and I'm sure breathed in our fair share of the green dust that flavoured the air cinnamon).

The previous summer, we'd discovered a small population of bats in the valley. Bat numbers were nationally critical at the time so it was all hands on deck to protect their precarious population, mostly by laying bait for the rats that predate on the wee creatures. I had my doubts about the effectiveness of this plan, partly because the bait had a tendency to go mouldy and dissolve in the wet Fiordland winters, and partly because the possums would hoover up the bait before the rats got a look-in. But that was all above my pay grade; I was a lowly ranger and didn't know anything about anything so here I was lugging toxins around in the bush because it looked good on paper.

Early afternoon on a fine day, I'd just loaded up with my sixth twenty-kilogram sack of pindone for the day and I was getting a little weary. We hadn't stopped for lunch as my hands were covered in green smoodge and to stop would mean being mauled by sandflies. My respirator had long since become sodden and to breathe through it was like trying to breathe in a fish tank. My gloves had been torn on all manner of scratchy bushes and had fallen apart. P.P.E. just doesn't tend to work in the bush. I was however wearing a high-vis shirt as it was the roar and who knows what muppets with guns were cruising around the scrub this time of year.

Carrying a twenty-kilogram pack through crown fern is a noisy business and as I came up over a particular rise in the hill — ZZZZZZIIIIMM — a bullet came screeching past me. Some douchebag had shot at me, thinking I was a deer. I yelled out 'Oi!' but the guy just ran off through the crown fern, never to be seen again. Bloody bad bastard that.

I reckon that he must have been hunting the same spur I was on, and having heard a 'deer' coming towards him he would have just sat and waited. The orange of my high-vis on that drab Fiordland winter's day must have flickered red like a deer in the green of the bush, and that was enough to squeeze the trigger.

I'm not pulling the trigger on a stag if I don't know its antler quality. They taste terrible in the roar. So if it's not going on the wall or in the freezer, I'm not shooting it.

In a way I don't mind the shot being fired. I didn't die, but I bloody could have. I figure that's a mistake that fella will have to live with for the rest of his life. Hopefully it was the wake-up call he needed to identify his target. The bit I despise is the cowardice of running away afterwards. The bit that goes 'I'd rather sneak away than apologise for almost claiming someone's life in pursuit of a stag'. To me that's some bad bugger stuff, and somewhat unforgivable.

What if I'd been injured? What then?

I had a lot of time to think about that moment while filling bait stations over the winter. A lot of time to reflect. The thing I don't understand is: if that person was roar hunting, why is he shooting stags he hadn't first assessed anyway? I'm not pulling the trigger on a stag if I don't know its antler quality. They taste terrible in the roar. So if it's not going on the wall or in the freezer, I'm not shooting it.

I was shot at three times that year. The next time occurred in spring. I was rebaiting traps in the foothills of the Kepler and it was the same scenario: I was pushing through crown fern with a pack on my back, sweating my way up a hill, stopping every 50 metres to service a trap and then quietly moving on. Again I was wearing high-vis and singing to myself every now and then. I would often sing songs from home while out by myself in the hills. Songs that I know by heart, country music and waiata from Te Tairāwhiti, where I come from. They welled up in my mouth as I worked, giving me comfort and a sense of home in what was often a lonely and culturally desolate landscape.

Then — PFFFZZZZEOW — a bullet raced past my head. You know a projectile is close when you hear that whistle. Again I yelled out 'Oi!' then started singing even louder. Again no answer but a rustle of crown fern as the marksman slunk off into the bush.

This time I had the shakes. This time I sat down and cried. It had been a long, hard winter, living in awful, health-damaging conditions. We'd been wet all the time, day and night. I was lonely, I was exhausted and I had given everything I had to the ngahere, to Tāne. I'd given every ounce of my being and my energy to help bring our native species back to abundance. I felt like this was the task given to me in life by my mentors and one I had accepted. Why was I being shot at? Was I prepared to die for my principles? Was I prepared to leave no other legacy other than a few traplines and bird populations clinging on to existence?

I just didn't know anymore. Maybe I needed a change of path or a holiday.

The third time was less of a close call but it was just as confronting. We'd been tasked with clearing the tracks after a 1080 drop. When the DOC campaign promoting its use of the toxic drops was announced as 'Battle for our Birds', I had a lot of soul searching to do. For me, and where I come from, predator control is necessary, but we had been raised to uphold the mana of the animal we killed through the process of death. Taking life has always been a part of our culture; it doesn't matter which culture you come from. Whether we hunt, trap or partake in war it has always been part of human existence.

A hunter works to perfect his craft so he can take an animal quickly and cleanly. He is grateful for the life he has taken, as it provides life for his whānau through kai. My first deer had suffered and I had vowed not to let that happen again.

As a trapper, the process is similar. We work at perfecting our craft, our trap sets and our tools so that we can take an animal's life as quickly as possible. Ideally the animal doesn't know what's hit them. We strive to eliminate non-target species and feel terrible if we take an unnecessary life. We feel gratitude when we find a dead animal in our traps, gratitude that this predator has given its life so that our taonga species can survive and flourish. We honour the whakapapa of the animal whether it be stoat, possum, ferret or rat. We honour their abilities as master predators and we honour the people who consider these animals their taonga species in their homelands many kilometres away.

This is my approach to trapping and to predator control: a predator is not a 'pest' and is worthy of respect even though I know that its life must be taken all the same.

We feel gratitude when we find a dead animal in our traps, gratitude that this predator has given its life so that our taonga species can survive and flourish.

So, I struggled with the idea of being asked to participate in a 1080 drop. This poison is a tool that takes life slowly and disconnects people from the process of predator control. There is no space for gratitude. No space to greet the body of each animal we take and to honour it. There's no relationship.

But I had been sent to Fiordland to learn. I was seeking to learn a different way and to take home a different understanding. I wanted to keep an open mind. If I didn't experience it with my own eyes and hands, then how would I really know the impact of this efficient tool?

I signed up as a track clearer and monitor, so I could be on the ground and gain as in-depth an understanding of how 1080 worked as possible.

As summer turned to autumn, one drop turned to several and the community blowback was, as we'd expected, fairly gnarly. We had death threats, and our usually casual office was now locked down with a secure-entry, buzz-in-buzz-out system. We had a crew of security guards at each drop. These massive, thickset bouncers looked severely out of place in the bush; it was pretty comical to see their gym bodies falling apart on the first hill they encountered.

But worse was to come. We were out there clearing the tracks so the tourists didn't have to look at green pellets or dead critters as they walked, and we cleaned the pellets off hut roofs and gutters so no one could claim 1080 was in the huts' water supply. As we walked the tracks, we heard gunshots firing into the bush from the lake. It seemed strange as hunting had been banned during the drop and tourism had been put on hold. So we got on the radio and called in this activity.

It turned out that a bunch of 1080 protesters were out on their boat in the lake, shooting off their rifles towards the Great Walks Kepler Track we were clearing. I want to be generous and give them the benefit of the doubt that they weren't aiming directly at us but it was close enough to freak us all out and a pretty stink thing to do.

Maybe they were trying to scare us — I knew some of the people involved and they definitely had a reputation for getting worked up about topics like 1080.

While I thought the way they were protesting was totally beyond the pale, I could understand the frustration that led to it. I would much rather be out on the ground doing the work in the field and we had shown we could achieve excellent rat, possum and stoat control throughout Fiordland's steepest mountains without the use of aerial toxin. However, the financial maths for that method didn't stack up.

The protests scared the crap out of me. I'd heard the stories and seen the outcomes of wheel nuts being loosened on DOC trucks and sugar allegedly being poured into helicopter gas tanks, and now bullets were flying into the bush while we were clearing tracks.

The order came over the radio to pause work and take cover while the police who were on standby quickly boarded a DOC boat and nipped out to suppress the protesters. I think they had their guns confiscated and were issued a fine but no jail time was served. We were then given the all-clear on the radio and told to resume work just as a helicopter flew over and spewed 1080 over the top of us as we walked so we had to backtrack and start our job all over again.

The final time I was shot at was years later, while doing an ecology job monitoring seabirds on my wife's cousin's farm on the East Cape. It was dusk after a full day on the hill and as per usual my mate Paddy and I had bitten off a little more work than we could chew. We were climbing our way up through deer tunnels in the tight mānuka scrub, heading for a prominent knob and pā site to deploy acoustic recorders. We wanted to find out if seabirds were using the old pā site as an orientation point to mob up with other seabirds before making their way to their nesting sites inland.

We snuck towards a clearing; Paddy, a vegetarian of the best variety, was hoping to spot bats and I was hoping to spot deer. As we peered through the last row of tangled mānuka branches we saw a stunning ten-point velvet stag feeding away quietly. We stopped for a while and watched, never one to rush an animal from its evening meal. Out came the camera and I received a couple of out-of-focus shots for my effort.

Then the stag winded us and bounded off into the scrub and we carried on with our work. It was getting dark, the time when shapes blur and tones become dull. Paddy and I pushed up through a series of clearings on old tracks. It's peaceful at this time of night, the air cool, the insects humming as they wake and the birds calling their last territorial tones. Paddy and I tended to work in silence when the bush quieted.

> In my experience orange high-vis does little to deter the shooter from pulling the trigger. If I can point to one thing that I reckon contributes to these incidents it's expecting that you're the only person in the bush.

Shockingly, the still was broken by a barrage of shots. Many misses. Many lucky targets. The bullets whistled past us, far enough away to hope we weren't the target, but close enough to raise the question. This time it was Paddy and I who snuck off quietly into the dark safety of the bush. We lay down, hearts beating out of our chests, and gave the hunters time to disappear.

After ten or so minutes we retreated. Down the tracks through the mānuka, down to the homestead, the remainder of our work left for another day. Here we were met by the farmer, my uncle-in-law. He asked about our day and, cagily, we told him about our experience.

The guy was ropeable, having not a lot of tolerance for poachers on his patch. In a flurry of stones and a cloud of dust, his ute rattled down the road to cut off the interlopers before they could get to their vehicle, which he knew would be stashed along the road on the other side of the headland.

Sure enough, the hunters were at their vehicle when the farmer turned up. When asked point blank whether they were poaching his property, they admitted they had been. In true East Coast fashion, they were reminded that no farmer would let a whānau go hungry but if they wanted to hunt a property they needed to pick up the phone and ask permission first. This way everyone knows who's where and situations like that evening could be avoided.

The real disappointment for me was that they came from a whānau I respect greatly. Their grandfather is a legendary bushman who knows so much about our ecosystems and whenua. He's a man of principle, and it would be sad if this way of being has been watered down over the generations. Let's hope it hasn't.

I've been shot at or shot near more times than I'm comfortable with. In my experience orange high-vis does little to deter the shooter from pulling the trigger. If I can point to one thing that I reckon contributes to these incidents it's expecting that you're the only person in the bush. Each time, aside from the protesters, I've been pushing through noisy scrub and I reckon the hunters heard me coming. Each time that the trigger's been pulled, the target hasn't been identified correctly and each time the shooting area hasn't been safe.

Maybe I'm just lucky. Maybe my time will come. But one thing I know is that I will keep returning to the bush, no matter the dangers. But please, when you're out there, take your time, uphold the mana of the life you are taking and please don't let that life be mine.

10. **HOROPITO AND GREEN DEER**

It was green. Dark green, the colour of fungus decomposing on the forest floor. Definitely not the kind of green you want to see on the outside of a steak you're about to eat.

But that's how it was in Te Urewera. Dad and I had been walking all day. Our beat-up and rust-splattered Austin Montego station wagon had bounced its way up the potholed road late the previous evening. We'd made camp in the DOC hut and had listened to kākā and kiwi calling all night through the open window. When we woke in the morning, pepetuna had lined the deck, trailing short lines of pale yellow eggs behind them.

I was seven years old and one of my favourite morning activities was to collect these large fighter planes of moths as they clung to their last glimmers of energy, having distributed their eggs into the soil the night before. I'd line them up along the corrugated timbers of the damp deck: first the green-, then the yellow- and finally the brown-winged moths. I'd sit back and admire their patterns, no two alike, each reminding me of the mataora of rangatira in the pictures lining wharenui walls in this deep, dark, damp valley of the Waimana.

There were thirteen marae in this valley in total. Dad was here to suss the place out for a school camp he was running in a few weeks. I was here to spend time on an adventure with my dad. With plastic bags lining my ill-fitting boots to stop me getting blisters, we crossed the first stream. The road seemed to fizzle out into a paddock then a track down to the riverbed. No official end, no car park, simply merging into the dense bush it cut through.

As we ambled up the riverbed, we met horses roaming the river flats and bush clearings, loosely belonging to someone but belonging more to the landscape around them. The track dipped into the river then back up along the river flats, narrowing to a tight, overgrown quad-bike track through the

TOP I was growing so fast as a kid that I used to get hangry if I didn't eat. Regular muesli bar breaks were necessary if we were going to have a good trip.

BOTTOM Dad was a teacher and took me on lots of his school camps. He was such an incredible story teller, he made the whole ecosystem come alive in his students' imaginations.

bush. Every few kilometres it'd open up onto a grassy river terrace with a homestead or a scrubby bend in the river with a whare and its ponga fence.

At each new clearing, skinny dogs would emerge from holes dug deep into banks to bark and sniff for food. Their kennels were the dark, warm caverns of earth. The favourite dogs would have a piece of wood hammered into the dirt above their hole with their name carved into it, a high honour for a deer-chasing dog. There were horses with rope halters, chewing circles in the grassy clearings around a strong steel peg, and skinned deer were often found hanging in a shady spot from a tree. There was almost never anyone about, as folks rose early to spend their days in the bush possum-trapping, hunting and gathering kai.

This was a different existence, one my grandfather had told me of many times. He used to hunt and fish these valleys in his younger days and had taught me the ways of green meat and of horopito.

Electricity and fridges still hadn't reached the ends of these deep bush valleys. Possum skins and fur were carted out in bales on horseback or quad bike to be sold in town. Flour, salt, sugar and kerosene for lanterns were carted back in, as well as ammunition and household items. The valley's hunting dogs would be identified as pig dogs by most hunters but in this neck of the woods they were bred to also run down deer, flushing them into the shingle-covered riverbeds for an open shot.

There always seemed to be a carcass or two hanging from a nearby tree and more often than not it was starting to turn. My grandfather reckoned the locals would just cut a leg down, trim off any green meat, then rub the leg with crushed horopito leaves and let it sit for a while before cooking it, letting the flavour work into the meat.

As a young fella I'd grown up with stories of medieval knights and castles, and how highly valued spices were used to disguise the putrid flavour of old meat. To me it made sense to use the peppery flavour of horopito to disguise old meat. But later, as a trapper in Te Urewera, I learned that we also coat older meat with horopito because of its incredible antibacterial properties.

It always blows my mind how the bush provides solutions to many of life's problems. Everything has a balance and plays a role in the ecosystem. Every plant is connected to another plant, and plays a role in the life of birds and in the landscape. Thankfully for us humans, the bush has a lot to offer us if we know how to ask the right questions and take the time to build a relationship.

Horopito is an incredibly generous tree. It grows in disturbed landscapes such as river flats, slips, bush edges or areas that have been cleared by fire or selectively logged. Horopito is a mender of landscapes as well as a cleaner of bacteria. It helps convert scarred, broken country from ferns and herbs into shrubs and then forest. It creates shade, allows dampness to stay hidden in the soil, and allows slow-growing rangatira rākau, our fruiting trees, to not be smothered by energetic and fast-growing ferns and grasses. Horopito plays a similar role in the ngahere as it does with meat, taking damaged whenua and transforming it into an abundant food forest rich in fruit, manu and diverse trees.

> The valley's hunting dogs would be identified as pig dogs by most hunters but in this neck of the woods they were bred to also run down deer, flushing them into the shingle-covered riverbeds for an open shot.

Horopito is very generous but as a young trapper I didn't really develop a strong relationship with it until I was taught how it helps us when washing our hands. I was always pulling month-old smelly possums out of traps, and cleaning out maggoty rats and stoats. No matter what your friendly city dweller tells you about wearing gloves to avoid disease, the truth is gloves last about five minutes in the sharp, prickly bush.

Every day trappers touch the unclean of death with our bare hands, on behalf of the manu and rākau around us. And every day about lunchtime, we search for a way to clean our hands so we can eat. Many trappers refuse lunch and work all day without food. Others carry small bottles of alcoholic gel. But true bushmen have been taught a relationship with the plants around us. There are many plants that can help us to clean ourselves. Moss is antimicrobial, stopping things from smelling, and it's also soft and damp, a natural wet wipe in the forest. Kawakawa is antibacterial and tastes good as well, a perfect replacement for a toothbrush if you leave yours at home. Horopito is strong and powerful, a 'knock your socks off' peppery-flavoured cleaner.

When I'm on my trapline and lunchtime's getting closer I start to keep my eyes peeled. In each creek bed, on each bush edge, I look for my friend horopito. When I find him he's usually growing in a grove; I search for the tallest and fullest in foliage. I ask if I can take a small handful of leaves to clean myself before kai and I sit back and listen.

In te reo Māori, the language of our nation, the word 'rongo' means 'to listen'. But if we look deeper, 'rongo' means not just to listen with our ears but to listen with our eyes, our nose, our feeling and the internal knowing we each have within us. I call it a tapping . . . When I'm asking plants a question, the reply often feels like someone has gently tapped on my shoulder and whispered in my ear. A knowing comes into me.

The plant may tell me: Yes I can offer you some leaves, but please take them from my sunny side, I can grow faster there. You can have a small handful, but please don't take too many. I have important work to do growing forests so we can all eat.

Sometimes the plant says: No, I am too tired, I need all the energy I can muster to establish myself here and do my work. Please look somewhere else, to another horopito or another species instead. I can't help you now but don't forget me. Maybe we will meet again and the answer might be different.

When the trees answer no, it's our job to listen. Instead I might look for kawakawa, who is fast growing, or moss, who is slow. They can also help me to clean my hands. On this day, maybe it is they I should be sharing lunch with rather than horopito.

When I'm asking plants a question, the reply often feels like someone has gently tapped on my shoulder and whispered in my ear. A knowing comes into me.

As a hunter and keen bush cook, I often collect horopito leaves. I dry them, grind them and use them in meat rubs to make pepper steaks. When I'm hunting or fishing, I wash my hands with the crushed leaves of horopito after field-dressing animals or butchering. In my farm-advisory work I introduce farmers to horopito and the role it plays in regenerating native forests. But overall I like to think of horopito as a friend, a tree I have a relationship with and who helps me in the bush. A tree with a very important job to do: growing forests.

11. THE TĪTĪ HARVEST

There are very few traditional harvests left to us here in Aotearoa. Many of our landscapes have lost their abundance to the myriad of introduced animals our forefathers, however well-intentioned, saw fit to bestow on our land and waterways.

But the tītī harvest is one. A glimmering beacon of hope, a line in the sand. It's one of the last great traditions of bird gathering we have left in Aotearoa that is truly ours. A seasonal harvest, where multigenerational whānau return to the same huts, scale the same cliffs and are chased by the same seals as the many generations before.

Once there were kererū camps, kākāpō camps, takahē camps and moa camps. The tītī were so abundant that they inhabited high points from the coast right up to inland mountain ranges. Their flight paths were so regular that songs were used to guide people through the landscape, a kind of oral map. Tītī burrows pocked the ground like golf balls and in an act of absolute generosity the birds fertilised both forests and fields with nutrients they gathered from the sea and pooped out across the whenua.

Tītī are a cornerstone of an abundant forest; this is the story of how harvesting a bird can benefit an entire ecosystem.

One warm autumn morning I was invited to help the people of the Tītī Islands rid a small rocky island of rats, off the southeastern coast of Rakiura. Rakiura is lucky enough not to have stoats or ferrets, but rats were having a big impact on tītī chicks, eating them in their burrows.

Tītī nest in burrows; back in the old days many coastal-nesting birds shared their holes with tuatara. When the tītī parents left to patrol the oceans in search of food, the tuatara would stand at the burrow's entrance, waiting for a wayward wētā or skink to pass by. I like to think of them as a kind of reptilian babysitter with a sharp, serrated jaw that any no-good

ABOVE To be able to witness one of our few traditional harvests of manu in Aotearoa is an absolute highlight of my career. I had no idea I would later be raising kids that whakapapa to these islands and this activity.

burrow browser wouldn't want to mess with.

The real value in the tītī harvest today as a conservation tool is not found in the tītī at all. It's in the relationship between land, people and kai. Every year hundreds of Rakiura Māori flock to these remote islands from all over the country. They take months off from workplaces that have no choice but to be understanding: for many the tītī harvest is more important than any job or commitment. It's their identity, a part of Ngāi Tahutanga and a practice that enriches lives, brings whānau together from all corners of Aotearoa and keeps traditional mahinga kai practices alive.

The birders wait for dark, stormy nights when the young birds emerge from burrows to flap their wings, building all-important muscles that will carry them across the oceans in years to come. As the tamariki fan out through the undergrowth they bring the birds back to the adult birders, who are content to walk on the tracks. The tamariki eagerly wait in anticipation to see if their bird is fat enough to be added to the hui or if it's a kiaka that must be taken back to its hole to put on more weight and possibly be ready later in the season. If the bird is caught in the open, the tamariki will gently pounce, cradling it in their arms to bring to an adult for quality control, never taking a chick that isn't fat enough and releasing those almost ready to fledge so the next generation of tītī can thrive. It's a fine line, but over the course of the evening many hui of birds are taken. Once dispatched between thumb and forefinger, they're plucked and bundled then loaded onto strings and sent down a metal flying fox from the high cliffs to the workhouses below.

A thwack resounds across the island as each hui of birds bounces off a tītī feather pillow at the end of the flying fox and all the māmā and tāua (Ngāi Tahu lingo for gardener) come outside to hang them in the workhouse.

Some time after midnight a procession of head torches winds its way down the cliffs and tired tamariki are coaxed into bunks, each with a look of accomplishment on their face.

As the morning comes quick and early it's down to the workhouse before breakfast. The youngsters snip flappers and scratchers from the birds with sharp shears while the adults dip fresh birds into wax to be hung for the day. Yesterday's birds are hoisted down from their hooks where they swing in bundles of four or five and are laid on a sack on the earthen floor. Now the youngsters set about peeling wax from birds, taking with it the soft down feathers that nobody wants to find in their evening meal. An adult then guts the birds, taking care to keep the big glob of hinu aside for cooking potatoes in throughout the year. This delicacy is like duck fat. Then the pōua sort and pack the birds into buckets — A's, B's and C's, ranked by fatness — and preserve them in salt. Lastly each pōua signs the top of the bucket with his initials, the grade and the quantity of birds inside. Buckets will be handed out to whānau, traded and in some cases sold to pay for the cost of the helicopters to get to and from the islands.

The Tītī Islanders love their islands. They are often more 'home' to them than their houses in town. And it's this love for the islands that the tītī is responsible for. In recent generations rats have ravaged these coastal paradises; the tuatara who guarded the burrows are gone and the tīeke that once nested in the workhouses and became family pets quickly disappeared as rats marauded the islands. Even the tītī suffered predation.

But that's just the thing. Without the presence of people, the rise of the rat may have gone unnoticed. But because tītī draws the islanders each year to this isolated corner of the South Seas, something could be done. The islanders missed their tīeke friends, and they sure as anything didn't want rats eating tītī chicks in their burrows. If possible it would be incredible to reinstate tuatara to their clifftop holes.

People have raised an entire generation to understand that mahinga kai is a cornerstone of conservation and that people's connection to their landscapes through kai is key . . .

So the islanders started to remove the rats, first with poison and later with traps. Their efforts were successful and in many cases tīeke returned to a point of abundance, where you almost have to hustle them out of the way as you climb up the meandering tracks and are greeted by their song in the mornings. But what's even more impressive is that these people have raised an entire generation to understand that mahinga kai is a cornerstone of conservation and that people's connection to their landscapes through kai is key to retaining an abundance of native biodiversity.

I was in my mid-twenties when I was so lucky to be given the opportunity to be a small part of this journey and to gain a glimpse into the world of the tītī harvest. Little did I know that later in my life I would marry a Ngāi Tahu woman from Tītī Island lines and my kids would inherit the right to protect such a unique mahinga kai practice and an understanding of conservation unique to Aotearoa.

12. STANFIELD HUT AND BATTLING THE BLUES

We looked like the Beverly Hillbillies as we bounced our way up the country in our dinky little Corolla station wagon. We were loaded to the gunnels: bags, books, hunting gear and deer skulls all jumbled in the boot while Moss the dog, prone to car sickness and smelling like vomit, sat up front on the knee of my girlfriend at the time, Sacha. We had a long plywood box I'd made especially for the trip strapped to the roof which was jam-packed with chickens of all descriptions, and as we drove along, hay and cracked egg yolks littered the road behind us. It was moving day and we were both looking forward to the warm climate of home. Although we'd loved our southern adventures, we were craving the North Island. The land of fruit, vegetables and family.

Over the past year, DOC and I had drifted apart. DOC was heading in the direction of contractors rather than field staff, which I felt compromised what to me seemed like the key to preserving our wild places: having people on the ground caring for ecosystems and retaining our connection with the whenua. Fiordland had been the last stronghold for the old model, but then my boss announced that here too they were going to start phasing out field staff. Bugger it, I'd had enough — heading north was the next logical step. I'd learned a lot from my time in Fiordland and hopefully I could bring some of that experience to projects in the North Island.

Thankfully my boss in Fiordland had opened a door for me and I'd ended up with a job managing predator control at Cape Sanctuary, a privately owned conservation project in Hawke's Bay. When I arrived they had an old trap network of rusted-out, fenn traps inherited from DOC many moons ago. Someone had decided to open up the mesh on the ends of the traps, the idea being to catch cats and rabbits, but the wider hole meant birds could also poke their heads inside the trap, where a succulent, fresh piece of meat in a trap box was only too tempting.

It always makes you feel absolutely terrible, but every trapper will at some point catch the wrong creature - we had accidentally caught the odd native bird in other projects down South, especially toutouwai in winter when the insects disappear and the birds are hungry. A starving robin will take a lot of risks to investigate a potential food source, and a piece of meat in a trap box is exactly that. But while I could understand wanting to catch the feral cats which do incredible damage to native birdlife, when you're operating a trap network you always want the risk to be as low as possible. My whole working life had been spent helping endangered species flourish and helping to design traps that reduced the risk to non-target species. So, job number one was making the ends of the trap boxes smaller.

After that I ordered hundreds of stainless-steel DOC200 traps, the crème de la crème of traps at the time. I spent the next month replacing old rusty fenns with DOC200s and refreshing the mesh ends on the trap boxes.

I was running around like a blue-arsed fly trying to get this project running in a way I felt happy with, but in my opinion I wasn't getting the support I needed to do the job properly.

It felt like internal politics and tensions in the workplace were making it hard for me and other people to do our jobs well, and my relationship with my boss was souring as we just couldn't seem to agree on how to do anything. It felt to me like a lot of my time and energy was being used to manage relationships, rather than do the job I had been hired for, and I couldn't seem to make it all work. Things were starting to get me down.

Each night I would bounce my way home in my newly acquired old Mitsubishi L200 ute to our pretty little rental house and get stuck into the vegetable garden. We had a big greenhouse and grew a stack of our own veggies. I had tomatoes, beans, leeks, spring onions, beetroot, carrots and a berry patch to die for. Sacha's nephew Carlos and niece Ruby would come round after 5 p.m. and 'help' in the garden. They ate so many strawberries, blackberries and tomatoes that most nights they were too full for dinner.

The garden was my happy place. I had trained Moss to herd the chickens into a particular corner of the garden and keep them there. Each time a bold chicken wanted to leave their designated foraging space, Moss would gently nudge them back into line with her nose. That's how I did the weeding — just cycling the chickens round the garden with the dog. They would turn the soil and poop in some extra nutrients in exchange for the odd worm or beetle.

TOP LEFT I picked Moss up from an old hunter called Hunter in Fiordland. She was the last of a litter because she had a broken leg. It healed fast and she became my best mate.

TOP RIGHT When things got really dark for mc it felt like Moss was the only one who really got it. She hardly left my side. In the end that was more critical than I could imagine. © Sacha van den Berg

BOTTOM As well as finding deer, Moss would tag along on my traplines. I reckon she considered herself a trapper too and would catch stoats every chance she got.

Unfortunately the dog had the same approach with Carlos and Ruby as she did with the chickens. If the kids were foraging in the strawberry patch and tried to wander off, Moss would nudge them back to their strawberries. If they were playing outside and wanted to come in for a drink of water, Moss wouldn't let them come up the stairs. If they were in the greenhouse they definitely weren't to come out. As far as she was concerned the kids were her responsibility, just like the chickens, and they had to stay in the place that I'd put them.

As much as I loved working in my veggie garden, the troubles at work were getting me down and as work got worse so did my mental health. The worse my relationship got with my boss, the less I wanted to be there. I had come straight from the pristine wilderness of Fiordland, a wild, remote sanctuary of self-reliance where beautiful snow-capped mountains and crystal-clear streams surround you at every step, and where, apart from helicopters and jetboats, the only form of transport was my own two legs. Now I was driving a quad around a dry, rabbit-infested farm with just kānuka gullies and a smattering of pine trees for bush. To top things off, I wasn't allowed to have my dog at work.

Before I knew it, at 27 I found myself battling depression for the first time in my life. I lost all motivation to go to work.

My motivation waned, but there weren't many other conservation jobs in the region. Sacha wasn't keen to move out of Hawke's Bay because her family was there but things weren't getting any easier for me. Before I knew it, at 27 I found myself battling depression for the first time in my life. I lost all motivation to go to work. I'd bounce my way up the windy farm track to the sanctuary but often I just couldn't bring myself to go through the gate. I stopped surfing and wanting to spend time with our family. To be honest I became a bit of a negative arsehole to Sacha and slowly but surely my life started to fall apart.

I wasn't sleeping at night, I'd just sit there worrying, running scenarios in my mind about life that inevitably convinced me I was a loser. One morning at 4 a.m. I'd just had enough. I packed up my hunting gear and the dog and went bush. Stanfield Hut was a solid two-hour drive away and a three-hour walk in, a place I'd track-cut in summer and trapped possums in winter many moons ago. I'd helped renovate the small orange hut with a new plywood floor and walls, a new hearth for the fire, an awesome kitchen bench with a sink and even dug the long drop. It was a bit of a freezing old hut, nestled in the headwaters of an easy little creek. It wasn't the most comfortable place in the world but if there was anywhere that felt like home for me at that point, it was Stanfield Hut.

So off we set, Moss and I, the light of my head torch bobbing away in front of me picking up the dog's white tail as we ambled through the scrub. I carried my Tikka .308 over my shoulder and a knife belt round my waist. Stanfield was an incredible place to hunt. Harsh, steep gullies flowed out onto grassy river flats. There was plenty of tree lucerne about so without a dog you walked straight past plenty of hiding deer. But most mornings there was a hind or a yearling silly enough to be caught feeding when the grey of morning emerged through the trees and that's when a dog and a Leupold scope came into their own.

This morning was no exception. As we wound our way up the creek, slipping on icy boulders and crunching through frozen river gravel, Moss came to a screeching halt, her brown head locked in place and white tail stiff and erect in the air, a telltale sign that whatever she was looking at wasn't a possum. As I searched fruitlessly in the half-light for the deer, Moss glanced at me with a look that said, 'Why aren't you shooting the bloody thing? It's right in front of me.'

Using a trick I'd learned from an old hunter named Hunter in Fiordland, I snuck up right behind Moss, lined my rifle up directly along her back and over her tail and head and let the light-capturing abilities of the scope do the work. Sure enough, illuminated behind a patch of lucerne was a yearling hind feeding out on the frosty river grass.

WHACK!

At close range the yearling was pole-axed and fell into the creek. The hole left by the .308 was turning the small tributary red in quite a biblical moment. Moss, as usual, was nowhere to be seen. She'd be tucked up safe in the bush, still distrustful of the stick that goes 'bang'. Being a German short-haired pointer, and highly strung like many of her breed, in a few moments her separation anxiety would kick in and she'd be at my side once more, unable to stay away for long.

Usually I'd come to the bush to escape the stresses of the urban world and to find some clarity. But today I just felt numb. Usually the bush was

TOP My old Mitsubishi L200 ute. A thirsty beast of a vehicle but I could load all manner of trees, deer or trapping gear on the long tray, while Moss and I bounced along on sheepskin rugs in the front.

BOTTOM Spending time in the garden with Sacha's nephew and niece was a real positive for me when not much else was.

the one place I could go and just be me. For the first time in my life, as I sat watching a beautiful pastel sunrise top through the trees, I just felt nothing. I felt a total disconnection to myself, to my work and the world.

Everything I'd worked for in life seemed to be slipping away, and I didn't know how to stop it. I'd been told when I started in the bush that they needed good keen men and if I worked hard, that in return I'd get a steady job and a decent life. Now, DOC was tendering most jobs out for contract, an insecure employment arrangement which didn't offer enough to make ends meet or even offer holiday pay, let alone the free house that was once part of the package for DOC's field staff. Jobs were becoming more specialised and I was being boxed into being a 'killer', which was all hard graft and very little thanks. I had been raised on the stories of the Forest Service, the Wildlife Service and deer cullers — the generalist bushmen with a finger in every pie.

That was the life I'd pursued and now due to DOC's new model it seemed they had little use for a bushman like me. Like an injured football player, I felt I'd been relegated to the sideline, to the minor leagues. The pride I felt for my work as a bushman had been stripped away and I just felt ashamed that I wasn't good enough for conservation anymore.

Usually the bush was the one place I could go and just be me. For the first time in my life, as I sat watching a beautiful pastel sunrise top through the trees, I just felt nothing. I felt a total disconnection to myself, to my work and the world.

That morning in the bush, the penny dropped like a sling-load of traps from under a chopper and I realised I was depressed. It dawned on me that somehow, in the back recesses of my exhausted brain, I'd subconsciously gone bush with the potential option of ending it all. That thought really scared me, but at the same time I still felt nothing. Nothing good anyway. I didn't much care about how my family would take it; I rationalised they'd be better off without me. Same for Sacha; I'd be freeing her up to get on with her life. But as Moss the dog looked up at me, I just couldn't bring myself to put her through this — a confused dog left in the bush by herself. So I didn't.

But the stark reality of the situation was that everything I'd put down to a bad spell wasn't going away in a hurry and I needed help. I sat there with that dead deer, the creek running red with its blood, and just cried. I cried for me and the hopelessness I felt. I'd come from having an awesome career and being good at what I did to failing dismally at turning a project around. I cried for the way I had distanced myself from Sacha and my family, and the arguments I had caused. And I cried with gratitude for the unconditional love of my dog and the bush. Somehow the bush had reminded me that I wasn't a total failure — I could still shoot a deer, I was still a provider. I still had something to offer the world and just maybe I knew a few things that others didn't that the world still needed.

A walk that had started with the possibility of ending it all had instead ended with me crying into the fur of a damp dog, knowing how unfair it would be to leave her stranded in the bush alone after she had just done a stellar job finding a deer. She didn't have to do that; she didn't even like the cold water of the creek or the slippery rocks in the morning. She was just there to give me a hand and if I was up for a walk she was going to be there, right beside me all the way.

All of the love from my girlfriend, my family and my friends came with an expectation that things would come right in the end, and for me that felt like a pressure I couldn't live up to. I didn't know whether things would come right.

But with Moss it was different. She was just there, in the moment, because it was her role as dog to be there. My role was to drive the truck and shoot the deer. It was pretty simple. A relationship passed down to us through generations of dogs and humans.

So that's what we did that day. The deer went on my back, Moss proudly paraded up the creek in front of me, pointing at everything she came into contact with including butterflies, sheep and poop, like the great indicator dog she was, and we loaded our kill onto the back of the ute. With the heater on full blast, Moss then curled up on her sheepskin rug in the front seat with her head on my lap and fell asleep as I drove us home.

In truth, that wasn't the end of depression for me. It was a long, hard road to recovery but that day I made a decision to work my way out of it rather than end it. I dabbled with work for a while, even managing to go two or three times a week. But the biggest part of the battle was admitting to Sacha and my family that I was struggling. They were struggling too, struggling with me struggling. I had been acting like an arsehole, defensive, angry, cruel with my words. What's more, my parents also had my sister living with them, and she was even more depressed than me. I felt like if I admitted my depression

ABOVE When things got tough I would often find solace in the words of Barry Crump. An author that battled his own demons but a great writer nonetheless.

it would just send my folks over the edge. But something had to change.

Then Sacha in her wisdom suggested quitting work, since that was what had got me down in the first place. She'd looked into a one-year teacher-training course that I could do from home and maybe that would give me the space I needed to come right. Sacha usually knew what I needed in my life, so I trusted she could see a path through this and signed up.

Over the next few months I studied when I felt up to it. I grew food in our garden when I needed a break and hunted with my mates when I needed to escape. I didn't have to see anyone if I didn't want to and although the black dog still firmly had its teeth sunk deep into my brain, the release of pressure from work meant I could be nicer to those around me. With the support of my family I also met a pretty incredible counsellor who helped me make a plan to climb out of the deep dark hole I was experiencing. I wasn't into medication — I never even took Panadol, preferring to feel the pain and deal with it than dull it behind a pill. Antidepressants were off the table for me at the time, though in retrospect they could have helped. My lack of feelings at the time allowed me to be really black and white about things. Each week felt a little easier, with time in the garden, counselling and study starting to bring me out of the fog. Slowly I started to feel again, started to interact with people and started to hunt. We had some brilliant hunts while I was studying; just about every time we went to Stanfield Hut.

Each week felt a little easier, with time in the garden, counselling and study starting to bring me out of the fog. Slowly I started to feel again, started to interact with people and started to hunt. We had some brilliant hunts while I was studying; just about every time we went to Stanfield Hut.

And that's how it was for me. Stanfield Hut helped me hold the tattered shreds of my life together for a while. Every morning was a battle, every social interaction awkward and difficult. Study was a drag but brought in a student allowance that paid the rent, and my relationship had turned into more of a friendship than anything romantic.

For a while now Sacha and I had been passing like ships in the night. I'd started to be able to sleep, and I was eating and exercising again, but the rift my depression had caused in our relationship was huge. I'd also lost my sex drive. We really cared about each other, and we cared about each other's families, but after a while Sacha just woke up one morning and said, 'We aren't in love anymore, are we? I don't think I can do this.'

Sadly, she was right. I mumbled a half-hearted 'Do you think it's fixable?'

I received a flat 'No' in reply, which I knew in myself to be true.

It wasn't emotional. It wasn't difficult. It was just a factual assessment of the situation. Sacha and I had known each other for six years. We'd grown with each other and been each other's safe space for a good chunk of our lives, and now it was going to end. We needed a plan.

The plan took about three minutes to come up with. Sacha would keep the flat and hold on to Moss the dog for now. I'd take the station wagon and move to Gisborne. For us to both be in Hawke's Bay would be torture; neither of us wanted to witness the next stage of each other's lives first-hand, and to be honest, if we were to pull off a break-up we needed to have distance. The familiar comfort of each other's arms would be all too enticing in the lonely months to follow. We'd been down this track more times than one but this time it felt different. It was final.

For our families, however, the turmoils of the last six years and the on-again off-again nature of our relationship had made them a little gun-shy about what a break-up might mean. They figured we'd be back together in a matter of months and life would carry on as normal. But that was not to be the case. Aside from a number of lustful moments when I'd return home from a day's work to my Gisborne flat to find a mischievous Sacha in my bed or the odd cup of tea catch-up when we slipped while hugging and stumbled into bed, things went pretty much to plan. We kept our distance and stayed good friends as we supported each other in our new lives and, as time went on, into our next relationships.

Sacha, thank you for helping me through this bloody difficult time in my life. I know I was a proper arsehole and made you feel like crap a lot of the time. You are a pretty incredible human. As much as we had some amazing times in our relationship, I'm really proud of how we managed to part ways. It fills me with great happiness to see you raising your daughter and living an awesome life.

To anyone suffering from depression, or even thinking that they aren't coping, please hear that tapping out isn't an option. I know it feels like the only viable path, but the gap you leave behind will be massive. If you decide to succumb to the hurt and the dull, aching non-feeling of depression, it doesn't just end your life. It ends the lives of those around you. This too shall pass. There's a road out. It won't be easy. Chances are you will be visited again by the black dog. But each time you'll build more skills and resilience.

For me, being able to focus on the small things I didn't hate (they didn't feel good at the time but they were a welcome respite from feeling bad) like gardening, patting the dog or being in the bush got me through. The more time I spent in these places, the more I could cope. Getting some exercise helped me to sleep better and made me hungry, and in time, like a dead leg, feeling came back into my life and I was able to find happiness again. When you're dealing with loved ones trying to help, try to replace saying 'I'm sorry' with 'Thank you'. It's positive and keeps their support around you.

To my family and friends, I apologise for being vacant, angry and defensive. The very fact that you wanted to help put too much pressure on me. Your being invested in my wellbeing was too much for me to cope with. I didn't feel like I could get better. I just felt like I'd let you down. My career had gone to tatters, my relationship was on the rocks. Everything I felt like I was had been questioned.

Thank you for being there and thank you for forgiving me.

13. THE GREATEST LITTLE CONSERVATION PROJECT IN THE WORLD

Months after returning to the East Coast, the place I was raised, I was still trying to claw my way out from under the dark fog of depression. I was studying, surfing a little and I even picked up a part-time job at a local winery cleaning the vats. I was still figuring out who I was post-Sacha, building myself up using things that felt okay to find little glimmers of joy.

Being home once more and living just a stone's throw from the Hamanatua Stream and the Lockwood house I'd grown up in had given me a sense of belonging that I held on to with white knuckles. Everywhere I went there was family and memories. I had uncles, aunties, cousins and no end of family friends nearby. Instead of feeling the pressure of expectation, I felt at home.

These memories of things I enjoyed as a kid led me to seek out the rivers of my youth. The places Dad and Poppa had taken me to teach me who I was. Maybe now was as good a time as any to be reminded of that.

I'd sold the L200 ute before moving north; it ran on unleaded 95 and my student allowance simply couldn't foot that bill. Instead the white Corolla station wagon would have to clamber its way up the potholed forest roads to the Waioeka, loaded up with fishing rods, a rifle and all manner of gear. There was no excuse not to have an adventure and before long I was heading back across a familiar swing bridge on my way to Koranga Forks Hut.

The Waioeka was much how I remembered it: plenty of rainbow trout in the rivers, lots of skinny deer in the bush and the odd pig kicking around in the scrub. There were just two things that were missing.

Somewhere in the recesses of my mind I remembered seeing whio bobbing their way down the mountain streams in front of us as we fished. That's how we knew whether the fishing would be good in a stretch of river. If the whio were feeding, that meant the river was loaded with insect life, and a pool loaded with insect life was a likely home for trout. But the ducks, whose colouring flirts between grey and blue, were nowhere to be seen.

I also remembered being able to hear kiwi calling at night as I lay in my bunk as a kid, tired from the day's adventures. But now there was silence, save for the friendly call of the ruru. Something was off, and over the next few months I bounced the idea that our whio and kiwi were missing off my uncles, Dad and a few hunting mates. The consensus was that they'd been gone for a while and it was a real shame nobody had done something about it.

Well, that was it. Why hadn't DOC protected our birds in my absence? I'd been gone for some time now, sixteen years in fact, looking after the birds in somebody else's mountains but had anyone been looking after the birds in mine? So I visited the local DOC office. Sure enough, the same '-itis' that had affected DOC Fiordland had reached DOC Gisborne also. It appeared they simply didn't have the financial resources to look after the wildlife across the entire region; it looked to me like they barely had enough to keep the tracks and huts open and the whio and kiwi of the Waioeka weren't a priority.

Next I visited the council to ask the same questions, but I got the same answers. The Waioeka wasn't a priority for anyone but me, my family and my hunting mates.

Disappointed, I called up Uncle Kerry, to complain about the injustice of the situation. Kerry had spent much of his twenties wandering the hills of the Waioeka with a dog named Pig. In his wise and gentle way, he reminded me that those who spend time in the bush feel connected to it and feel like they want to look after it.

The penny dropped . . . Maybe it was up to us! I mean, we had the skills. My hunting mate Geoff and I had both been doing conservation work and between us we knew a whole lot about bringing back threatened species. Our hunting and fishing mates had all the bush skills to make a project happen in the backcountry. Someone had to bring back the whio and kiwi of the Waioeka. We had no idea how we were going to pay for it all, but someone had to do it.

So back to the DOC office I went. 'Hey team, if I wanted to establish a community conservation project on DOC land, how would I do it?' Turns out all I needed was a community group agreement and to be able to generate our own funding, and away we'd go. It didn't sound too difficult to me. DOC

ABOVE It felt really good to be looking after the rivers and bush that I had learned to fish and hunt in as a kid. © Cam Henderson, *Hunters Journal*

TOP One of our volunteers, Alan Barry Robinson, warming himself by the fire after a big day's trapping.

BOTTOM Uncle Kerry has had my back since day dot. So, when it came to starting a conservation project in the Waioeka, a place he had hunted since the 70s, he was in boots and all.

also had one really critical piece of information — their report showing there were four pairs of whio left in the area we were looking to trap. They reckoned the whio hadn't bred properly for ten years but the report showed where their home ranges were and gave us a pretty good indication of where we should focus our efforts.

> It always feels funny to me speaking about other people's taonga. I feel like my whānau have walked these hills and rivers just about more than anyone. We have eaten from the whenua, we know each kink in the river, each pool and each tree we pass. But regardless of the depth of connection I am not mana whenua to Mātāwai and the Waioeka.

In a flap of importance and enthusiasm, off I set to establish a conservation project. I had seen community-led projects in action in Fiordland and Wellington. Quite a few had popped up across the country but word hadn't quite reached the back eddies of the East Coast that we could do our own conservation work.

Hunters are one of the most useful tools we have in New Zealand when it comes to sighting rare and at-risk species. As hunters we are slowly taking responsibility for the areas we hunt, and many hunters are incorporating predator control into our range of activities. We are the people with boots on the ground, so if we see something out of the ordinary, it's on us to let someone know. Entire species that we assumed were extinct have come back from the brink after hunters spotted them in a far-off place.

What's more, there were a few glistening examples of what hunter-led conservation might look like. I had helped with the Fiordland Wapiti Foundation's whio conservation project when I was living there in 2015, and I'd helped establish the hugely successful Sika Foundation's whio project in the Kaimanawa Forest in 2017. Both those projects focused on increasing whio populations in their regions, but they were led by trophy hunters. For our project, which we named the Eastern Whio Link, our relationship with the bush was through kai rather than trophies. I saw an absolute niche in the conservation world for a project that held bush knowledge and mātauranga as its core values, things our hunters and fishers knew well. Mahinga kai and conservation fit perfectly together as both are focused on abundance. If your conservation model is the same as mine, abundance means achieving a sustainable harvest of our native species.

I also visited the local marae and awkwardly stood and spoke about the decline of whio in the area and how we wanted to do something about bringing them back. It always feels funny to me speaking about other people's taonga. I feel like my whānau have walked these hills and rivers just about more than anyone. We have eaten from the whenua, we know each kink in the river, each pool and each tree we pass. But regardless of the depth of connection I am not mana whenua to Mātāwai and the Waioeka. I always feel embarrassed that it could be seen as not my place to be caring for these awa. But I do. They have fed our whānau for generations. That and the lack of reo I hold always makes speaking at the marae a daunting experience.

But no matter how nervous I was, no matter my lack of reo Māori, my intent must have shown through. They knew we weren't turning up asking for sign-off on a preconceived plan; we were turning up wanting to create something together for the taiao and the community. Everyone in the room was on board — hunters and tangata whenua agreed that we didn't quite know how to achieve our goal but we were really happy to learn alongside each other to get there.

For the next couple of weeks, between lectures and work, I phoned people — hunters, fishers, conservation connections and so on — until finally I got a lead that could help. A friend knew of 250 traps sitting in a workshop that weren't being used. A couple of cheeky phone calls later and a few pallet-loads of free traps arrived on my doorstep. We were almost in business.

These were super-lightweight, gas-powered traps that could kill 24 animals before needing to be reset. I had run a scientific trial in Fiordland using them a few years earlier where we had absolutely cleaned up the local stoat population. I was over the moon with excitement. This was exactly what we needed for our project as the small rabble of hunters I had managed to wrangle together were happy to donate two weekends a year to the project but anymore than that might prove to be a stretch.

Now we needed some money. The lures and the gas it took to run these fancy traps weren't cheap and it was looking like it might cost us around $5000 a year to keep them operational. A friend with a clothing company called Game Gear was prepared to front the first $2500 to see if we could get the project off the ground, and we would go from there.

TOP Grant Cowley, Joel Dickson and myself that first freezing winter. Joel owned the outdoor brand Game Gear and was our first big sponsor for the Eastern Whio Link.

BOTTOM Geoff Mclaughlan, a good mate and cofounder of Eastern Whio Link. Nothing quite beats a day of fishing, hunting and checking traps along the beautiful rivers of the Waioeka.

So, in the winter of 2019 we took to the bush. Uncle Kerry, my mate Joel, his mate Grant and me in one direction, and Geoff and a bow hunter called Nigel in the other direction. It was hard graft. The rivers were icy cold and we had to keep stopping to build fires by the side of the river to warm up our legs and the pig dogs. Whoever's idea it had been to walk up these rivers in winter (it was mine) hadn't done their homework. It was a lesson we wouldn't repeat in a hurry.

But we got it done. In the end I had to carry my old, wet dog Bonnie across my shoulders back to the hut and for once in her life she was invited inside to sit by the fire to warm up. Partway through the afternoon she'd given up the ghost and just stopped on the opposite bank one river crossing. She was beat. Us would-be trappers weren't much better, but we now had a 25-kilometre trapping project to our names just ahead of the whio breeding season.

In an effort to bring in more funding I decided we needed to go on a media rampage. We wrote stories for the hunting magazines and the local paper, did a few interviews with Jesse Mulligan on National Radio, wrote notes in all the hut books and even started a social-media platform. We'd come up with the name 'Eastern Whio Link' as our vision was to link whio genetics from the thriving population in Te Urewera right up to the East Cape. Te Urewera, Waioeka and Raukūmara were the areas where we liked to fish and hunt, so it just kind of made sense.

All of a sudden we had a surge of volunteer interest. Schools wanted to send their kids into the bush with us to learn about conservation, folks wanted to come down from Auckland to reconnect with the bush, and we even had one hunter fly his private plane up from the South Island to volunteer on the project. There was no shortage of volunteer trappers on Eastern Whio Link that first year, but we still had no money to run the project.

Eventually, we carved out a point of difference in the conservation world by talking about the link between mahinga kai and conservation. We spoke about how kōhia fruit can be used as detector cards to measure rat impact, how tawa kernels can be used to measure possum impact, how trout condition and abundance are indicators of good whio habitat and how we can use kareao and pikopiko browse to measure the impact deer are having on the ecosystems — all stuff us hunters and fishers know but don't really talk about. We started to see some financial support coming in. Opotiki Helicopters offered us free helicopter time, Crispi Boots came on board to support the project and good old Uncle Kerry put his money where his mouth was and made a pretty incredible donation after selling his dairy herd.

What's more, we had Dog & Gun sending free coffee for the volunteers and Radix Nutrition sending us dehydrated meals. Somewhere in the mix I'd ended up with a decent job working for Goodnature Traps as a technical expert (whatever that meant) and was now in the position to buy us woollen bushman T-shirts with our logo embroidered in yellow on the front. It gave us a great sense of pride to be able to send our volunteers into the bush with a bundle of food and coffee, and when they returned from checking their traps, usually with a deer in their packs or a brace of trout swinging from a cord at their hips, we'd greet them with a black-and-yellow woollen top as a thank you and a welcome to the team of Eastern Whio Link trappers.

> Whoever's idea it had been to walk up these rivers in winter (it was mine) hadn't done their homework. It was a lesson we wouldn't repeat in a hurry.

That year the ducks did us proud. We killed so many stoats with our A24 traps that the team could have almost made a hat out of them. That might not sound like much, but an individual stoat does so much damage that if we catch ten to twenty stoats a year, we can almost entirely avoid stoat predation on whio. The result was twenty fluffy wee whio chicks fledged across the project, with each pair achieving an even five fledglings.

They reckon whio conservation is a bit like painting by numbers. Most other species need huge landscape projects across rugged terrain, but for whio a single line of traps up a river at 100-metre spacing does a great job at controlling stoats to a level that the ducks can breed. But we were so proud.

The second year, some of the kids who had visited with their schools were now fully-fledged trappers, and we were throwing them in helicopters with an older hunter as a guide and putting them into some incredible backcountry hunting and fishing. The only requirement was that they checked a few traps as they hunted and the whio kept breeding.

Year two saw 26 fledged chicks and we started to make the news in the international hunting sector. This ragtag group of bushmen who ate from the land and just wanted to look after the ecosystems that looked after us was of interest to folks for some reason. People from the cities were keen to get back to a connected way of living and they wanted to learn a trendy thing called

TOP The way the kahikatea protrude through blankets of mist is a truly stunning Waioeka vista.

BOTTOM In the first four years we fledged over 80 whio chicks. Not bad for a rabble of hunting mates.

'foraging' from people who knew plants. Hunters around the world wanted to better understand their ecosystems and how they could look after the areas they hunted. Eastern Whio Link was soon becoming a university and the vision of a small crew of mates checking traps in the bush was quickly slipping through our fingers, replaced by managing people, sponsors and media requests.

Now it wasn't just the conservation we were interested in. We had somehow done a good enough job of the trapping for the whio to breed successfully and now these little ducks were popping up all across the Waioeka and bobbing down the rapids in front of us as we fished again. The community's interest made us want to use the conservation project as a vehicle for social change. Then we met an incredible woman called Tui Keenan.

> This ragtag group of bushmen who ate from the land and just wanted to look after the ecosystems that looked after us was of interest to folks for some reason.

Tui had had her own TV show, *Hunting with Tui*, which documented her journey into hunting and how it had impacted her life. She was now working at a local school where 70 per cent of kids came from a household where Mum or Nanna were working really hard to put food on the table and Dad often wasn't in the picture. Tui was keen to run parenting courses through the Eastern Whio Link project, including taking women and kids into the bush. We'd seen kids really benefit from our education programmes, especially those who learnt better outside the classroom, so we worked with Tui to deliver her courses.

Sometimes folks would turn up in jandals, with ten-dollar Warehouse sleeping bags and shopping bags instead of packs. We removed those obstacles by building a gear library where anyone who was new to the bush could borrow raincoats, tents, cookers, boots and other basic kit. If a volunteer showed commitment and was keen to come on board in a more permanent capacity, we would work with our newfound sponsors to help them buy the necessary gear at a discounted rate. The impact we were seeing in people's lives was huge, and the project developed into something that benefitted the community as well as conservation.

Unfortunately after two years, Covid-19 brought our community programmes to a screeching halt and we weren't allowed into the bush to check our traps. We were more than a little concerned for the whio and that year's breeding success definitely showed the impact of our people not being present in the landscape, with just sixteen whio chicks fledging in 2022. But with every cloud comes a silver lining: the good folks in government saw fit to accept our application to the Jobs for Nature fund to employ people whose jobs had been impacted by Covid-19 as trappers. What a silver lining that turned out to be.

We could now employ the highly practical Geoff, my good hunting mate and cofounder of Eastern Whio Link, as a project manager and a couple of our other volunteers as trappers. What's more, we were given a large enough budget to service our existing network and expand the project to include 5000 hectares of kiwi habitat as well. Our vision of whio bobbing down the streams as we fished and hearing kiwi calling as we lay in our bunks at night was coming to fruition.

Having a project manager in place meant I could step back into the volunteer coordination and storytelling space and Geoff could manage the day-to-day running of the traps. Other leaders began to emerge from our now hundred-strong team of volunteers. Sam Henderson put her hand up to help us form a trust as a legal entity so we could more easily handle our finances; Tom, an ex-bank manager, put his hand up to be our treasurer; and Donovan, a graphic designer, came on board to manage the brand. Eastern Whio Link was slowly becoming official.

As it turned out, being a charitable trust was the missing link for sponsors. They could now donate money to us directly and receive a tax credit for the donation. We started to receive funds from hunting advocacy groups such as Blood Origins, big corporates like Westpac and even the District Council. We were able to purchase quad bikes and a side-by-side vehicle so our trappers no longer had to walk everywhere, and far out it made a difference to how far we had to carry hunted deer.

Now the Eastern Whio Link is in its fourth breeding season. We have a new project manager and crew of trappers in place, all of whom have come through the project as volunteers. Geoff and I, along with the rest of the trustees, are starting to see a little bit more balance in our lives, a few more hunting trips, a few more fish puffing away in the smoker. Others are stepping up to the plate to lead volunteer weekends and education programmes.

TOP The three stickers of credibility when you park at a back country road end in Waioeka. Be sure to have your 'Kiwi Aversion Trained Dogs', 'Trout Country is Whio Country' and your Eastern Whio Link 'supporters' sticker'.

BOTTOM There's something about these majestic wee warriors of the waterways that is really endearing. Each one has its own personality and they are all surprisingly more fierce than they look.

There are even people keen on starting a second Eastern Whio Link project further up the coast.

As far as I'm concerned we've come a long way since we first started the project with those four remaining pairs of ducks, and our crew of six hunters wading through icy rivers. We've successfully achieved our vision of bringing whio back to the rivers and we're even starting to hear the odd kiwi calling at night. But what makes me most proud is how many people now care about the Waioeka, the way that Dad and Poppa instilled that care in me. Now there's a whole community, generations deep, that won't let the whio or kiwi disappear anytime soon. In a few short years we were able to bring the whio population back to a level where my kids can experience the same normal I had as a kid.

We've successfully achieved our vision of bringing whio back to the rivers and we're even starting to hear the odd kiwi calling at night.

In a way, establishing the Eastern Whio Link allowed me to emerge from what was a pretty tough period of my life, a period where depression and a sense of failure in my career had been eating away at me. By pouring my creative energy into a project that was more than just conservation, but also a vehicle for community change and in a place that valued our model of working with te taiao, I was able to reinvent myself in my own eyes. I felt a sense of purpose and belonging and I felt valued within the community I had come from. I felt a sense of coming home to who I was, as I walked the rivers I was raised in carrying traps, catching fish and hunting deer.

As they say, ka ora te ngahere, ka ora te tangata. When the ngahere thrives, we thrive as people.

ABOVE I reckon we mould to the environments around us. We can't help but slow down and be happy if we spend enough time in the bush. It's really good for us. That's what Eastern Whio Link is all about, looking after those environments that look after us. © Strike Photography

I WAS RAISED AMONGST THE WAVES

I was raised
Amongst the waves
Like any other man.

I'll get my kicks
And get 'er done
Like any other man.

But there is one girl
Who gives me home
Like only one girl can.

And when I'm home
She lets me know
I am indeed her man.

14. A DATE LIKE NO OTHER

Within the first month of meeting the future mother of my children, I was heading away hunting for the weekend and asked if she wanted to come along. Having been raised on the West Coast and then having lived in Christchurch, Roimata hadn't been exposed to activities like hunting and backcountry adventures. She thought it sounded like an exciting idea.

The trip started off alright, until five minutes into our trek. We were descending a rather steep hill to the river when she ended up coming unstuck in a very dramatic manner. It hadn't occurred to me that some folk have never carried a pack on uneven ground and that the combination of an unusual weight, coupled with uneven footing, might result in a less-than-dignified tumble. After a short break to compose ourselves, and me pointing out a hind and yearling feeding on a distant clearing, we were back on track for our 'romantic' weekend away.

Roi will kill me for sharing this with you: we'd only recently met one another, on none other than the esteemed dating app Tinder.

That's right. The love of my life, my pride and joy and the mother of my kids came into my life as a result of two swipes right on a phone screen. She was a glistening star in the otherwise slightly grim world of Tinder, a quiet-looking artist that somehow, touch wood, I wasn't related to.

It was a stunning November day, blue sky, white sandy beach, warm water. We met at the beach just a stone's throw from where I'd grown up. I sat nervously in my white Corolla station wagon with a mattress in the back (not for that reason, you dirty buggers, it was a first date). My palms were sweating and I was wondering if she would even show up.

Then into the car park rolls a weird little silver Toyota Opa (still not a cool car whichever way you look at it) and out steps this tall (like Silver Ferns-netball tall), dark-haired, slender 'woman of substance', as my grandmother

ABOVE They say it's a hard road finding the perfect woman, but in my books Roi comes pretty close. © Strike Photography

likes to call her. Slightly detracting from her poise and class was her East Coast fashion sense. I'm not sure who turns up to a first date in baggy basketball shorts and an oversized black Rasta singlet but that's what she had chosen. Maybe it was an artist thing? What did capture my attention was the chic way the bagginess of the basketball singlet showed not too much but just enough of the very stylish, forest-green, lacy bralette she had on underneath.

To say Roimata was a catch was an understatement. We managed to go for a long walk where she said very little and I chewed her ear off at a million miles an hour. We both deleted our Tinder accounts and I managed to talk her into coming to a blues night at a local bar later that evening.

Apparently Roi showed up and then left again, texting to say she couldn't find me. I was right up the front with one of my loud, boozy mates so she can't have looked too hard. (He's one of Roi's cousins, actually. Told you Gizzy is a small place.) But we managed to find one another and in the end Roi avoided the long drive home to her flat by deciding to move in with me that night. Two kids later, she still hasn't left. I still don't know how a classy woman from Christchurch sees past a mattress on the floor of a beach shack full of sand that the wind's blown through the cracks in the walls, but there you go. I guess every dog does have its day.

But back to our romantic getaway. Once we entered the river we needed to have a quick conversation about the fact that there was no actual track. This was a minor detail I had apparently managed not to communicate. Pointing out that the river was quite navigable, with very few sections over waist-deep, was not met with enthusiasm. However, the vehicle was back at the top of a steep hill and the river seemed like the more appealing option, so on we went.

After a few bends in the river, we came across cow sign — I mean serious amounts of pugging and steaming cow patties covering the otherwise beautiful river terraces. I'd heard wild cattle inhabited the area seasonally but I'd never seen any myself. Wild cattle aren't common around the country; this herd originated from escaped animals from the back of farms and had managed to establish large breeding populations in the Raukūmara. Strong enough to push over young trees in search of food and heavy enough to churn up the forest floor, resulting in large-scale erosion, they do incredible damage to vegetation in the valley floors. Areas with wild cattle are instantly recognisable by the lack of undergrowth and the pugged-up soil.

More on instinct than anything, I dropped to the ground as we emerged

TOP Roimata outside the old Ruatahanga Hut, one of the places you could still hunt wild cattle, red deer and catch huge rainbow trout all in one day.

BOTTOM What's not to like when she is walking towards you in a sleeping bag? We had known each other less than a month and this adventure was either going to make or break us.

from the thick cover, with Roi following suit. Ahead of us on the other side of the river was a mob of about ten cattle bedded down on a grassy terrace in the sun. We set up a nice little rest on my pack, tucked in beside a mānuka sapling, and glassed our options. The trophy hunter in me came out as I searched fruitlessly for a bull, then a cow with horns. I was later to learn that bulls often stay distant to the main herd and that the cattle in the Raukūmara were mostly polled.

> I had a vision of me stuffing up the shot and a wounded cattle beast charging across the river, spray flying everywhere, and mowing us over. Roi's dad would kill me if something ever happened to his much-loved youngest daughter.

I hesitantly offered Roi a shooting opportunity, which she flatly turned down. Hugely relieved but also pretty nervous, I settled in to select an animal. Stories of wounded cattle charging hunters and dogs, and people being stampeded by angry beasts, raced through my mind. I had a vision of me stuffing up the shot and a wounded cattle beast charging across the river, spray flying everywhere, and mowing us over. Roi's dad would kill me if something ever happened to his much-loved youngest daughter.

On the other hand, an opportunity like this does not occur often, and as the saying goes, you don't look a gift horse in the mouth. The animals were all bedded down, the wind was in our favour, but one young cow kept looking our way, a sure sign that they'd soon be on to us. She seemed in good nick compared to the others, many of which I guessed were older animals and looked a little skinny. I was keen to get the best eating animal we could find. After a while the young cow must have seen or heard us and stood up broadside, looking in our direction.

It was the opportunity I'd been waiting for. I knew shot placement was going to be key and I wasn't sure how quickly an organ-shot cow would go down, so I chose a bead on the lower neck. CRACK, the .308 spoke. Cattle disappeared in all directions and for a few seconds the place sounded like we were trying to load a stock truck, with bellowing and thundering hooves adding to the chaos. As things settled, I saw my cow (which Roi later affectionately named 'Daisy') lying on the ground. A quick head shot finished what we'd started as the reality of our situation sunk in.

I'd shot my first wild cattle beast, we were all still in one piece, Roi's dad wasn't going to kill me, and we still had plenty of daylight for the butchering. On the other hand, we were still an hour from the hut and a long hard slog from the truck down a bouldery river and up a huge hill. To top it all off, we had an immense amount of meat to pack out as well as our already generous packs of gear.

We planned to butcher the animal on site, bone out the two back legs, and take the back steaks. We'd then hang the meat in a shady spot and continue up to the hut to have our 'romantic' weekend away. On our return we'd load the meat into our hopefully lighter packs, and carry it all out.

Butchering was going to be a big job and as I started skinning the cow, Roi stood about five metres back. It became apparent that I wasn't going to get a whole lot of help; seeing her first animal killed was going to take some processing for Roi. I stopped, took a step back, and had a yarn about Daisy. We talked about how she was a beautiful animal, about how she'd lived an amazing life out in the bush, and how by harvesting her we were not only going to feed ourselves and our families but the environmental benefits of not having her in the ecosystem were significant. Roi was keen to make a handbag from the skin but I knew the weight of green cowhide. It is heavy and we would have enough of a carry with the meat.

After talking this out and allowing time between seeing Daisy shot and cutting her up, Roi was happy to lend a hand with butchering. She was fascinated to see the different layers of skin, fat and muscle. She had to hold up the still twitching back steak while I cut it out and we talked about nerves and muscle groups. Roi stated that a back steak looks just like a steak from the supermarket, but it was strange seeing it come straight off the animal. It was a great moment, and I was proud as punch to be able to create such important shared memories and understandings as a couple.

We hung the meat, made sure it was fly proof, and carried on up to the hut. It rained all night but with candles, a meal cooked over the fire and a little rum, it did make for a rather romantic setting. However, in the morning it was obvious the river was on the rise and if we hoped to get out, now was our opportunity, so we packed up fast. Once the rivers come up on the East Coast it can be weeks before they subside again.

After reaching the meat stash, I loaded a back leg into Roi's pack and a back leg and back steaks into mine. A back leg may not sound like much, but the back leg of a cattle beast is huge and weighs a tonne. Add this to

ABOVE The wild cow Roimata affectionately named 'Daisy'. There aren't many places you can still hunt wild cattle in Aotearoa but the East Coast is one.

your overnight kit and that is an incredibly heavy pack for anyone, let alone someone who isn't used to hauling out loads.

On seeing Roi struggle in the first river crossing, we made a deal. There would be no tears until we reached the hill at the end. She stoically agreed and did an incredible job through the river crossings. The hill was a different story, however. We climbed out of the river in the dark, both exhausted, hungry, and pulling on our last stores of energy. It had taken us five hours so far, with lots of stops.

I pulled out a block of chocolate I had hidden for this exact moment and we took a ten-minute spell. Looking upward, we could see the truck gleaming white in the distance, but from where we were, it seemed like an impossible task. The hill was steep and long, but we somehow mustered the energy to get going again.

I won't write in detail about the climb to the truck other than to note that:

- There were tears.
- My ongoing positive attitude and encouragement can at times be considered 'patronising' and 'not helpful'.
- An agreement was made that we would never shoot a cow so far from the truck again.

All in all, we made the seven-hour carry with 40-kilogram packs. I decided right there and then that Roi was a keeper and had more stamina than most of my hunting mates. We got engaged a couple of months later and she signed up for a ten-day roar trip in the Southern Alps. She now names every animal we shoot together — it's kind of strange, but it does add a personal touch when pulling meat from the freezer.

15. HUNTING HAAST: THE MISSED DEER

When I first met Roimata I knew she had a bit of go in her. I'd already managed to corrupt her with my bushman lifestyle by taking her on a wild cattle hunt, and asking her to spend seven hours carrying half of it out to the truck. She hadn't left me yet and things were getting serious, so I thought I'd try her out on a roar trip to see if she could really cut the mustard as a bushman's wife . . .

Plans were made for a trip to Haast, a place where I'd guided a mate into a cracker stag a few years prior. We would drive almost the entire length of the country to chase roaring reds in one of New Zealand's most remote and rugged environments. The helicopter could take three people and gear, so we made a quick phone call to Uncle Kirk to see if he was keen. Without needing much convincing, he was in.

Uncle Kirk is easily my favourite hunting companion ever. He's super easy-going and would give you the shirt off his back in a snowstorm. He reliably pulls the trigger when he needs to and feels terrible about taking the shot even when it's his turn, almost like he's depriving you of something. He turns up with heaps of tucker and isn't into drinking much booze on the hill. These are all qualities I admire in a hunting companion and that's the reason Kirk is top of the phone list for every mission.

A couple of things worth noting about hunting with Kirk. Firstly, you need to be up early, much earlier than you otherwise would. He's a bit like your first truck; he takes a little while to get going on a cold morning but once he's warmed up, he'll go all day and coffee definitely helps. Secondly, he uses my grandfather's old rifle so any time I hunt with him I feel connected to the man who introduced me to hunting in the first place.

As April rolled around, we found ourselves at a road end on a sunny morning in Haast waiting on the helicopter we'd booked to ferry us up to our

TOP How Roimata manages to still look stylish on day six of a trip, I have no idea.

BOTTOM LEFT Kirk's bush stag. Good hunting mates are hard to come by but Kirk is one of the best.

BOTTOM RIGHT It wasn't all blue skies and we were beyond happy when we greeted the helicopter sodden and hungry on the last day.

ABOVE There's something about the cold open tops that is just invigorating. Maybe it's how far we can see or how exposed we are to the weather but there's a certain thrill to hunting in these remote environments.

desired camp spot. Already a couple of things hadn't gone to plan. Somehow Roi's boots had been left on the roof of the car as we had driven off the morning before, each of us pointing the finger at the other for this foolish mistake. We'd made a mercy dash to Wānaka for a new pair. To top it off, somehow between Wānaka and Haast, Roi's vape had also gone missing. With no general store in sight this was looking like a nicotine-free trip, which could be interesting. It was 11 a.m. . . . the agreed meeting time. But by 3 p.m. there was still no sign of a helicopter and the hills were starting to clag in with cloud.

Having paid our blood tax to the local sandfly population many times over, we were getting worried. Maybe the helicopter pilot had forgotten us? A quick drive to the nearest house and a rather abrupt phone conversation later, I was able to confirm that the pilot had gone hunting himself that morning and must have forgotten we were in his calendar. The confirmation phone call I'd made the night before obviously hadn't reached the pilot, but the office lady promised she would contact our pilot as soon as he flew back into reception and hopefully get us on the hill before the storm struck. Once again, we were left to swat sandflies and watch the clouds continue to envelop much of the mountains before us.

After some time, we heard the unmistakable sound of a Hughes 500 and soon we were hurtling through squalls of rain and hail, racing before the storm to a beautiful alpine tarn I had seen once before. Under any other weather conditions, that stunning vista would be our home for the next week. We hastily erected tents and flies and burrowed into surprisingly dry sleeping bags to wait out the worst of the rain.

After a tumultuous night, Tāwhirimātea finally blew himself out and we awoke to a crisp, clear, somewhat silent morning. From our vantage point we could see right out across Aotearoa's western ocean and to the east the Arawhata Valley. This was the type of country where legends were made. These tops were grazed by some of the early settlers, a breed of farmer who used to push their merino sheep up near-vertical faces from the valley floor below to the lush summertime grazing amongst the tussock on the tops. J.J. Nolan's grandfather had cut a sheep track up a more navigable ridge generations prior and having climbed it a few years earlier, I struggled to see how sheep could traverse such rugged country.

But that is where the big boys live. Stags don't get old hanging out in accessible places during the roar and I was keen to find the steepest, nastiest spur I could find this trip and hopefully the big boy living on it.

That morning I was eager to get away but quickly realised the team needed coffee and breakfast, so I set about making camp more comfortable. After the third cup of coffee, my companions looked like they might finally consider going for a walk and so seizing the opportunity we set off. We found ourselves meandering along a familiar ridge where I had got the wind wrong on a good stag a few years prior and roared intermittently, searching for some form of reply.

There were signs of early rubbing and scrapes but the wallows we came across were relatively unused. But it was the silence that finally got to us. My memories of this place told me that with every new spur there should be fresh eruptions of guttural moans. I expected to be dodging scrubby, testosterone-filled satellite stags while quietly moving in on the roars of the big boy. The hills should have been resounding with a complex array of sound. I should have been confused about which stag to home in on, listening to the personalities of their roars and trying to figure out who had the raspiest tone. It's not always the loudest or most worked up, just the deepest and fullest sound.

Sadly there was nothing but disappointment. We slowly reached the conclusion that we might have been a few weeks too early for the roar this year. Who knew whether it was the warmer weather or some other reason beyond our grasp. One thing was certain — this ridge was a lot less inspiring than the last time I'd been here.

Oh well, we were here now, and we figured there was no harm in trying so we continued on. After arriving at a promising wallow and letting out some rather non-committal moans, Roi and I were startled upright by the ear-piercing crack of my grandfather's rifle. Kirk had noticed something we hadn't. A young stag feeding slowly towards our moans had copped it, and rolling down the hill in front of us, there he was — and was he fat. All that beautiful summer condition confirmed our fears that yes, we were definitely too early for the roar. However, we were on the board and Kirk, true to his gentlemanly nature, was incredibly apologetic, having wanted to give me the first stag of the trip. But meat is meat and a stag in this good a condition was venison to take home, a win in my book.

After a disappointing morning, this was just the morale booster we needed to keep us motivated. That evening we were chipper with meat hanging in the tree, a happy trio making plans for the next day.

That night it rained, and it did not stop. It bucketed down for a solid 24 hours in the way that only happens in Haast. Those familiar with the area will know how heavy it can rain, like a swimming pool has been upturned on your tent. The wind flattened the fly against our sleeping bags, guy ropes ripped from tussock and pegs tore from sodden ground. For a full day we tried to read and sleep amongst damp sleeping bags and, with chocolate having recently replaced nicotine, we took turns running to a quickly dwindling snack pile to fuel Roi's cravings. Thankfully by morning the second storm of the trip had blown itself out.

> Stags don't get old hanging out in accessible places during the roar and I was keen to find the steepest, nastiest spur I could find this trip and hopefully the big boy living on it.

Again, we put our camp back to some form of order and set off in search of a public-land stag of the standard we knew this inhospitable country was capable of producing. Lunchtime saw us sunburnt and seeking shelter, a stark contrast to the day before. No roars had been heard and our glassing bore no fruit. Then, suddenly, Roi heard it — a subtle moan. I didn't believe her at first (always believe your women, team) but Kirk confirmed it. Far across the tussock tops in a small hollow were two stags of undetermined quality. They were some distance away but they were the first roaring animals we'd heard all trip, so the chase was on.

We made a plan to dip down out of sight from the animals, creep our way up a creek and hopefully pop up on a tussock mound close enough so that we could determine what we were looking at. All went to plan. We popped up where we said we would and spent some time glassing the stags in their little hollow.

One stag was a spiker, that was easy to determine. The other had less clear characteristics, with good solid tops and looking like it could be a ten- or twelve-pointer, possibly with smaller or non-existent bez tines. To me that was close to a wall hanger. I've always thought, based on aesthetics, a wide symmetrical ten or twelve is the lowest-qualifying cutoff for my wall.

I was new to tussock country, but the stags were well within shooting range based on the shots I'd taken on slips and clearings in the North Island.

TOP In between storms, Roi built us a lovely fire to warm our spirits if not our bodies.

BOTTOM A woman that can work dogs and sing is hard to come by, but one that isn't scared to carry out a deer or live in the bush with you is an absolute treasure.

As the animal was bedded down, I decided to find a rest and settle in for a shot. I must have been overthinking it at the time and from memory I'm sure I'd been watching a lot of mountain-goat hunting videos leading up to this trip, as I asked Kirk to take a bead on the animal for a backup shot in case I muffed my one.

The next part happened really fast. I asked Kirk if he was good. He said 'No'. I waited, the stag stood up, I asked if Kirk was good but again he said 'No'. The stag started to move off quickly, obviously aware something in its surroundings was not quite right. It stopped broadside for a second. I readjusted to a slightly awkward shooting position and then it struck, that inexcusable moment of greed. The unfounded glory that shooting a trophy stag would bring. Of making amends for missing out last time, for getting the wind wrong on a potential beauty, the jealousy of guiding my mate into the best public-land stag I'd ever seen and allowing him to take the shot. There was the drive to succeed and the notion that every good hunter needs a trophy on his wall.

I pulled the trigger despite knowing full well I didn't have the rest I needed and that the animal wasn't settled enough for me to take that shot. Instead of the expected thump of bullet hitting flesh I heard a crack. The crack of a tree splintering just above the stag's shoulder. The sound of failure and the relief of not injuring this creature rolled over me all in one moment.

In retrospect, I would have done many things differently. I would have gone closer, using the bush for cover, and found a shooting rest I was more comfortable with. I still find it awkward shooting amongst long tussock. I should have backed my own shooting and not relied on Kirk for a backup shot. He later confirmed he'd said 'Go', not 'No'. But most importantly, I should have never pulled the trigger without feeling comfortable with the situation. In the end, letting a deer walk away was far better than running the risk of wounding it.

The next day was stormy again, rain and sleet. I was being tough on myself for stuffing up the opportunity the day before and couldn't face sitting in a tent replaying scenes of what could have been. I somehow convinced Roi to explore some new country with me in the rain and sleet. I just needed some kilometres under my boots to process what had happened. We took off to a far ridge, knowing full well there would be nothing out and about in this weather. It was to be our last full day on the hill as the chopper would arrive in the morning. We found some great wallows and some excellent areas to explore and I managed to come to terms with myself as a hunter once more.

The day of our planned extraction came and went. We sat around under a tarp, our main camp packed up earlier that morning. It was Easter but the Easter eggs were long gone. It rained all day and we kept hoping the sky would clear so the helicopter could haul us out. Back then we hunted with no comms, no inReach or cell service. It was just sit in the rain and wait until the clouds cleared. Finally night fell, and we set about rebuilding camp. We had no dry clothes and only two dryish sleeping bags between us, so we pitched just one tent and the three of us jammed in together. We managed to use the last of our laughter chuckling at ourselves for putting ourselves in such a sodden situation before falling asleep.

The next morning dawned crisp and clear. The helicopter arrived bright and early and we were flicked out of the bush cold, wet and keen on a burger. Roi's tobacco cravings had disappeared; perhaps she'd walked them away in the mud. I hadn't shot a stag but that was an achievement in its own right.

Some trips are more successful than others. This was a particularly sodden one. We totally mistimed the roar by taking the dates from the last hunt I'd done in this part of the country and putting them into the new calendar. I had blown the shot on the only decent stag we had seen, and we'd been smashed by three storms in one week. But I guess that's what you can expect from Haast and that's the fickleness of roar hunting. We had to see the funny side in it all and walk away with good memories and a half-decent yarn. Kirk's still my best hunting companion and Roi solidified her place as the bushman's wife. She even got a ring out of it a few weeks later. But I was still in search of my stag.

16. TE KAHIKA PIGS

Maybe it was the glimpses Roi was getting into the bush life. Maybe she was just getting bored of my over-excited stories and needed me to find other people to talk to. But one day she suggested that I start communicating the excitement I had for the bush through social media.

She reckoned I was always complaining about how the next generation of young people, the would-be bushmen (and -women, of course), were always staring at their phones and weren't turning up to look after the ngahere. She suggested if I made really interesting content about the bush, they might see it and want to be involved. Meet them where they were, she reckoned, and teach them in the format they're used to.

She had a point. My little cousins already called me 'Sam the Trap Man' so we created an Instagram handle and I started making videos and taking photos to upload to my 120-follower-strong social-media platform. I just started documenting what we did in the bush and the things I thought were pretty cool. Turns out people really enjoyed seeing wholesome content on the internet — and it wasn't just kids who were interested. The social-media page started to take off and before too long it was so big that my work started to get a little concerned about it. Nothing a little contract variation couldn't solve though, ae.

Then one day at Fieldays, a little ankle-biter of a pig hunter came up to me and said, 'Hey, I recognise you. You do plant videos on Instagram.' Turns out he owned a clothing company called Game Gear and was keen for me to wear his clothes and represent the brand. Free gear for the bush . . . that sounded good to me. I was still kicking around in woollen singlets scrounged from op shops for three bucks and some old, worn fleecy trousers from back when I was trapping in Fiordland.

Joel became a pretty good mate over the coming months and before I

ABOVE A Te Kahika tusker, not a giant boar but he had good hooks. © Fez, courtesy of Game Gear

knew it we were flying into the middle of the Raukūmara to chase pigs with his pack of bailing dogs.

For those of you who don't know the Raukūmara, it's like a miniature Fiordland. Flat, grassy river terraces with tall-sided valleys that are straight up and down like a power pole. Pigs are pretty easy to hunt in this type of country, especially when the tawa is fruiting. It's a simple game of find the tawa to find the pigs. Pigs will travel huge distances to find tawa fruit, and when they find it they gorge themselves, turning their puku into a mashed porridge of tawa kernels. Their meat even takes on a sweet, fruity aroma and the hinu is delicious. That's what makes helicopter pig-hunting trips so worth it.

With helicopter unloaded and a hammock camp established we were off up the creek to check the river flats. We weren't disappointed. About a kilometre upstream of camp the dogs hit fresh scent. They were gone a matter of seconds before the entire hill face above us erupted in barking as pigs dashed from heavily clad bush and escaped across slip faces. There were heaps of them.

We had three dogs with us that trip. Bear was our main finder bailer. She was smart with a good nose and nine times out of ten she was the one fast enough to keep up with an escaping pig. She'd nip it on the backside when there was no risk to her and as it spun around to protect itself she would back off and bark. Her game was to slow it down enough for the reinforcements to arrive. Bear was the kind of dog that asserts herself as head of the pack even when it's not her pack. She wouldn't let anyone else near the boss for a cuddle or a pat and she wouldn't let any other dog near the pig when it's on the ground. It's her pig. She was a bit of a black-and-white princess and if there's a camera out you can guarantee Bear would be in front of it.

Reinforcements came in the way of Hooch, a scarred-up ginger dog that reminded me of Horse, the cat from *Footrot Flats*. She bailed well but had a nasty streak in her, too. She was less risk averse than Bear; while they took turns dashing in to bark at the pig, if Hooch thought there was a chance of the pig running she would nip in and tag it on the bum to let it know it had to stay put. Hooch was a little insular and aloof, but she was my favourite. Tough as nails but polite and dependable. Nothing flashy but she put a solid effort in no matter how big the pig was.

Then there was a useless whippet cross named Mocha, who was afraid of her own shadow and showed zero interest in pigs. She looked like the

TOP After chasing pigs it only felt right to have a look around for a deer at the same time. © Fez, courtesy of Game Gear

BOTTOM The rivers of the Raukūmara are pretty easy to navigate making the hunting user friendly. © Fez courtesy of Game Gear

OVERLEAF While hunting is definitely about bringing food home for the whānau I do really enjoy cooking in cast iron over an open fire. Being able to operate a bush kitchen using hunted, foraged and fished ingredients from the environment around me is one of my favourite things about being a bushman. © Fez courtesy of Game Gear

fancy swirl on the top of a soy latte and acted like it too. This trip was her last chance to make something of herself as a pig dog before finding a home as a pet or if no one wanted her . . . well, let's just say we often joked that Mocha was fairly lead-deficient.

Crossing the creek at speed to the first bail-up, old poto Joel went tits up in the river and sprained his ankle. Not a great start to the trip. But with stick in one hand and rifle in the other we hobbled him up the hill to the hooky black bristler of a boar the dogs were dancing with in a tangle of kareao. Down went the stick and up came the gun. A quick 'Git outside' made the dogs back off momentarily, giving Joel enough time to get a shot away before his ankle crumpled. A snarl of dogs and pig came tumbling down towards us.

Nothing quite beats cast iron and fire in the scrub and my days of backcountry dehydrated meals were long gone. Nope, it's all about fresh meat and fresh vegetables gathered from the bush around us.

That night we built a big bonfire and let it burn down to embers. I butterflied each of the fat boar's back steaks and stuffed them with dried apricots, apple and cream cheese, then rolled them into a spiral and wrapped the tasty balls in bacon. A quick sear in the camp oven then it was left to cook in a bath of port and cider.

If there's one thing I know about pork, it's that it loves to stay moist, and if there's one thing I know about Joel and me, it's that we like to bring a few luxuries to allow us to really get our cook on in the bush, especially when the helicopter is carrying it. Nothing quite beats cast iron and fire in the scrub and my days of backcountry dehydrated meals were long gone. Nope, it's all about fresh meat and fresh vegetables gathered from the bush around us. As we rolled a succulent joint of flavoursome meat onto a bed of fresh kareao shoots foraged while we were hunting, both of us agreed this was the way food is meant to be done.

Next morning, with a boar hanging from the tree, and Joel's ankle strapped and feeling a lot better, we hobbled our way downstream where the dogs didn't waste time thwacking into another mob of pigs. Raukūmara boars aren't huge in stature but far out, they are tusky. This time the pig had given the dogs the slip on the river flats. They'd only just managed to get a rolling bail going when they caught up with him high up in the bluffy, tight

heights of the face above us.

Joel feigned a sorer ankle than he otherwise might have and sent me up the hill with the rifle and the useless Mocha to deal with the pig. It was a dirty, tight scramble of horopito and kareao, and when I finally made it to the dogs, I came down on top of them because the shooting's always better that way, and they were getting pretty tired.

The dogs saw me and squared the pig up so it was facing directly towards me. It's absolutely incredible how dogs that know their trade are aware of such subtleties. Then with a 'Git outside', they backed off and I pulled the trigger . . . NOTHING. My brain panicked. Oh crap, it's not my gun . . . Where's the safety? . . . Hope the pig doesn't break . . .

In a split second the dogs leapt back in with a desperate tone in their barking. They must have been absolutely shattered by now. They were expecting a dead pig on the deck and I was asking them to do more work while I fiddled around with the rifle like a numpty.

Where is that bloody safety? Then I see it . . . click . . . 'Git outside' . . . I see the square front of the pig's skull . . . WHACK . . . rifle slams into shoulder . . . and the dogs leap on the pig as it slides down the hill.

A little stunned, I fumble my way down to the dogs and the boar to find Bear already telling Hooch it's her pig. Mocha, typically, is nowhere to be found. Turns out she's afraid of rifles, too. Then out of the scrub comes Joel, with all signs of a sore ankle evaporated. 'Nah mate, I just wanted you to get your first pig at the bail and when I heard the dogs bark, I knew it was a goodie.'

He'd faked it this morning and sent me up the hill without him, knowing that I'd be too nervous to pull the trigger over his dogs if he was there. Instead he'd snuck up behind me and watched the whole thing unfold, including the mucking around trying to find the safety on the gun. He was just sitting back in the bush, laughing his head off at my follies.

This pig-hunting game was a real rush.

TOP It's worth getting up early to see the way the dew clings to branches in the morning, making leaves and spider webs shimmer. © Fez, courtesy of Game Gear

BOTTOM As I get older I am often more content to let the binos do the walking for me. © Fez, courtesy of Game Gear

17. RAUKOKORE REDS

Not long after our successful foray into the Te Kahika, we once again decided to try our luck in the Raukūmara. Joel had the heads-up on a handy spot called the Raukokore, a wide, rambling river system with a good number of productive wee side creeks.

So one Friday morning at the crack of dawn, the utes pulled in to the Ōpōtiki helicopter hangar. Big billows of breath from excited dogs puffing out of an old, recycled road-sign dog box. No Mocha this time — she'd been given the sack after her rotten, pig-avoiding, gun-shy, food-stealing performance in Te Kahika and had gone to a whānau in Te Puke who needed a pet. Lucky for her because that's about all she was good for. No, this time we had the A-Team on board — just Bear and Hooch. We weren't here to put bridles on giraffes.

A stunning heli trip over the blue coastline of the East Cape had us on the ground in about twenty minutes. As we set about slinging the hammocks, the dogs, both chained to a tree, started to get fidgety and tug at their chains. 'They're keen,' Joel reckoned. 'Must be something close by.' So, leaving the hammocks until later, he released the hounds.

Straight across the river they scampered and not ten metres into the bush they had a solid bail going. 'Little pigs,' Joel reckoned. He could tell by the tone of the bark. 'We better get over there before Hooch grabs one of them.' Although Hooch was my favourite, she did have a terrible habit of overpowering small pigs and switching from a bailer to a holder anytime she wasn't scared of something.

Across the creek we ran, Joel up to his waist, me up to my knees. Rivers must be tough if you're a short-ass like him. I beat Joel up the bank in a couple of strides but he took the lead back as his little frame found the gaps in the kareao while my gangly arms and legs got caught in everything.

ABOVE A fat velvet stag all plump from summer grass. © Fez, courtesy of Game Gear

TOP It's tough rocky riverbeds like these that wear a dog's feet out after a few days. © Ben Vercauteren, courtesy of Game Gear

BOTTOM Joel was testing a prototype sleeping mat so after a hot day's hunting I had the idea to float down the river on it to test it for leaks. © Fez, courtesy of Game Gear

Sure enough, Bear and Hooch had a skinny wee sow and her piglet doing the dog dance in a small clearing where an old forest giant of a rimu had fallen down a few years earlier. The sow was horribly skinny and would make terrible chewing if we took her, but she sure had a lot of spirit and was giving the dogs hell. Not wanting anyone to get hurt and still under the influence of the pig hunters' catch-and-release mentality, I grabbed the dogs while Joel grabbed the pigs. Like boxers, we marched each back to their respective corners of the clearing to go their separate ways. While I held the dogs back Joel released the sow in the opposite direction. But the cheeky bloody thing still had more scrap left in her and turned around with a squeal to rush Joel in an open-mouthed charge. Baffled by her confidence, he gave her a well-placed boot in the ribs and off she wandered back into the scrub.

Our pride only just intact, we retreated back across the river to our half-made camp where the dogs were chained back to the tree and told in no uncertain terms that there would be no more chasing of skinny old sows. We had it on good authority there were some great donkey boars in the area and that's exactly what we were after.

That evening I snuck off for a sneaky little deer stalk while Joel prepped dinner, leaving the dogs back at camp. Joel wasn't terribly excited about the idea of stalking deer but judging by the amount of sign around camp, the potential to nail a red skin was pretty good. The dogs' chains had been checked and resecured. Nothing ruins a good deer stalk more than an over-enthusiastic dog chasing pigs.

Choosing a friendly-looking side creek with a slow breeze blowing out of it I parted from the main river. Wide river flats broken by tutu and māhoe made a shark-tooth pattern up the gravelled stream bed. There was no shortage of grass and no shortage of sign, in fact there was poo and hoofprints everywhere. I hadn't gone 500 metres before the smell of deer wafted down the stream towards me.

I poked my nose through a tight, bouldery section of the creek and saw a young stag, the red of its coat bright against the green evening bush. It hadn't seen me and continued to feed unperturbed. Knowing the value of a decent rest even at close range, I crawled across the piripiri-infested grass to a big, smooth boulder that would make the ideal shooting platform. I could feel the familiar discomfort of piripiri stuck to my leg hairs with its little brown hooks.

Finding the stag in the scope, an easy twenty-metre shot sat him down quick. But before I knew it a second stag sprang from cover, hidden by the tutu it ran through. As it took off upstream I could see a bare section of gravel it needed to cross in order to escape. I don't mind running shots at close range but I let the deer angle a little far away from me. Aww well, meat is meat, I thought and squeezed the trigger. Over he went, a broken leg and punctured lung. I had him tidied up in a quick minute.

Not a bad start to the trip — two fat six-point velvet stags down. Just about the best eating we could hope for, so I trussed the bigger of the two stags and carried him back to camp on my back. Knowing that once gutted, the second one wouldn't spoil hanging from a tree overnight in the cool evening breeze, I left it there.

Swinging gently in our hammocks that night, rocked to sleep by the odd gust of wind, we couldn't help but dream of the potential of day two and the adventures to be had. I've always quite enjoyed hammock-sleeping and Joel had designed a really decent one. No uneven ground under your back, no cold hard soil, just the softness of air and a sheet of parachute material that moulds to your back. Couple this with an inbuilt mosquito net and a fly suspended high above you, that clammy feeling of tent camping is replaced by the space and peacefulness of mountain air. If you get real tricky, you can even manage to roll the hammock on its side and pee out the side zip without leaving your sleeping bag. Just make sure your dog's not sleeping underneath otherwise they get one hell of a fright and are liable to act sulkily during the next day's hunt.

Day two had us up early to retrieve the second deer. We slung it up in a Joel-designed portable meat safe. It's handy having mates with this kind of kit.

With eyes on an evening meal of venison we still needed some vegetables from the bush so off we set on a foraging mission. Kareao, kōwaowao, pikopiko . . . It was all potentially on the menu but strangely so far we had seen very little greenery to sustain us. The bush had been completely chewed out by deer, and the pigs turning over the huruhuru layer weren't helping much either. This is often the case in areas of high deer numbers and we had to work pretty hard to find us a feed.

In the end Joel and I had to climb high up into a bluff system and there hanging out over the precipice, beyond the stretch of a deer's neck, were the fresh shoots of kareao we were searching for. There were heaps of them, the plants knowing that in order for them to grow they needed to stretch away

TOP I have always enjoyed hammock sleeping. Between a hammock, a fire and a cast iron pan there's not too much more I need from a good campsite. © Fez, courtesy of Game Gear

BOTTOM Bear always guarded any kill as if it were her own. She wouldn't let any other dog near it. © Fez, courtesy of Game Gear

OVERLEAF My Raukokore camp kitchen. Venison eye fillets, port sauce and kareao shoots were the flavour of that trip. © Fez, courtesy of Game Gear

from the nip of deer teeth and lean out into the abyss.

To be honest we felt a little bad picking those shoots, even though we left plenty behind. We knew that not many were getting away and slowly but surely the forest was starting to collapse in this area. We definitely weren't doing our job keeping on top of the deer numbers in the Raukokore. The balance is definitely out of kilter when it takes half an hour to shoot two deer and two hours to pick a handful of supplejack tips.

No matter, we had a feed and in finding it we had a better understanding of the state of the ecosystem. We set about building a big fire from fallen tawa and tōtara logs and started to cook our feed. Tender, fat back steaks crusted in a sweet cocoa and coffee rub, seared in cast iron and left pink in the middle, laid across a bed of kareao tips fried in butter and garlic. That's exactly how we liked to eat. Once again we retired to our hammocks, this time a little heavier than the night before.

With the dogs well rested from a light day of foraging and carrying deer, we decided to chase pigs in earnest on our last day's hunting in the Raukokore. Joel had his sights set on the steep hills above us. Up we climbed, losing cupfuls of sweat in the sweltering February heat. The dogs found an old stag wallow in a spring and dived straight in, muddying it before we could get there for a drink.

Out of the valley floor the forest was barren. The fruiting podocarps were long gone, hammered by possums; the palatable undergrowth had been devoured by deer; and the tawa that was left fruits just once a year. No wonder the sow we saw on the first day was so skinny. There just wasn't any tucker on the hills. With no food around, the pigs weren't hanging out this high up so we clambered back down to the river valley to hunt the cool, grassy side creeks instead.

Demoralised after a long, pigless day, Hooch had given up the ghost. The rocks and hard ground of the Raukokore had taken their toll on this stoic dog's feet; she just laid down and refused to walk any further. On closer inspection the pads on her feet were worn raw and she had a horrible cut on one of her paws. Graciously she allowed herself to be slung over our shoulders and we carried the poor dog back to camp.

With Hooch tied up, we set off again with Bear in tow. It was getting pretty late but since it was the last opportunity for a hunt on that trip, we figured there was nothing to lose. We poked our noses up a side creek handy to camp, keen on whatever meat was on offer. The last day of a hunt is known as meat day. With the chopper coming we knew any meat from the last day was the freshest and best to take home to the whānau, so any deer or pig that had the misfortune of stepping in front of us that evening would be copping a slug and filling our freezers. Or at least that's what I thought . . .

As we took a turn in the river, I held up my hand. There, on the opposite bank, was a big old black boar sliding down the gravel bank to get a drink from the creek. I settled down on my knees to take a shot. He still hadn't seen us even though we were super close; pigs do tend to have poor eyesight.

With the chopper coming we knew any meat from the last day was the freshest and best to take home to the whānau, so any deer or pig that had the misfortune of stepping in front of us that evening would be copping a slug and filling our freezers. Or at least that's what I thought . . .

I felt a hand on my shoulder and Joel let the dog go. Hitting the boar at full pace, a short-lived bail ensued. Bear was totally under-gunned as a single dog against this big old tusker and he broke for the hills indignantly. He almost scoffed at our inadequacies as hunters as he ambled past us, grinding his tusks at being pursued by our little black-and-white dog.

For the next few hours Joel ran around the hills after Bear and the pig. I could hear the intermittent bail-up as the dog tried its darnedest to stop a boar way beyond her calibre. I sat in the creek, refusing outright to partake in such a folly. I was a little dark that I hadn't been allowed to take the shot. It was 30 metres and there was no way I would have missed. But I guess pig hunters will be pig hunters and the temptation of giving Bear a run on a decent boar had been too much to resist. It would have been different if we'd had Hooch with us, but those were the cards we'd been dealt. Joel was a mate so I could forgive him his eagerness.

Dejected, damp and dirty, Bear hobbled back down the creek following her sheepish leader. They hadn't managed to stop the boar but at least we knew there were a few good ones about should we come back next year.

When the chopper arrived the next day, two exhausted dogs and two weary hunters climbed in. We had a decent load of venison with us but we both couldn't help thinking of the boar that got away.

18. DANGERMAN AND THE DEER

Some hunting trips are an absolute disaster but are saved by good fishing, and some fishing trips are totally derailed by the distraction of venison. This particular morning, we found ourselves sitting in darkness at 5 a.m. with gusts of frozen clag driven into our exposed faces as we questioned our decision to pick up the rifle rather than stick with the rod.

We'd been in the midst of a boys' fishing weekend when we received an invitation to hunt on a much-sought-after hunting block neighbouring Te Urewera. The block's abundance of reds, fallow and pigs is famed across the North Island and to be offered the opportunity to hunt here was something we couldn't pass up, no matter how good the fishing had been over the last couple of days.

Our crew consisted of Dangerman, Geoff, Slam Safari and me. We'd been parked up at the Wairata Shearers' Quarters for the opening weekend of the new fishing season and what a time we'd had. Slam Safari, a world-famous musician named Samuel R. Saffery, was the brother of my good mate Jess, and having recently returned from the U.S. of A. he was keen to get amongst everything the New Zealand backcountry had to offer. We decked our musical mate out in boots, raincoat and a spinning rod then thrust him into one of the country's most bountiful fisheries, the Waioeka Gorge. And Geoff is Geoff. Knowledgeable, practical and about as good a bushman as you could imagine. If there's a job, Geoff's done it; a problem, Geoff's fixed it; or a joke, Geoff's heard it. He's exactly the guy you want in your corner when the shit hits the fan and the rest of the time he's just a good bloke.

Then there was Dangerman. For those of you who haven't met Dangerman, he is an upstanding citizen. He has rocked a mullet and wispy moustache since being forcibly evicted from the warm climes of his mother's womb many years ago. Dangerman is a national surfing champion and one heck of a trout

ABOVE George Zame AKA Dangerman, pretty stoked with his first deer.

fisherman on both spinner and fly. Not one to be caught up in his own hype, this Joe Dirt lookalike usually has a tin in one hand and a durry between his lips. Not exactly the type of individual fathers-in-law approve of or mothers-in-law welcome with open arms. But for all his rugged posturing, he's a bit of a softy underneath it all and he's always up for a laugh. Not a bad bloke to be stuck in the hills with for any length of time.

The last couple of days' rain had the river running brown but the fish in the side streams, undisturbed since last season, were swallowing everything. We threw spinners, soft baits and flies and each day we had our limit puffing away in the smoker back at camp. On day one Danger and Slam both hooked into some excellent fish up the Wairata, Slam on the spinner and Danger on the fly. Both landed donkeys of rainbows; the lads' hooting and hollering drowned out the screech of their reels as the big fish darted about the mountain stream on tight lines.

In the afternoon we changed streams and I hooked into a real solid brown jack that fought so hard I thought he was going to break my line. But after a tussle that had me drenched in the cold winter water, he ended up in my net and was destined for an existence between crackers, cheese and chutney. That's exactly why we love opening weekend. We were fishing right next to the main highway and the honey holes of the Opato were producing fish that would get way too smart for our amateur efforts later on in the season.

We usually carry a rifle when we're fishing (not by the highway but just about everywhere else). The number of times deer have stepped out of the bush while we fish is ridiculous and we're definitely not opposed to a feed of venison when it presents itself. Earlier in the trip, Danger had mentioned in passing that for all his rugged bushman looks, he'd never shot a deer. Geoff and I, knowing we had an ace hunting invitation up our sleeve, decided to lay down the fishing rods and get Danger his deer.

That's how we found ourselves at 5 a.m. in the pitch dark, peering into an absolute white-out with icy mist being driven into our already numb faces. This was proper Te Urewera weather and on an exposed ridge it could be frigid.

As we sat and waited for the day to break, curled up side by side in raincoats and puffer jackets, faces hidden to block the wind, we heard a sound we hadn't expected. No more than 30 metres away, the piercing sound of a male kiwi cut through the fog. I knew the area well, thanks to my work with

TOP Some trips the fishing is just incredible. I managed to catch this brown not 20 metres from the main road.

BOTTOM George with a good rainbow from the Koranga River.

TOP As soon as we heard that kiwi we knew it was going to be a good day.

BOTTOM One of my favourite fishing buddies, George is as good on the fly rod as he is on the spinner. He even ties many of his own flies.

the Eastern Whio Link, and knew it was home to just a handful of kiwi that had been clinging on in the bush. To hear one up close was a really unusual occurrence. As hunters we are always looking for tohu in the bush; call us superstitious but Danger and I knew this was our tohu that we were going to get him a deer today.

With next to no visibility, the clag had turned from black to grey, announcing dawn. We started our descent through the thick folds of scrub along the creeks. The clouds came and went, offering brief glimpses of promising spurs and clearings a hundred metres in front of us. More than once, we witnessed dark shapes bound off, only to be engulfed in the mist once more. There was no shortage of deer on this block and before long we'd seen six, but with no shooting opportunities presenting themselves.

The clag was just too solid, and while the deer couldn't see us, we also couldn't see the deer until we were practically on top of them. They were being spooked left and right and I was hesitant to have Danger take a running shot on his first deer. Witnessing the consequences of a bad hit is enough to put any new hunter off hunting and we weren't about to let that happen.

Our frustrations were interrupted by the report of Geoff's .243. Having cut his teeth hunting in the Kaimai Range, Geoff is no stranger to getting up close and personal with deer in the tight stuff, so this fog was playing straight to his strengths. A nice fat animal was nestled in a ponga grove not far from our grinning mate and a quick drag to a recoverable site for later had us continuing on our search for Danger's first deer.

As we lost elevation the morning mist cleared and what it left behind was a stunning scene of grassy clearings amongst mānuka scrub and old native growth. As we edged along, feeling exposed after our morning's clag hunting, Danger quickly motioned a halt. I crouched. He fired from the standing position in an instant and the old .308 bushpig dropped a fat bundle of steaks to the ground.

With Danger there was no carefully found rest for the rifle, no talking a new hunter through his breathing and shot placement. Just a confident and comfortable standing shot and a big-bodied hind down. It's not exactly the scenario I had planned for in my mind, but it worked out surprisingly well. Danger had heart-shot his deer and it had collapsed immediately.

We counted 28 other deer bolting for cover amongst the broken vegetation of the gully. This place really did have an abundance of deer, maybe even bordering on a problem. One thing was for sure, Old Mate had ticked another first off the list, and by the way he was carrying on it obviously meant something to him.

After a scramble down a near-vertical bluff system, where the deer had conveniently rolled, and a quick game of 'follow the red patches', we found the slightly bedraggled yet impressive animal. We set about field-dressing and managed to tick off another first in the Dangerman chronicles. Turns out gutting a deer is a little different to gutting a trout, and while Danger had schooled me successfully in boneless trout-filleting techniques over the last few days, it was now my turn to return the favour.

It's amazing how ingrained your natural sequences and processes are. Over the years we finely tune our repertoire of tricks of effectively and efficiently breaking down deer. We pick up a little from this mate or that old, timer until we are proficient. It's not until we need to articulate what our hands know to do, and unpack the reasoning why we do it this way, that we finally start to appreciate what an artform we've mastered.

Alongside gutting came the obligatory anatomy lesson. Everything seems a whole lot different in a deer when you're used to cutting open fish. The hind was in fawn, which, while it may make some of us squeamish, makes me wonder if this is how male hunters have learned about childbirth and female anatomy since the beginning of time. There are many lessons to be learned while hunting and today the bush and the deer was Danger's classroom and mine too.

I reckon it's almost compulsory to do a backpack carry on your first animal, so that's what we did. We can always drop down to a less exhausting method as time goes on and age takes its toll on knees, hips and backs, but if you can do a half-decent job of carrying a whole animal the first time then you've earned your stripes in my books. So off we set, back up the bluff system at more of a trudge than a scamper.

Danger had successfully joined the rank of deer hunter. We bagged three deer that morning, and while the local marae got one for an upcoming event, the other two would be filling our freezers and feeding our families over the summer barbecue season.

As we headed back to Wairata to pick up Slam and check how his day's fishing had gone, we knew the chilly bins would be full; the crew would all be heading home with venison for the freezer and a load of smoked trout as well. It had been a great weekend away and one we vowed to repeat again next year.

19. MUSHROOM HUNTING

On the first day I met Roimata I called my dad to say the search was off. Like the Danish Viking stock I come from, I'd been searching for a shield-maiden of my own my entire life, someone tall, strong and uncompromising in their values. That was the type of woman I wanted to raise children with. Sure enough, before long we were joined by Rehua, our blond-haired keeper of manu after which he was named. Three years after that we met our quiet watcher of a daughter, Te Kōtuku, whose personality matches the poise and decisiveness of her heron namesake.

The first night after Rehua was born, he slept on my chest. Roimata was pretty exhausted from a long labour and I was more than happy to have this little creature curled up like a puppy on top of me. I was besotted. Every now and then he would wake and I would pass him up to his mother for a feed.

I couldn't shake an overwhelming, nagging fear that I simply didn't know how to do justice to the role of being a dad. I'd been hit with a feeling immediately that this was the most important role in the world and kids, as the saying goes, don't come with a handbook. So, with encouragement from my parents, I decided to just be me and to dad the way I thought it should be done. I knew I was going to fail at some things, but I figured with a little confidence and by sharing the things I loved when I grew up with my kids, we would learn how to do it along the way. I'd been raised in the wholesome embrace of nature and I figured if that's what I enjoyed about my childhood, then why not try to bring that into my children's lives.

So we took them bush. At first Rehua was in a frontpack as we 'gave his mum a break' but as he grew older he would crawl around in the undergrowth, chasing my gumboots, and we would go at his pace. After crawling came walking and he pretty much learned to walk in the bush while navigating roots, fallen branches and ferns. My shoulders were always there to carry him when he was tired and we covered a lot of country just ambling through the trees in this way.

With a fresh palate yet to be colonised by the tastes of sweet and salty, Rehua soon developed a love for what we call 'bush lollies', the fruits of Haumia that fall to the forest floor. There was tawa, kōnini, kahikatea, tōtara, kōhia, tītoki . . . the forest always managed to provide a snack and Rehua was always hungry. I figured the more he ate from the ngahere, the closer the connection he would feel with the bush. Being a big believer that we mould to our environments, I was really proud that my son was moulding to be in balance with the bush.

By the time he could walk, Rehua could recognise just about every edible fruit in the forest. More importantly, he knew how to recognise the poisonous ones too and would point at them, saying 'yuck!' at the top of his lungs.

Eventually there came a time when his sense of being a provider emerged with a strength I hadn't expected. He would come home from the bush with stained pockets full of squished bush lollies for his māmā. Not as excited as he was by the slightly dishevelled fruit, his māmā would do her best to feign pleasure in eating them. Roimata has always struggled to be anything but honest; she has the incredibly endearing quality of showing exactly how she feels on her face. It's one of the first things I really liked about her. In a world of false pretences, with Roimata you get a straight read on how she's feeling no matter the situation.

So, we needed to find a different way for young Rehua to play out his desire to provide and that came in the form of mushrooms. It's no secret that many of our native mushrooms are delicious, and that many of their cousins can make us very sick. As bushmen we like nothing more than adding a brace of fungi to our packs as we stroll through the bush as a welcome addition to the evening meal. Whether it's venison stew, smoked trout or an array of fried, foraged vegetables, mushrooms always enhance the table fare.

But many of our city-dwelling friends haven't grown up around the bush and are rightly hesitant around identifying which mushrooms are safe to eat. Rehua, however, had one distinct advantage. He already knew the trees through his puku. Tītoki and tawa both gave him bush lollies and he could recognise their leaves on the ground, kind of like a clue in a treasure hunt. Rehua would follow them until he found the fruit. He recognised the twisted trunks of the tītoki and the way lichen clings in circles to the trunk of the tawa, and therefore he was well placed to know them as host trees of the smooth, giant tāwaka mushroom we were now searching for.

> Being a big believer that we mould to our environments, I was really proud that my son was moulding to be in balance with the bush.

Tāwaka have a way of growing at three heights on the tree. These are known in our family as Rehua height, Māmā height and Pāpā height. Any mushroom growing on the roots are designated as Rehua height and he will pick them quickly and with great pride and stuff them in the kete that his tāua made him. Anything above Rehua height and still reachable by hand is called Māmā height, as this is the level Roimata picks when she is foraging with us. And anything growing in the canopy is Pāpā height. Rehua gets a great laugh from my attempts to coax these mushrooms down from their treetop perches with a long stick or when I try, with all the clumsiness of a dog, to climb for them. We don't mind Rehua tucking any tāwaka into his kete. We reckon this is the role of tamariki; he loves the tāwaka and the tāwaka often grow big, juicy and fat at his height so we figure the more he picks, the more he loves tāwaka, the bush and the types of trees they come from. For Roi and me though, with the tāwaka higher up the tree we try to wait until they have dropped their spores so that they can reseed the forest with new tāwaka for the year to come.

Tāwaka are our favourite late summer and autumn mushroom. We love to slice them into chunky strips and fry them until they start to crisp on the outside but stay juicy in the middle. Their nutty flavour makes them an absolute favourite and they're received with much more gratitude than bush lollies when Rehua walks through the door bursting with pride.

When he was two and three, tāwaka were an easy mushroom to identify. Rehua knew the trees and where they lived. But as he reached the ripe old age of four he started to think a little more about what made things different and his mind was suddenly interested in how to identify each unusual fungi. It was a perfect time to start foraging for enoki, the velvet shank mushroom. With his new fervour for mushrooming deeply linked to his identity as a provider, we needed a mushroom that was available in winter, and enoki are one of the few true winter mushrooms in Aotearoa. We admire these little golden umbrellas of the forest for their beauty as well as their flavour. Rehua has a checklist as he forages:

1. Are they orange? Yes, check.
2. Do they have a fuzzy stem? Check.
3. Do they have a skirt? No.
4. Can I see any white spores on the mushrooms? Check.

'Pāpā, I found velvet shank!'

'Good boy, son,' I reply, making sure I do one last check before we add his mushrooms to the kete. Velvet shank has a cousin that we don't want to tangle with and a little quality control never hurts.

These tasty wee treats come home to be added to risotto, a stir fry or pasta. They're much more delicate than tāwaka and have their own unique flavour.

As he's got older, Rehua has a map in his head where he keeps all the trees, tracks and birds tucked away in the pockets of his mind. Somehow he knows where each bird's territory starts and ends, and he has a way of chatting with them to get them to show him things.

On a spring day he'll come running up to me . . . 'Pāpā, I had karakia with pīwakawaka and it's going to show me where tawa is because I'm hungry.'

'Boy, it's spring! Tawa don't fruit in spring,' I say, not wanting him to get his hopes up.

'You wrong,' he reckons and wanders off into the undergrowth, led by the flitting pīwakawaka.

In 50 metres or so, sure enough, there's pīwakawaka dancing about on a forest floor littered with tawa fruit and there's Rehua stuffing his face with a bounty of fruit that has dropped totally out of season. As his teeth gnaw the flesh from the outside of the kernel, his hands dart from mouth to overalls as he stuffs the tawa kernels in his pocket for roasting over the fire later. Trust Rehua and his forest friends to find the one in a thousand tawa tree that decides to fruit in spring rather than autumn. But that's just the way he's been since day dot. He always had insects and birds hanging out with him in his cradle and telling him stories.

Rehua has the same skill at finding brown oyster mushrooms. Somehow he retains a map in his mind where the dead trees grow these tasty, fish-flavoured furls. In spring after rain, when the soil starts to warm, we venture into the bush in search of oyster mushrooms. I follow Rehua and we

ABOVE The flavour-filled velvet shank. Not to be confused with several other poisonous lookalikes.

take turns checking the trees etched into his three-year-old memory. There are tī kōuka and tītoki tucked just inside the bush edge, still very much alive but holding on to dead standing wood. It is here that the oyster mushrooms grow. With just enough warmth from the sun and just enough moisture from the bush, they burst forth as the fruiting bodies of a mycelium busy doing its job in breaking down decaying wood and returning it to the forest floor as soil.

Mushrooms have a way of slowing us down in the bush. They help us notice which trees are sick and which are healthy. They help us to understand the seasons, and the seasons of life.

Oyster mushrooms start out small as little buttons but grow rapidly to a very delectable size in just a couple of days. During oyster season it is our job to circle the trees and choose exactly the right time to pick the mushrooms. Unlike other mushrooms I find oysters to be a little slow at repopulating in the wild so we try to find the perfect window between when they have dropped their spores and when they turn soft, old and mushy. The oysters we harvest are destined for a hot cast-iron pan then laid across a bed of buttery pikopiko on brioche bread. Who said a bushman can't have fancy bread?

Mushrooms have a way of slowing us down in the bush. They help us notice which trees are sick and which are healthy. They help us to understand the seasons, and the seasons of life. We wonder if the forest under a fallen tree has enough saplings to take its place and, if not, whether we need to fence the bush off or shoot more deer to ensure succession. To me, mushrooms are the way the bush invites us to be part of the conversation of what happens after a mighty rangatira rākau falls and who takes its place.

In the last year, we have also been joined on our mushrooming adventures by Te Kōtuku, Rehua's little sister. She is bundled in the frontpack, wagging her legs excitedly every time we find mushrooms and yelling at Rehua each time he stops to eat the kai he finds scattered across the forest floor until he gives her some. While the challenges of ten-day helicopter trips chasing deer in remote corners of Aotearoa may be parked for me during this season of life, I find it even more satisfying to see the joy on my kids' faces as the wonders of the bush provide for them. Dad life is all about micro adventures.

20. REHUA'S FIRST TROUT

It was an overcast June day right towards the end of the fishing season when Rehua and I took the long winding drive from our home in Gisborne to the Koranga River.

Spending time at this river has been somewhat of a rite of passage in our whānau for generations. It's the place my grandfather taught me to fish trout, the place my father took me on my first overnight tramp and the place we choose to raise our children. It's through this place that they have a strong connection with the taiao.

It's here that we teach our tamariki about the great big guardians of the awa, the tuna. We swim with these muscular giants in deep, slow-flowing mountain pools. They often swim right up to us, nibbling on our feet, and if they are particularly hungry we may have to convince them not to take a bite from our pale legs or bottoms when we are bathing in the deep, dark pools of the river. We teach our kids to feed the tuna the puku from trout we catch. We see the tuna as kaitiaki of this awa, an awa that has been encroached upon by trout, an introduced species. Now the tuna must compete with these large predatory fish for their food of the small fishes and insects of the stream. As we gut our trout, the least we can do is to feed the tuna a share of our catch in a gesture of solidarity. The people and the tuna sharing a hākari together and hoping for an abundance of all things native once more.

It's not that we dislike the trout. It's not the fault of the shiny rainbow or the dull spotted brown that they have such a big impact on our awa. It is an error of man. My grandfather was a keen sportsfisher, trout high on his list of weekend excursions. He was a purist, a fly-fishing, catch-and-release-type guy in his older days. Open-minded in many ways but of a different generation to me, a different orientation with the world. He taught us to fish, taught us a love of the awa, taught us about the interconnectedness of things

ABOVE Rehua and his first fish. We were both super proud of this moment.

and taught us of conservation, of gratefulness.

Here I am with my son, Rehua, a three-year-old from a long line of fishers. A line of fishers that return to the same stream to teach the next generation our ways. As we sit observing the insects rising in the cool air above the riffles and pools, I feel the other fishers with us. My poppa is there with his cane basket, a black plastic Thermos, tall and protruding from the kete of food my nanna would always pack for us. Without fail there would be fruitcake, bathed for weeks in brandy, a knife-cut revealing the array of dried fruit inside, us kids always searching for the green and red glazed cherries. There would be tea and Milo, each in their own worn-out old Marmite jars with no label. Bacon-and-egg pie sat in its soft Tupperware container with a paper serviette blanket. This was the way of my grandparents, the kai basket, a gesture of love and support for the fisher.

As I hoist Rehua onto my shoulders, his bum nestling softly into the top of my day bag, we cross the first waist-deep river. You never do get used to the sharp, crisp cold of winter streams, but the water welcomes me nonetheless. It's the welcome of life, of alertness, of energy, of cleanliness. A zing of waking shoots to my head as my thighs enter the water and I feel the presence of my father, a man whose shoulders I remember well. My small fingers found comfort as they scraped across the prickles of his bald head and investigated the soft wrinkles at the corner of his eyes as I bobbed precariously above the river's rocks on his strong shoulders. Rehua, too, works his fingers into the curls of my beard, finding bravery in the familiar pāhau that he has gripped since birth.

The worries of our mothers, grandmothers and wives are with us too as they anxiously trust us with their prized sons and daughters. They know that the tamariki, the mokopuna must go to the awa to learn but they're concerned nevertheless for their safety.

There is expectation, too. To teach the children the art of listening. The art of listening with ears, eyes and heart to the awa. Understanding what it can part with and when, understanding when it needs support. This is the way I endeavour to teach Rehua.

Safe on the far bank of the river, Rehua finds himself a kahikatea tree laden with koroī. He sets about plucking these fat juicy red fruit, safe in the knowledge that the lower branches are for the kids, the mid branches for adults and the higher branches for the manu, wētā and mokomoko. At least that's how it is for our whānau. His delicate fingers pluck each fruit, bursting with juice as it pops from the tree. Holding each black kākano, he slips the sweet red flesh of the fruit past his teeth and tugs. The black seed tears from the fruit and is discarded onto the ground to grow another tree.

I notice a wet patch spreading at the base of Rehua's pocket and enquire gently, 'Son, why is your pocket wet?'

'I take koroī home for Māmā,' comes his earnest reply. My heart thumps with pride. This boy is still in touch with the truths of the world. He knows that it is his role to provide kai for his whānau. Unfortunately, as is the way with koroī stored in pockets, they become squished and the juice tends to leak everywhere.

I suggest that his māmā likes smoked trout just as much as a squished pocketful of koroī from the kahikatea tree. He lights up . . . 'I take both?' he asks. 'Good idea,' I reckon. It's not worth arguing with a determined three-year-old.

Moving on, Rehua spots the bright orange glow of kōhia fruit in the canopy above him. Pointing and jumping he asks if I can pick some for him. Obligingly I do, explaining the role kōhia plays in the bush, how it binds the canopy together, filling the gaps between the trees and not allowing the sometimes destructive Tāwhirimātea in between the branches. I explain that is why we find kōhia far up in the canopy straddled between trees or on the edges of the bush where wind can often sneak in unobstructed.

The wind can push entire forests over if it gets a foothold. We see it time and again in beech or rewarewa forest. Even tall, straight kahikatea can succumb to the power of Tāwhirimātea. That is the role of kōhia; even the often-overlooked vines have a role to play in our ngahere.

But Rehua is mostly interested in the sweet red flesh that sits beneath the layers of orange and white shell, so naturally that's where our conversation drifts. He wants to know why we don't crunch the seeds with our teeth. I speak with him about their bitterness. Inquisitively, with a cheeky grin on his face, I see him position a shiny seed just right between two white teeth, then crack his teeth right through it. His face puckers in disgust and he has learned first-hand (again) the reason we don't crunch kōhia seeds.

Rehua wears his hair in long, beautiful blonde curls as a nod to my father's Scottish ancestry. So, I speak to Rehua about hair oil, of how kōhia seeds were once crushed by his tīpuna to extract a sweet-smelling, glossy hair oil that was highly valued for keeping hair clean and smelling good. There was no Pantene Pro-V back in those days. Later I notice him putting the black seeds in his pockets after he's sucked the red flesh from them, I'm guessing to make himself a concoction of hair oil.

ABOVE Rehua decided he would carry his fish all the way to the truck with no help. He has always been a committed provider.

TOP Koroī, the fruit of the kahikatea, are always a welcome snack while we are fishing.

BOTTOM Rehua will often eat handfuls of fruit harvested from the bush around him on any given adventure. Even at three years old he could usually find enough food to keep him full. Of course, I always had a picnic on hand as well.

Finally Rehua tires of kōhia. Maybe he is full, but I suspect he tires of my stories of plants. He asks sheepishly, 'Pāpā, we fish now?'

I see in his tone that he is trying not to offend me. 'Yes son, now we fish.'

Sitting well back from a likely-looking pool, we extend our telescopic spinning rod, a tool I have grown to love over my years in the bush. This style of rod shrinks down and is great for the tight forest-clad rivers in which we fish. They are cheap, and as a dad of a young family, that makes a difference. I think I purchased my first telescopic rod-and-reel combo for 60 dollars in a sports shop in Gore many years ago, and I've repurchased the same model over and over again since. I hold nothing against fly fishers with their fancy rods and beautiful hand-crafted gear; I quite admire the artistry of their chosen method if I'm honest. But when it comes to putting fish in the smoker I can't go past the no-frills effectiveness of a telescopic spinning rod.

Pulling thin nylon through eyelets, we attach our classic rainbow Veltic spinner. Again, nothing fancy, no swivels, no shiny gadgets, just the knot my poppa taught me and a ten-dollar spinner. Then we sneak to the head of the pool, Rehua standing well back as I cast.

We made a deal in the car earlier that I would cast and try to hook a fish and he would try to fight it and wind it in. At first the proud young hunter argued against this idea with the determination and belief that he could manage the entire process himself. With admiration I softened him into accepting that this was the way fishing was taught in our whānau, the same way Poppa taught me and the same way he was taught too.

We teach one part of fishing at a time. First, we teach the awa, then the ngāngara, then the fish. Next we learn how to fight the fish so as not to lose him, how to tire him so he drifts quietly into our net. We let our rod do the work rather than bringing him in fast and having to battle him on land. We learn about working the reel, about the crank handle and the drag. This is the first part of fishing we need our muscles to understand before we learn to cast and manipulate a lure.

It takes three casts to coax a decent-sized rainbow from the still waters behind a rock. With a screech of the reel the big jack is off downstream, knowing all too well the dance he must play if he is to spit the hook from his mouth. A surge of excitement runs through my arms as the rod quivers with tension as the fish darts this way and that in search of slack line. I squash the primal urge to fight this fish myself, knowing the disappointment Rehua would feel if I don't give him his shot.

As I call Rehua over I see stern anticipation written all over his face. He has a lot riding on this moment. I want to press pause, to take him aside and explain that there is no pressure, that this fish is a big one and there's a good chance we will lose him. But we don't have time. This fish needs to be fought now and to be honest I'm pretty sure Rehua's concerns aren't about me at all. I'm pretty sure it's about his love for his māmā, about his desire to bring home a fish, to smoke it and provide kai for the one he loves the way every young boy loves his māmā.

I hand the fishing rod over. The fish tugs. It's too heavy for Rehua's little arms and he struggles to keep the tip in the air. As Rehua winds, the fish skudders in circular runs around the pool then decides to leap. Line pressure releases from the hook and 'Pop!', out it comes. That's the thing with these big old jacks, it's never their first rodeo. They don't get old by being caught. But Rehua is standing there defeated, almost in tears.

'Not to worry, boy. We all lose our first fish. Let's nip up the river to the next pool and get back amongst it, āe?'

The next pool was deep and dark and while dropping a spinner into the depths proved fruitless, a quick cast into the boisterous rapids at the head of the pool soon had a pan-sized bullet of a rainbow trout doing circles in the main pool.

Once again I handed the rod to Rehua and once again he fought the fish with a totally different result. This fish was well matched to Rehua's strength: not so small he could overpower it but not strong enough to tug the rod from his grasp. With quiet determination and skill gleaned from keen observation, he tuckered that fish out until it was spent, sliding silently over to my net in the shallows.

Proud as punch he grinned at me and in true three-year-old fashion his jaw started to flap, telling and retelling the story of what happened and about all the people he was going to feed with his fish. I was so proud!

I'd learned from my dad that it's always good to go out on a high note so we called it quits. Rehua insisted on carrying his fish over his shoulder all the way back to the truck. He might have had big intentions of feeding half the community with that one fish, but once it was smoked, he and his māmā demolished it in one sitting with satisfied grins on their faces. I didn't even get a look-in.

21. THE SKINNY HIND

It was New Year's morning and my in-laws were visiting from Christchurch, so Roi had graciously given me a three-day pass to go bush and fill our freezer. Christmas had left us sparse with only two packets of stewing meat and some goat, and that wasn't going to satisfy the New Year visitors.

With the truck full of gear and my old dog Bonnie running around in circles, excited to be going hunting, I hurtled out of Gisborne at 4 a.m. towards the bush. It didn't take long before the first major hurdle; groups of drunken revellers from Rhythm and Vines staggered across the road, falling into ditches and bringing the small trickle of traffic to a complete standstill.

Usually this time of the morning offers the quiet tranquillity of anticipation, with country music playing through the car speakers and some banana cake handily sitting on a plate in the passenger's seat as the truck rolls towards the sunrise. But today I would have to endure delays, something I'm not good at tolerating at the best of times let alone at 4 a.m. when I want to go hunting.

In my experience there are two kinds of hunters: the ones who are waiting kerbside with their gear and a hot brew in hand waiting for the pickup, and the ones you need to prise out of bed by knocking on windows and doors, before waiting an extra half-hour while they pack. I identify with the first lot.

After the annoying delay en route, I arrived at my chosen road end, which was already full of trucks, but I took no notice of the packed car park. I knew from experience that most of these hunters and fishermen would be content stalking the frontcountry, while I would be pushing on to a more remote location.

My dog and I headed up the first hill as the sun rose, casting a soft pastel-pink light across the dry farmland.

At the top, as we left the expanse of farmland and dropped through a series of ponga gullies, my dog started to wind hard. Bonnie, an SPCA rescue, has an odd way of indicating. As with many Muggle-blood mixes she doesn't lock up like a pointer, but rather slows right down and looks behind to see if I'm seeing what she's seeing. It's a 'soft point', as I like to call it. A sniff of the air, an inconsistent cock of the paw, a slight shiver through the spine. If you didn't know her, you wouldn't see it, but she was hunting alright and if you learn to slow down and listen she would show you where the deer were. We made a series of stalks following her nose but didn't come up with the goods so we moved on downriver. Fresh pig sign had ploughed up the river terraces, so I tucked that away in my memory and we kept moving.

After three hours we hit our turn-off to the upper Kahunui. There were many reasons for choosing this catchment on this day: the deer numbers were usually high; pigs were known to inhabit the upper valley; and better still, there was a remnant whio population that I was keen to assess. It had been a dream of mine for years to protect whio in this area. The rivers hold a great trout population, which is usually a good indicator of whio habitat, and ever since I was a kid, there have been birds holding on despite a lack of stoat trapping. I wanted to conduct a reconnaissance mission to assess the whio habitat of this catchment and figure out the on-the-ground logistics of extending the Eastern Whio Link project into the Kahunui.

Almost on cue, while I was dreaming about abundant whio, a stoat ran up the river within two metres of Bonnie and me. It hardly touched the ground as it moved, bouncing along and investigating the creek for food. Stoats are amazing; their hearts are able to beat three times faster than the human heart and the fact that they only have to eat every ten days makes them the ultimate predator. The damage these creatures can do to whio is devastating: raiding nests, predating on both eggs and chicks, even nailing adult birds during the moult. If pest control is not in place, very few birds make it to adulthood, and this has resulted in a slowly dwindling whio population across the country. As hunters, that's why we established the Eastern Whio Link project. We quite liked seeing our native birds while we hunted and fished.

Further upstream, we came across more deer sign but Bonnie hadn't shown any indication of winding yet. It was also getting a little late in the day for deer to be active, so we decided to stalk a few trout instead. Unfortunately, they were too smart to fall for my feeble attempts at trying to catch them in the shallow, clear-watered stream.

ABOVE The skinny hind. I felt quite torn about having shot this animal.

Suddenly, Bonnie put on the brakes, her heckles up, front paw folded, looking around as if to say, 'Do you see what I see?' I stare back, 'Nope, it's one o'clock, the deer are in cover by now. You're bonkers, you funny old dog, but go on, have a closer look.'

She edged forward, not usually that reliable at wind-scenting, but she seemed certain that she was on to something. After what seemed like an eternity, an ongaonga bush started to shake and out stepped an animal browsing along the river flat. I couldn't tell if it was a yearling or a hind, but we needed the meat. Quickly I chambered a round and at ten metres I could hardly miss. CRACK!

> Trying to communicate the lack of meat to a disappointed dog was also a challenge. Bonnie was expecting a feed and sulked for a good hour afterward. She had done her job and I had done mine, but neither of us were walking away with meat.

A quick stumble from the deer and then all went quiet. The little side creek she'd landed in started flowing bright red, indicating that the hind must have fallen straight in the creek with the bullet wound opening an artery.

We moved in and discovered that the hind had been neck shot. But she was in shocking condition. Serious muscle wastage had resulted in ribs showing through where her back steaks should be, and the ridge of her spine jutted out prominently. There was definitely something wrong with this deer. Her back legs were emaciated and would hardly provide a feed for the dog, let alone a family of visitors. She reminded me of a Tongan street dog I'd once seen on holiday with Dad, and it pulled on the same sympathetic heartstrings.

It was then that I noticed that one of her back legs had been broken and had healed in a bulbous mess, leaving a slightly open wound. Curious, I gutted her to see how healthy she was inside. As I suspected, she was barren of fawn and had incredibly pale kidneys, which usually signifies poor health. Not knowing what to make of this, I decided to let her lay without butchering her. I suspected that the muscle wastage was due to the injury on her leg, but I wasn't about to risk diseased meat for me or the dog. After a quick rub of the hands from my handy-dandy pocket bottle of antiseptic handwash, I felt a little rough having pulled the trigger on an animal I didn't intend to eat, but hopefully I had ended what would have been a difficult existence in the wild. Still, I hate leaving meat in the bush and not being able to harvest anything from a kill. It really does leave me with a bad feeling.

Trying to communicate the lack of meat to a disappointed dog was also a challenge. Bonnie was expecting a feed and sulked for a good hour afterward. She had done her job and I had done mine, but neither of us were walking away with meat. Explaining to my wife that we'd shot a deer but had come home with no venison was going to be equally difficult; the in-laws were visiting and sending them home with meat is a family tradition. Mindful of this, I decided to continue in search of a fatter, healthier deer.

That evening, after slinging the hammock and enjoying a meal of rice supplemented with kāreao shoots, we went for another stalk. Unfortunately, the only deer to be seen were three carcasses maybe a month old, highlighting that someone had obviously given the area a good working-over before Christmas. Bonnie was showing signs of being footsore and had developed a limp after eight hours on river stones, so things weren't looking too promising for a morning stalk.

After waking up to the sounds of kākā, I poured some biscuits onto the ground for the dog and happily rolled over to read my book. 'Good on you for having soft feet, dog,' I said. With a baby at home it had been a while since I'd enjoyed a sleep-in.

Midday arrived and it was clear that Bonnie's feet weren't improving much. Knowing how long these ailments can take to come right, I decided to pull the pin and head for home where she could rest up properly. It'd be alright if I had to carry her as we had no venison to haul out anyway.

Defeated, we headed out and met three groups of hunters en route to the car park. None had been successful. Maybe it was the heat, maybe it was disease, or maybe it was just our lack of skill. Whatever the cause, we were all heading home empty-handed to face our families and the gaping hole in the freezer left unfilled by the festive season and a failed hunt.

22. ADVENTURES OF THE KAHUNUI

As the chopper buzzed the hut clearing, we could see dogs, flies and possum carcasses littering the place. Our hearts sank as we realised our weekend in the remote backwaters of the Kahunui would have to be shared with some less-than-hygienic characters. We could almost smell the camp before we saw it and the repugnant scene before us was out of place in the serenity of the backcountry creek we knew well.

The little orange forest-service hut not only had someone in residence, but they had been there for quite some time. Every available bunk was covered in gear and there was bucket upon bucket of food supplies piled under the benches. Ironically the only empty box in the place was the one I'd had flown in the month before in anticipation of our trip. It'd been chocka with tinned fruit, creamed rice, biscuits, chocolate, beer and even a little bottle of whiskey, everything we needed for a well-stocked trip. But as I searched the crevices of the hut not even a biscuit could be found. The empty whiskey bottle would later be spotted being used as a candle holder above the main culprit's bunk, upon which lay a man who looked like any wealth he had acquired was gleaned off the back of others' misfortune.

He was as dirty as he was skinny, and his cheekbones leered forward in a kind of smug grin that didn't exactly inspire trust. Yep, if anyone had eaten our tucker, I guessed it would have been this greasy bush rat.

I'm not a stickler for rules and my wife will attest to my lack of house proudness, but there's one thing you just don't do in the bush, and that's eat another man's food. Especially when his name and the date of when he's coming for it is written in large, bold letters across the top of the box. I was ropeable and in need of a walk to cool down so off I set, rifle in hand, but with every new corner of the creek there seemed to be a rotting, green deer carcass hung up in a handy tree. Yep, the bush rat had been in residence for

TOP Rani was either working or hunting during the day. He just didn't have an off button. But at night he crashed, having to be shaken awake again in the morning.

BOTTOM Rani with one of the deer chasing dogs.

a while now, judging by the number of deer hung in trees, a familiar sign of long-term summer-hut living. The meat turns bad before you and your dogs can get through a whole animal so you make sure to hang the carcasses a long way from camp to give the flies somewhere else to be. The place stunk of death and the only upside to having company was the large pile of firewood stacked outside the hut to fuel the constantly smouldering, smoky fire.

> I'm not a stickler for rules and my wife will attest to my lack of house proudness, but there's one thing you just don't do in the bush, and that's eat another man's food.

We had flown in to lay out traps on the Kahunui Stream. There had been whio sighted in this section of the river, and we had finally found enough money to put stoat traps around the area. On this trip we had my uncle, Kerry Gibson, who is a top man on the Eastern Whio Link and has been part of the project since its inception. The second member of the crew was Rani Moran, of local farming stock. Rani was a gangly bugger; at fifteen years of age he was all go. If you could keep the tucker and work coming, he wouldn't stop from dawn till dusk, when he would upend his great frame and crash out in a pile on his bunk. Give him two minutes sitting down and he'd get bored and take off on the next adventure, trapping, fishing or hunting every waking minute of the day. Then there was me, a slightly broken-down bushman with a bit of a podgy dad bod brought on by a kid and a mortgage to pay.

As for our hut mates; well, one was an ex-deer culler whose pride and joy was his chasing dogs. He's the one I reckon ate our food. He was living in the bush after losing his flat in town to some behavioural disagreement or another. A typical 'hideout in the bush until it blows over' situation from the looks of it. Aside from the lack of cleanliness around camp and the empty box of food, he wasn't a bad bugger. He had good dogs and although it took me a while to shine to him, by the end of the trip we got on well enough.

The other fella was his brother, freshly relieved from a Covid-19 quarantine hotel room in Auckland. He'd been teaching English in Singapore and had flown home. It seemed a bit random that he was so far from a road end, but his not being a bushman explained the yoga mats in the surrounding clearings and circus acrobatic rings hung from a nearby tarata tree.

The two brothers were yin and yang. One was talkative and loud with

TOP I walked 16 kilometres to catch this trout. We smoked it over the Kahunui Hut fireplace that evening.

BOTTOM Deer-chasing dogs live on a lean diet of venison and possum. Always hungry and grateful for any scraps that are discarded, hurtling out the hut door.

endless stories, a bit of a rough diamond and showing the toll of years of hard living. The other was softly spoken and rather tidy, and was a practitioner of acupuncture. They'd both grown up in the scrub with their father, who was a meat shooter, deer culler and possum trapper back in the day, but each had chosen a different path.

The two brothers were yin and yang. One was talkative and loud with endless stories, a bit of a rough diamond and showing the toll of years of hard living. The other was softly spoken and rather tidy, and was a practitioner of acupuncture.

The first night, to escape the reek of camp, Rani and I shot off up a side creek for a hunt and although we spotted a young stag, we managed to spook him. The sound of my bolt sent him crashing off up the river flats and into dense undergrowth. I had the feeling most of the handy deer like this one would probably be easily spooked from our hut mates' chasing dogs and we would be doing well if we could shoot one this close to camp. We returned to camp late enough, only to have to put up with a mild session of storytelling and the odd video of chasing dogs from our new mate.

Day two had us up early and we ventured downstream, setting out the bulk of the traps. After a big morning on the hill, Uncle and I were more than content to retire to our hammocks to read books. Rani, on the other hand, took our hut mate up on his offer to take the chasing dogs for a run. A few hours later he was back covered in blood and grinning from ear to ear.

According to our hut mate's yarns, the dogs had managed to bail up two deer. One was cornered on a slip where Rani had managed to shoot it from quite a distance over the dogs, which our hut mate was quite excited about. The other, the dogs had scragged (by that I mean they started tearing it apart in the way of Te Urewera chasing dogs). By the time Rani got there, being a good rugby lad he thought he would leap in to tackle it and slit the deer's throat. There aren't many hunters who can say they've waded through a pack of growling, gnashing dogs to take down a deer and dispatch it. But that's what Rani did, an experience almost exclusive to the backwaters of Te Urewera and the Waioeka.

That evening we were subjected to more footage of dogs chasing deer out of the scrub to be shot with shotguns, rifles or taken with knives in riverbeds or hut clearings. Each story was told more excitedly than the last. Finally Uncle and I managed to sneak off to our hammocks far enough away from the dead possums on the hut clearing to not be bothered by the smell.

The next morning, Rani and I moseyed up the side creek to retrieve his second deer before heading off to finish the rest of our traps. Rani, being the unrelenting chap that he is, was keen to head further downstream in search of a trout. The trout were proving rather difficult to catch; maybe they had also experienced some excess pressure lately. We managed to land a couple of absolute whales as the light faded and headed back to camp to hang one in the chimney to smoke. It had been a return journey of over sixteen kilometres that day and I was shattered, retiring to bed without dinner.

> There aren't many hunters who can say they've waded through a pack of growling, gnashing dogs to take down a deer and dispatch it.

With the work done, the remainder of our time was spent butchering meat for the flight out and watching more videos of chasing dogs on our hut mate's phone. They had generously offered that we could take all the meat with us as they could get another deer whenever they needed it. Judging by the number of animals hanging in the bush, I believed it. There was enough going to waste as it was.

I was glad to get away from that place after a couple of days. The stench was bad. We decided to give the Kahunui a spell for a few months, give the bush rats a chance to find other lodgings, the carcasses an opportunity to rot away and the deer a wee while to calm down and filter back down from the ridges.

23. KORANGA FORKS HUT

In the dark depths of the Waioeka sits Koranga Forks Hut, nestled in a land of steep hills, grassy river terraces and bouldery gorges. You have to have your wits about you as a bushman to get around comfortably in country like this.

Mists roll through the early-morning forests, slow and wet. Your scent is masked from the flickering nostrils of deer. This is country that hasn't yet made up its mind whether it's Te Urewera or Raukūmara, whether it prefers wet, fog-covered podocarp forest or dry tawa slopes. But one thing's for certain: there's no shortage of deer, pigs and trout to keep the average bushman entertained for a lifetime.

Koranga Forks Hut was the site of my first great achievement in the bush. When I was seven, Dad decided it might be time to climb Hikurangi, one of the great mountains of our region, but thought it important to try me on an easier walk first. The Koranga was no stranger to us; up until that point in my life it'd been a place of whānau picnics and day walks. A place my grandfather would fish as I rambled along the stream banks after him. A place where Dad as a teacher held school camps.

But this day was different. As a precursor to climbing Hikurangi, we needed to test my fitness and resolve. We'd bounced our way down the rutted and potholed gravel track, pulling up to the muddied road end by 10 a.m. Dad's rusted-out old white station wagon got us everywhere we needed to go in those days. I had my sleeping bag and lunch box stuffed into a turquoise schoolbag with the entire load wrapped in rubbish bags to keep the rain out. It felt proper heavy and the straps weren't exactly comfortable. We set off at a pace that was a stretch for me and a hindrance to my father, but we were out there in the bush together spending time on an adventure, which is all that mattered to either of us. As a family we didn't have much

TOP Koranga Forks Hut was the first hut I ever walked to and is definitely the heart of the Waioeka in my opinion.

BOTTOM We had lots of amazing adventures together, Dad and me.

when I was a kid but any adventure with Dad was awesome.

Before long we came across a whānau camped on the river flats, a deer from the morning's hunt strapped to their quad bike. On the first big hill we smelt a pungent stank that managed to get right up inside your nostrils and felt like you could smell it in your tonsils. Dad reckoned it was goats, and before long we heard the distinct clacking of horns as two billy goats thrashed it out on the track in front of us. I remember hiding behind Dad, a little scared as those goats smacked their heads into one another.

Koranga Forks was a long way for a seven-year-old whose growing legs were still more bone than muscle. Although I willed them not to, they started to ache after a while and I was torn between wanting a rest and wanting to keep up with Dad. Seeing that my legs were tired, Dad told a story of when Poppa Lex was about my age and had to walk to school on frosty mornings. They couldn't afford shoes back in those days and Poppa Lex used to run from cowpat to cowpat, sticking his feet in the nice, gooey mess to warm his feet up on cold winter mornings. Dad reckoned Poppa Lex used to get told off pretty bad for having stinky feet when he got to school, but he didn't care. At least his feet were warm.

That made me laugh. Dad had a good way of taking your mind off things and reckoned the secret to walking was about sending your mind off into your imagination and telling yourself stories. If the story was good enough your mind would soon forget about how sore your legs were, and before you knew it you'd be at your destination. He was right, too. Before long we'd arrived at the swaying, old, wire swing bridge with a whiny, old black-and-white dog on our side of the river and smoke coming from the chimney of a rickety corrugated-iron hut on the other.

I patted the dog, who was skinny and covered in mud. It got all excited for a pat and I quite liked dogs. My other Poppa, GK, had English pointers that we used for hunting pheasants and ducks, and dogs always seemed to warm to me.

I had to work up a bit of courage to climb onto the creaky wire-meshed bridge that swayed from side to side high above the river. But Dad showed me how crossing a swing bridge has a certain rhythm to it. If you can time your steps with the bounce of the wire it won't throw you off balance. Even so, I felt a bit like the forlorn dog whining on the bank behind us. Being so high up with the river crashing over boulders below took all the willpower out of my young legs. But following Dad across, I eventually made it.

On arrival at the hut we were greeted by a pack of pig dogs, odds and sods of all descriptions. There were brindled bullies, heading-dog crosses and a whole lot of blue-heeler types. As the dogs kicked up a racket, the owners emerged from the hut, bringing with them a trail of curses that had the dogs disappearing back under the hut where they'd come from. The owners of the expletives were two long-haired, flannel-shirted, Rastafarian pig hunters, the type the East Coast is famous for.

> On the first big hill we smelt a pungent stank that managed to get right up inside your nostrils and felt like you could smell it in your tonsils. Dad reckoned it was goats, and before long we heard the distinct clacking of horns as two billy goats thrashed it out on the track in front of us.

I was slightly in awe of these rough-clad, rough-talking bushmen but they were friendly and fun and after pouring me a coffee from a billy swinging above the smoky fire (who in their right minds gives a seven-year-old coffee?) and loading it with dirty spoonfuls of sweetened condensed milk from an open tin sitting on a windowsill, they invited me to do a bit of eeling with them in the hut pool.

Dad was in agreement so we all wandered down to the hut pool where we built another fire and hooked giant hunks of possum guts left over from feeding the hungry-looking pig dogs onto oversized hooks, and hammered driftwood stakes through the round plastic reels of nylon into the shingle so a tuna couldn't drag them into the depths as we sat there and waited.

We didn't have to wait too long. As I cooked marshmallows on a stick in the embers of our fire, a plastic reel started to tug at the driftwood. Then it started to spin wildly. One of the dreadlocked bushmen ran over to the line and, using his Swanndri to shield his fingers from the cut of the nylon, he coaxed the eel away from rocks and log jams until it eventually came writhing up from the depths to wriggle and squirm on the grassy bank.

These fellas didn't muck around; soon after, it was cleaned of slime by fistfuls of bracken and hanging from a tree.

By this point I was reaching my expiry date. It had been a big day's walk and I was almost asleep on my feet. The track to Koranga Forks was meant to take three hours but we'd managed to take six; no wonder, considering all the stops we'd taken. Between Dad and I, we'd somehow forgotten my toothbrush, and with the amount of sweetened condensed milk and marshmallows I had ingested that evening, my pearly whites were in dire need of some attention. Dad showed me how to turn a kawakawa leaf into a toothbrush by chewing the spoon-shaped end into bristles. He explained how the leaf's antibacterial properties, when rubbed on my teeth, would leave them feeling smooth and clean rather than fuzzy. So with clean pegs I clambered into the top bunk to sink into the soft foam mattress of the DOC huts of that era.

I awoke to the smell of bacon wafting through the rafters. Another enamel mug of coffee was thrust into my hand and our adopted hosts soon slung a plate of squished white bread and wild pork bacon at me from the fireplace. I wasn't too sure about the bacon as the rind still had the remains of singed black hairs poking through, but I ate it, not wanting to offend our new friends.

They reckoned they were off for a hunt and if we were heading out, could we keep an eye out for their dog across the creek. It was one of their daughters' dogs and had been missing for a week or so. I told them we'd seen it the night before by the swing bridge and they laughed, saying the silly thing was afraid of heights. I felt too silly to admit that I was afraid of heights too and that I didn't blame the dog for not wanting to cross the bridge.

The hunters shook our hands vigorously before leaving, trailed by their pack of dogs that emerged somewhat reluctantly from under the hut. 'Good to meet you fellas,' they reckoned then off they went, leaving Dad, me and three eels that were pegged up on nails behind.

About a month later on a scorching summer's day, Dad and I set forth on a climb that was going to test my fortitude. The Hikurangi track is pretty much straight up, with no shade from the sun and no flat sections to give your burning calves a rest. What's more, on that day the track went through a paddock absolutely brimming with huge Angus bulls, and little curly-haired me was pretty intimidated by having to push through those colossal animals. Dad, on the other hand, wasn't scared one bit so I took up my usual spot slotted right in behind his orange-and-green Swanndri, thinking with any luck the bulls wouldn't notice I was there.

Once again Dad reminded me of how to go to a place in my imagination, and after a gigantic yet uneventful hike we made it to Hikurangi Hut. I was shattered, so shattered in fact that the rats that kept Dad awake in his bunk that night clambered and crawled all over me and I didn't even wake up.

In the morning I was woken to Dad saying, 'Do you want to watch the sunrise?'

It was freezing cold but bundled up in Dad's Swanndri with a mug of Milo in my hands I wandered outside to see the sun. Hikurangi Maunga is officially the first place in the world to see the sun and that day it was just me and my dad, the first on the entire planet.

I was shattered, so shattered in fact that the rats that kept Dad awake in his bunk that night clambered and crawled all over me and I didn't even wake up.

As I climbed back into my sleeping bag, Dad made us breakfast. I was still tired and sore from the walk the day before. But that was just the lemon next to the pie, as Dad liked to say. We weren't just content with seeing the sun rise; our mission for the day ahead was to crest the summit.

So with Dad carrying the daypack and camera, we scurried our way up through prickly alpine vegetation, just about jumping out of our socks when a wild bull burst from the scrub in front of us, tossing his head and running in the other direction.

Eventually we made it to the scree slope that fell from sheer rocks above. Scree is really difficult to climb when you're tramping, especially with little kids' legs. As I scampered up the moving rocks, they would all come tumbling down, taking me with them. It was two steps forward and one step back, and if you stopped you'd slide even further. It was like racing an escalator going in the wrong direction; the secret was to just keep going and eventually we reached the top.

The top, however, was a narrow path no more than two boot-lengths across and on each side a sheer cliff dropped away below us. I was petrified. My fear of heights that I'd become aware of crossing the swing bridge in the Koranga was back with a vengeance. My stomach was turning, my legs weren't working and as I looked down the cliffs to the valley below a metallic taste seeped into my mouth.

Dad sat me down and told me to rest. He could see I was panicking and needed a bit of a spell. Realising a little too late that crossing the ten metres of rocky tightrope to the summit was probably beyond me at that age, he very understandingly told me I didn't have to do it.

That moment of not having to do it changed everything for me that day. The pressure of living up to Dad's perceived expectations just washed away. I felt light and my legs started working again. Sensing a change in my energy, Dad reckoned that if we were going to do it, we should do it now. 'I can't hold your hand because the track is too narrow,' he told me, 'but if you make it I'll give you a lollipop.'

I remember thinking, 'A lollipop?' What a crap prize for risking my life on these rocky outcrops. But I wasn't doing it for the lollipop: I had a strange determination growing inside me, a feeling I didn't quite recognise. I was going to do it because the opportunity to achieve something was there and if I walked away from the challenge I knew I would spend hours running the scenario back through my head and wishing I'd done it.

I was never a brave kid, always soft, gentle and never competitive. But somehow that day I found the drive and motivation that comes from competitiveness with myself rather than with others. Two minutes later I was holding on to the flaky, white wooden trig station at the peak of Hikurangi Maunga, with the wind blowing through my hair. Dad took a bunch of photos of me that day and in every single one I'm clinging on to that wooden trig like the wind was going to blow us all away.

That day impacted the rest of my life. It was the day I discovered the ability to put my mind over my emotions and grit in, knuckle down and walk forward. An attribute that would serve me well for a life in the bush.

24. THE MIDDAY DEER

Feeling like a flea on a wet dog, the humidity in the bush was barely breathable. It was late morning in a block bordering the mist-clad Te Urewera. I'd woken early to discuss plans with fellow hut residents and concluded that the best call was to roll over in my sleeping bag and dissolve once again back into a pile of z's. As is common with public-land hunting, you either have the place to yourself or every man and his dog descends on the same block you'd hoped to hunt that weekend.

> Deer aren't stupid and they leave a twenty-metre buffer of untouched vegetation right around the track so that they don't get shot by unenthusiastic rifle walkers. As soon as you venture far from a track the vegetation is absolutely chewed out.

We had arrived in two trucks the day before. It was just after a severe storm, rivers were raging brown and massive trees had fallen across the road, adding an extra twenty-minute walk to our day. We thought no one else would be mad enough to head bush on such an unlikely weekend, but as night had fallen and cups of tea were being made, three more head torches could be seen bobbing along the track towards the hut.

The next morning, when I finally did emerge from my sleeping bag, dodging the hut rafters as I sat up, I set about getting my kit together for a foraging mission. I had opted to stay back from hunting to allow others enough options to find a spot. But even if I wasn't going to hunt, I definitely wouldn't be sitting around being useless. So off I set, rifle slung across the shoulder just in case and a bag on my belt so that I could harvest enough pikopiko for the crew's dinner. If they could bring home the venison, then

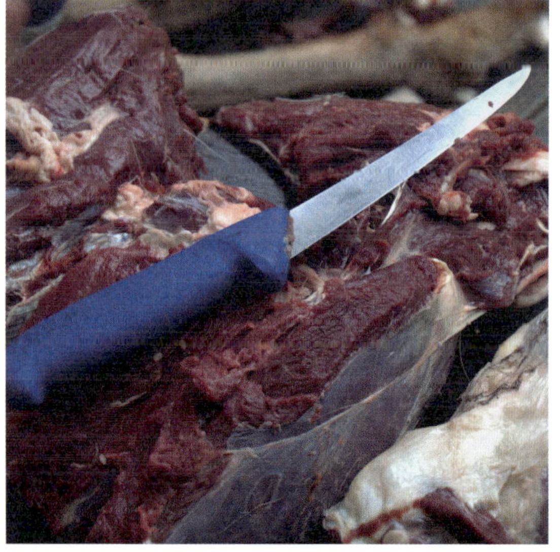

TOP LEFT I used to carry whole animals out from Koranga Forks Hut. Now as I've got older I tend to bone them out. Maybe it's my sore hips and knees; maybe I'm hunting smarter. One thing's for sure: I do miss the glory of the big carries.

BOTTOM LEFT By shooting more deer we grow more pikopiko. It's that simple.

TOP RIGHT Call me weird but instead of taking gory photos of dead deer I like to take pretty close-ups of their unique features; ears, swirls of hair, antlers and so on.

BOTTOM RIGHT Fresh venison back steaks for the crew.

I'd get the vegetables and no one would have to rely on freeze-dried meals.

So off I set. The interesting thing about foraging in the bush is that the best foraging is right on the tracks. Deer aren't stupid and they leave a twenty-metre buffer of untouched vegetation right around the track so that they don't get shot by unenthusiastic rifle walkers. As soon as you venture far from a track the vegetation is absolutely chewed out. As a result, people who don't venture far from the track tend to think the bush is in much better condition than it actually is.

Stooging along picking the curly wee taste sensations that are pikopiko, I bumped into some of the lads coming back from their hunt. They were empty-handed but as it was their first time hunting the block they remained in good spirits. They reckoned they were done for the day, which lit me up with a burst of excitement — I might get a quick hunt in after all.

I gained altitude via an easy spur that rose from the valley floor. My skin resembled that of a frog, constantly wet by the air around me. I like hunting in the mist; it keeps you cool so there's no need to sweat, and when there's no need to sweat, you don't have to drink as much. This allows me to climb high above the small seepages, streams and creeks of this rocky country in search of deer.

As I climbed, the deer sign became stronger and sucked me from my easy spur across harder country of steep, shingly guts and tight kiekie-filled gullies. As I pushed on, the sign became fresher. Soon I was in a bluff system high above the river where the ground was loose underfoot and mangled shrubs clung to the cliffs by their roots poked into deep cracks in the rock. It was here that the deer were eking out an existence, far from the prying eyes of the hunter. Deer are clever and will often put themselves into the toughest country when they're exposed to a lot of hunting pressure.

After taking a few unplanned slides and only just recovering before being sent over the edge to the river below, I was reminded of my time working as a trapper in Fiordland, where we'd spend our evenings recutting sharp edges onto our boot soles with our hunting knives for the day to come. It was imperative to have as much grip as possible and that sharp edge could be jammed into a rock crevice whereas a soft outer edge on your boot might slide free. Nowadays I have two kids to get home to and, having fallen off my share of bluffs over the years, it was starting to feel a little sketchy.

As I backed out slowly from this steep terrain, disappointed in my lack of bravery, I heard a clatter of rock. Searching with my feet for a steady foothold amongst the shale, like a robin searches for insects amongst the leaf litter, I looked up. Standing broadside on the other side of a gully system was a hind. Miraculously she had succumbed to the ultimate character flaw of red deer. She must have smelled me, become spooked, then ran a few metres before being overwhelmed by her sense of inquisitiveness. She'd stopped and was looking around for the source of that peculiar smell. It was surprising she didn't see me in my electric blue thermal (I hadn't planned on going for a hunt and had dressed for comfort rather than camouflage) but as they say, don't look a gift horse in the mouth. The sharp crack of the .308 bushpig had her tumbling down the scree slope doing cartwheels past me. Thankfully, she got caught up in one of the few decent trees in the vicinity, otherwise she would have tumbled to the gully floor.

Field-dressing a deer on a cliff face has its positives and negatives. The positive as I see it is that the gut bag falls away easily. The negative is that keeping the deer from tumbling after the gut bag can be difficult. This leads us to the next real challenge of the hunt.

The lads at the hut had heard my shot and were probably no more than 300 metres from me as the crow flies. But I was also possibly the same height in elevation as those imaginary crows. Retrieving this animal was going to be tricky, but I prided myself in going further and into sketchier country than most hunters will go to provide kai for the table.

Half an hour later, after a few head-scratching and bum-puckering moments, I wandered into camp with hind legs slung across my shoulders and back steaks swinging from my belt. There was also a bulging bag of pikopiko nestled in my pīkau. We would be eating like kings tonight. As the remainder of the hunting parties dribbled into camp empty-handed, we prepared our kai. The choice bits were for us in the field, with plenty to spare for the whānau at home.

Not bad for a midday hunt less than 300 metres from the hut. I guess it just goes to show the deer are there, it's just up to us to find them.

ABOVE It's scenes like these that don't change. We hunt and fish the same mist laden forests our grandfathers did all those years ago.

25. THE CORNER POOL

He went to the river in the pouring rain, knowing that to most, it would be unfishable. Fishing wasn't the reason he sought the water that day. He had a lot of thinking to do. Work was getting a bit much and his relationship was becoming strained because of it. The fishing was just an excuse. The Mrs had an insatiable appetite for smoked trout and a day off for fishing met no protest if the reward was a couple of rainbow-sided pan flappers.

Water streamed down the hood of his raincoat as he walked the banks of the main river, knowing it was much too dirty to fish. But the walking helped. Somehow the rhythmical plodding of squelching boots brought his thoughts into order, something he struggled to do from an office in town.

The ducks were all tucked up on the bank, beaks firmly nestled under wings as the rain pelted down. That's where most humans would be today, tucked up somewhere warm and dry. But as a fisherman he had never really minded the wet. There was no such thing as bad weather, his father used to say, just a bad choice of clothing. He'd been raised on these rivers, rain, hail or shine. His grandfather had taught him how to fish, how to read the river and how to dress.

There's nothing wrong with wool, he'd say. Wool is good for you. Keeps you warm when it's wet and breathes when it's hot. Not like this fancy synthetic stuff these days. Under his raincoat, that's what he had on. An old woollen jersey and a merino singlet.

As he wandered, he thought, and as he thought, he headed for the corner pool, the first in a side creek that other fishermen walked past, a side creek that almost never flooded even when the main river was in full rage. He'd stumbled across the corner pool one day in absolute frustration when he'd come to the river in search of a day's fishing but found it brown after unseasonable recent rains.

ABOVE A big rainbow jack I caught in the corner pool on a day the rest of the rivers were running brown.

Try as he might, that day he hadn't been able to find any clean water in which to throw a lure, so he resorted to spinning in that tight little gutter of a creek just as it cascaded down to join the main flow. To his amazement a huge jack pounced at his lure from the shadows almost immediately and put up a high-paced head-shaking resistance before eventually being coaxed from the shallow 60 centimetres of water that made up the creek bed.

That had been a few years back. Since then when it rained he made a habit of visiting the same corner pool and venturing up the stream to fossick through its other deeper depressions in search of fish. He'd found that when the main river ran brown, the trout would congregate in any clean-flowing water they could find, loading each pocket of the creek with hungry mouths eager to take a hook.

Almost on autopilot, his brain full of worries, he threw a lure, the silver Veltic bouncing off the hard cliff that fringed the pool then dropping into the creek with a pop. The creek was shallow so he was sure to keep it off the bottom as a pause in the action would let any suspecting trout in on the hoax, exposing metal to eye when it was otherwise disguised by movement. Nobody home today!

> There was no such thing as bad weather, his father used to say, just a bad choice of clothing.

Dodging blackberry and overhanging tutu, he clambered his way up boulders and took a shortcut through a kahikatea flat to reach the second pool. And there, stacked in with no place to go, were seven fat rainbows heavily laden with late-season spawn. Wedged between boulders at the head of the rapids he threw, receiving a follow for his efforts.

He threw again and saw a dominant hen cautiously nudge towards his lure. Flirting with disaster, he slowed his wind to allow her to catch up. Too slow and the blade would flicker, letting her know of the dangerous game afoot; too fast and this fat old girl wouldn't put in enough effort to keep up. Finally convinced, she lazily made a swallow and the game was on.

She raced around the circular arena of the pool, leaping into the air several times in an effort to dislodge the hook. She was strong and hefty. More than once he felt like she was going tear free as he played her. With the rod tip of his 60-dollar telescopic set-up almost bent in two, he manoeuvred her away from underwater boulders and that one niggly branch that threatened to snap the line. As she battled, the other fish fled the pool downstream.

Eventually she tired and with a last-ditch effort she floated across the surface, rolling into his waiting net. This was a fatty, a good-sized fish. The flesh would be pink with spawning colours, almost salmon-like. What's more, the bright orange roe she carried inside her could be battered in egg white and fried for a tasty snack. This fish really was a prize.

As he trudged his way back to the truck, he felt a lightness. Somehow the things he'd been jostling with in his mind had come to a place of clarity. A little rain, a little walking and that great tussle with a fish in the creek had put things into perspective. They reckon it's better to be a slay-up than a play-up, and he would soon be heading home to the warmth of the fire, a steaming mug of herbal tea and a good feed while his wife supped on smoked trout for dinner.

26. HUNTING WITH SWANNY

Like stepping into a scene from a mystical film, hunting with Swanny makes you second-guess the bounds of reality. On a midsummer Monday, I found myself being carted into the unknown, down a road I'd been on just once before. To a land where gigantic fallow deer are around every corner, where reds are a slightly less-desirable freezer filler, and where tusky boars amble through clearings, lethargically ploughing soil even in the middle of the day.

The roads seemed to point straight up to the sky (I'm really glad we weren't in my ute), plateauing out when the air thinned. It was clear that we were in another world. Mountain cabbage trees and gnarled beech thick with macrophytes marked the altitude. We were definitely in the Raukūmara Ranges, this place just felt different.

Swanny is a bit of an enigma. He used to play in rock bands with my uncles back in the day. In town he's a smooth-dressing, eloquent professional. He manages Gisborne's electricity network, making sure the hydro dams and power lines are functioning. But when he's transplanted into the backblocks and grown a little stubble on his chin, there's another facet to this well-rounded human. He's a bloody good horseman, an accomplished pig hunter and you should see his deer dogs — smooth, obedient and reliable. Yep, Swanny has all the charm of a gentleman cowboy and I guess that's why he's married to a model.

As I scrambled to force open a gate that wouldn't have been out of place in *Mad Max*, Swanny beamed from the ute window. He was quick to inform me that he'd made this gate himself and pointed out the elaborate network of cameras, 'to keep an eye on those bloody poachers'.

This is the home of River of Man Adventures (ROMA), a project with a difference. Mangaotāne, or River of Man for those with a slightly less

ABOVE Swanny and me hunting Mangaotāne. The steep river slips were home to numerous red deer and some of the biggest-bodied fallow deer I have ever encountered. © Paddy Stewart

developed understanding of our country's first language, is a large, privately owned forest spanning over 5500 hectares. Nearly half of this enormous spread is in native bush and the other half is first-generation pine plantation. Right through the centre runs a pristine river and along the boundary lies Raukūmara, the heartland of the mighty East Coast.

I'd been invited as a trapper to visit this block and I swear, as we passed through that rather imposing gate, the world took on a whole new meaning and pace. As we ground our way down out of the clouds on impeccably kept forestry tracks, a deer leapt in front of us. Swanny casually explained that it was the big black buck that always hangs out there; I was welcome to shoot him if I wanted. Maybe it was the way Swanny talked about him like he was speaking about a well-loved pet, or maybe it just felt too easy, but I just knew I needed to pass on this fella. I was here to trap stoats and protect the local whio population. If we were lucky, we might even be able to confirm the rumour that there were still kiwi present in the block.

As hunters we are starting to recognise that deer, pig and tahr numbers are getting out of hand and for us to retain the social licence to hunt we need to do something about it. In short, it's about quality not quantity.

The purpose of this trip wasn't hunting and I wanted to be really clear to Swanny that I wasn't here to take from the place, I just wanted to help. In that regard, ROMA is different though. There's a lot of talk on the wind about hunters being conservationists and keeping a lid on deer populations. Essentially there's a notion that hunters can and will manage large tracts of land to a level that not only allows native wildlife to flourish but also retains a healthy population of game species.

The intellectual argument goes that by keeping a lid on the breeding female population, hunters can both increase the carrying capacity of the land as well as improve the quality of the animals we harvest. As hunters we are starting to recognise that deer, pig and tahr numbers are getting out of hand and for us to retain the social licence to hunt we need to do something about it. In short, it's about quality not quantity.

And that's what it is in a lot of cases, just talk and intellectual brainstorming. True to his East Coast roots, however, Peter Swann was

ABOVE Paddy Stewart and Swanny setting up an acoustic recorder. We use these gadgets to monitor the places we hunt for kiwi, bats and many other endangered species.

quietly and humbly getting boots on the ground and walking the walk. For the last year or so ROMA had been running helicopter hunting ballots into their piece of paradise in the hope that recreational hunting pressure would reduce the number of deer and pigs to a point where the native forest would recover. Hunters were briefed on arrival and encouraged to shoot hinds as meat animals. In blocks where numbers have remained high, ROMA have brought in their own whānau-sourced cullers, and if that's not enough, the helicopters come through as a last resort.

And it was working. The people kept coming, booking trip after trip from all corners of the country. Why wouldn't you? Mangaotāne boasts some of the East Coast's finest red genetics, a fallow herd famed for its uncharacteristically large size and diversity of colours, extremely hooky boars, again in a full tapestry of colours, a trophy trout fishery, and even the odd wild Raukūmara cattle beast floating about. It's the kind of place where legends are made and tales have no need of exaggeration.

But that's just one arm of the operation. The income generated through hunting is then redirected into other conservation initiatives, such as purchasing the stoat traps we were here to establish. Mangaotāne had a very fragmented, very sensitive whio population, just teetering on the brink of collapse. That was the challenge to be quietly overcome by the ROMA team; we were here to protect the first three kilometres of river in a project that had the lofty goal of employing locals to protect whio and kiwi, if only we could find the manu.

So off we set, fortunately on foot. I'd been suspiciously watching an incredibly wild and aggressive grey stallion chase a small group of mares and yearlings around the homestead paddock, and was trying to figure out a way to tell Swanny there was no way in hell I'd be getting on one of those manic creatures. I usually like horses but these ones were pretty green. To my relief, he informed me that they were the remnant herd of old station horses that were left behind when the place was put into forestry.

As we wandered our way down to the river, we passed old, corrugated-iron musterers' huts in the process of being refurbished for hunters to stay in. We'd made a sound decision to leave the rifles at home as distractions were plentiful on every slip and clearing. According to Swanny, this was nothing; the numbers had been reduced significantly to get to this point. He reckoned that during the winter before they started their herd-management operation, the grass was chewed to the root and the deer were skinny as. His

TOP The old musterers hut on Mangaotāne Station.

BOTTOM After a day's trapping we would inevitably end up going for a hunt. Carrying deer out through the waterfalled canyons of the Mangaotāne River was a fitting way to end our day on such an awesome hunter-led conservation project.

eyes lit up whenever we saw a fat velvety; these were animals showing great potential for the roar.

Dusk came and went as we worked alongside this visionary bushman. Head torches were rummaged for in packs and we continued screwing the traps to trees. Summer nights have a way of being quiet, cool and still. At 11 p.m. we decided we were hungry. After retrieving a rifle from the homestead, we set about locating a feed. A handy red presented itself and soon eye fillets were sizzling in a pan.

When I'm in the bush, one of my favourite callings in life is to have a look just in case there are threatened species about. Often, by having a nosey, we can identify all manner of rare species far outside their known ranges.

Over a couple of Gizzy Golds, the East Coast's finest drop, conversation turned to kiwi. As with much of Aotearoa's far-flung reaches, we don't really know what's still present and what has been destroyed by the scourge of invasive predators our misinformed ancestors saw fit to grace our country with. When I'm in the bush, one of my favourite callings in life is to have a look just in case there are threatened species about. Often, by having a nosey, we can identify all manner of rare species far outside their known ranges. We just need to know how to look and then species like bats, kiwi, native frogs and insects reveal themselves. So off we set with a UE Boom and a kiwi call downloaded on our phones.

Monitoring kiwi is a slow-paced affair. We moved from high point to high point, catchment to catchment, blasting fake kiwi calls from our speaker and waiting for a reply. By 3 a.m. our hopes were fading, the cold was catching up with us, and the long periods of inactivity and listening had us nodding off. It had been a massive day, and a successful day too. We'd established a decent chunk of whio protection, shot a deer, and chewed the fat about this new movement of hunters for conservation.

Almost as if to affirm what we were doing, there it was: a call. A lone male kiwi with its long, ascending whistle repeating several times before disappearing into the night. We can read into these moments as much or as little as we like, but whatever your superstitious tendencies, a kiwi call offers yet another glimmer of hope. Another species that hasn't quite disappeared

TOP Boulder hopping laden down with traps is all part of protecting whio in the rivers of the East Coast. © Peter Swann

BOTTOM It always surprises me how pine forests and regenerating bush make such amazing kiwi habitat.

at Mangaotāne. Another opportunity for hunters to step up and to give back to conservation. They don't have to be greenies and they don't even have to check traps. Through the simple act of flying into the bush and hunting, hunters are protecting a unique and hugely valuable corner of New Zealand.

And you guessed right. Swanny wasn't going to let me leave without filling my freezer with venison. The next day we were up at sparrows' fart to check our traps and knock over a couple of fatties. That's just the kind of human Peter Swann is.

They don't have to be greenies and they don't even have to check traps. Through the simple act of flying into the bush and hunting, hunters are protecting a unique and hugely valuable corner of New Zealand.

Over the coming months we made it our mission to find every threatened species possible so that Swanny had as much ammunition in his belt as possible when it came to approaching funders for this conservation project. We had whio, tick, we now had kiwi, tick. But in order to really figure out what was going on we needed to call in my good mate, the gangly vegetarian Paddy Stewart.

Now Paddy is a proper finder of things. He knows where to look, how to look, and species just seem to pop up in his presence. If you have never seen a Hochstetter's frog or an Archey's frog for that matter, Paddy is the guy to show you. He has populations all over the bush where he knows where to look. One time he even showed me a pāua slug, a weird little purple geezer that crawls around the bush with a small pāua-like shell on its back. I never knew they existed until Paddy showed me. He was the guy to find our threatened species.

So, we set to work. Now, Paddy is a master of gadgetry. When he pulls up in his big blue Land Cruiser it's loaded to the gunnels with all kinds of recorders, monitors, listening devices and speakers. He has enough batteries to alter the earth's gravitational pull and stores everything in black foam-padded cases. Going to work with Paddy is like stepping inside a spy movie.

We drove around Mangaotāne in a side-by-side for most of a week deploying recorders for bats, monitors for kiwi and all manner of other gadgetry. As fate would have it we inevitably ran into deer that needed culling so we loaded up the back of the machine with animals as fast as poor vegetarian Paddy could unload it. That's sort of what happens when you're with Swanny on Mangaotāne. His way of showing you round sounds a bit like: 'I shot a deer here one day', 'Saw a monster stag here', 'There's an eleven-pointer that just needs a couple of years' growth before we take him living on that flat'. Then bang! 'Sorry team, that one was asking for it.'

There were times we were so loaded up with meat that a certain clunking sound stopped Swannie's usual rally-driving antics in their tracks. With him and Paddy both peering under the side-by-side looking at springy bits (I'm no good at mechanics), we found out that the plastic undercarriage of the bike had been laden down by the number of deer we were trying to cart back and had scraped on a rock in the track and come loose. Nothing a bit of bush mechanics and a cable tie couldn't fix, and we were soon back on our way.

Swanny and I did look for frogs, but we couldn't find any. After the first week, Paddy had to disappear to another job finding another critter but in a month he was back to retrieve his devices. Like two expectant dads, Swanny and I waited for our results. Paddy had to listen to all his recordings but the anticipation was getting to us. Every few days Swanny and I would flick each other little texts to check if the other had heard from Paddy yet.

After what seemed like forever, Paddy finally sent us a report. Yes we had kiwi, in really low numbers and hanging out in the high, regenerating native bush. We also had bats, both the long- and short-tailed species. We even had kārearea hanging about. This was a much better list than we'd anticipated and Swanny was rapt.

Now we would set about writing funding applications for a project along the same lines as the Eastern Whio Link for another group of hunters looking after the area they hunted in. With whio, kiwi and bats, Mangaotāne is a place of legend, that's for sure. A forgotten valley on the edge of Raukūmara.

27. MY STAG, WILL HE EVER COME?

Sunburn and sweat was not what I was expecting as I painstakingly crunched my way through tawa and ponga leaves, edging in on yet another guttural moan. The leaf litter of the southern Raukūmara resembled a dry bowl of cornflakes. It was just my luck, the first year I'd managed to get out for the roar since 2018 and try as I might, getting in on a big boy was proving challenging.

My roar history to date had been one of misadventure and bad timing.

2018: The last roar trip I had was with Roimata and Uncle Kirk. We'd chased reds in the freezing-cold mountains of Haast. The timing was a little off and we'd struck too early. I had an opportunity at a great stag and stuffed it up while Kirk took a real fatty for the freezer.

2019: We found ourselves the victim of poor maths skills and our son was born, you guessed it, on 12 April (I guess he's getting helicopter time for his birthday for the rest of his life).

2020: I was all prepped, block sorted, gear packed. It was going to be a cracker. Our son was one and we had the in-laws all sorted to come and stay while I was away and then oops! Global pandemic!

2021: Here we were. Six days solo in a distant pocket of private forest, all native, with nobody else around. On the agenda was finding 'my stag'. Anyone who knows me knows I am an idealist. I hunt purely for meat and I'm not interested in trophies or bragging rights. I just enjoy being in the bush and sneaking in on animals. I enjoy roaring in stags, but when it comes to shooting animals in the roar, I would much rather take a yearling or hind than a stinky, rutting stag.

However, with every bold statement comes a 'but' or a contradiction. I have given myself a hall pass. Having grown up with an absolute cracker Te Urewera red stag on my grandfather's wall, I've realised that shooting a

TOP A wee spiker. Not exactly the stag I was hoping to find.

BOTTOM Skinny hinds are a sign that there are too many deer in the bush and that an ecosystem is properly depleted. Deer management is something we need to do a lot better in Aotearoa.

trophy is something I want to do.

On day one, the Hughes 500 NOTAR dropped me through a tight hole in the canopy, into a small side creek. The original dot on the map I'd been given was covered in vegetation and although we'd searched up and down the river, this less-than-desirable landing site was the best spot we could find.

With the engine still running and the pilot keeping his foot on the juice, I unloaded hurriedly and with a quick signal to the chopper pilot he was off and on to the next mission.

I really enjoyed winding up young stags until they were just about popping, trying to hit the gruff, guttural undertones impersonating an older stag.

After setting up my hammock between two trees and ensuring camp was weatherproof, I set off on a hunt. Upstream was the place for me, a few plateaus on a likely-looking spur to check out. Sure enough at 700 metres elevation I was greeted by moans. It sounded like I was dealing with a satellite stag and a big boy who stank. I managed to get in close to the bigger stag, like real close. Unfortunately, his pad was in the middle of a ponga bench and I snapped a frond heading in. A crash announced he had packed up shop fast and a moment later I was left with flies buzzing around my head as I observed his empty stink hole of a wallow.

On day two I was up early and raring to go. I practically ran downstream to the start of the first spur and didn't stop climbing until I was at 500 metres elevation. Again, I had stags roaring, three of them, but none would move in to my moans. They were down on the slip edges of the opposite spur and I'm guessing their hinds weren't keen to move from where the food was.

A quick assessment of my options had me heading higher. If this block was anything like Haast, it would be smarter to drop down from the top rather than work them from my current position. So up I went. Spikers, eight-pointers, and no end of scrubby, uneducated stags came into my roars over the next few hours. It was super exciting. I would let out a moan and moments later a young stag would roar his head off and posture his way in, looking to steal my imaginary hinds.

I really enjoyed winding up young stags until they were just about popping, trying to hit the gruff, guttural undertones impersonating an older stag. I would hide behind a tree or in reasonably dense cover and bring them in to within ten metres. Their eyes would start to bulge as they came in tough and stiff-legged, like when two male dogs are trying to posture for dominance. Then there would be a moment when they would either smell me and stop — you could see them weighing up the risk of stepping towards this unknown creature — or they would charge past me as I sent them on their way with a bit of a yell.

This is the part of roar hunting I love. It's not the strategy or the hunt, it's seeing how different animals react to an incredibly intense, high-risk situation. In Haast I had a monster thirteen-pointer walk straight in on me, not a fear in the world, step out from behind a tight mess of scrub, look me in the eye, lower his antlers and shake them at me as if to say, 'I see you but I'm still going to take you on.' Thankfully we managed to drop that fella before he made good on his challenge and he now sits pride of place on my mate Ben's lounge-room wall.

Every time I roar hunt, I'm searching to relive that moment, a massive stag and an exciting challenge. But today was not that day.

By 2 p.m. I found myself on the other spur, dropping down on a gnarly-sounding animal. He was holding hinds on what the GPS told me was a steep slip. Taking every ounce of care I could muster and searching for each solid exposed root to step on, I descended onto the scene.

He was doing the typical 'turn his head so you can't quite pinpoint where the sound is coming from' trick. He had me guessing where exactly he was, and at the last minute, I realised I was heading down the wrong side of the slip. As far as vegetation goes, the trees on the sides of slips tend to resemble the inside of a scrubbing brush and one can't help but be a little noisy in the tight stuff. Again, I made it to where I thought he was and again I was left with just the pungent odour of stinky stag. I let out a roar and silence was my reply.

Defeated, I headed for the river and my highway back to camp.

Almost as consolation, a hind and a yearling stepped into the river in front of me. Grateful for camp meat, I drew a bead on the tender-looking yearling. The hind looked at me, looked at her fallen companion, and off she ambled.

With camp meat sorted, I arrived home and cooked up a tidy feed of back steaks.

Stiff and sore, the third day had me frowning at the boulders I had leapt between the day before. Roimata's cooking and the adventures of

TOP LEFT A huge wallow I stumbled across up high on the ridge. There was the odd young stag hanging about but I couldn't find the big boy.

TOP RIGHT The yearling I took for meat. There's nothing like fresh food on a long trip.

BOTTOM LEFT My .308 bush pig Tikka, CRISPI boots and a roaring horn. All cornerstones of a good roar hunting adventure.

BOTTOM RIGHT Camp meat hanging from the tree.

fatherhood hadn't been kind to my endurance fitness.

As I hobbled along, I saw a strange stag with no antlers feeding on a slip. Empty pedicles graced his skull. I let out a roar but he just stared back at me blankly, so I took a photo. Friends would later confirm this was a hummel, a stag that will never grow antlers. He was definitely safe for today as he wasn't 'my stag' so I moved on.

Day three played out much the same as day two. Stags roaring, the big ones not budging, and me stuffing them up left, right and centre. I bumped hinds, got the wind wrong when it swirled, and stepped on sticks. The ground was just too dry.

The only real difference in today's country was there was a bit of sign from wild cattle. I parked that information in mind for future trips. It's incredible to think that Raukūmara wild cattle descend from the very first cattle in Aotearoa. The stocky, horned, black Angus-looking cattle of southern Ireland are known as Kerry cattle and many of them escaped from European settler farms to establish a wild population in the bush. The herd today spans almost the entire Raukūmara, with pockets showing influences of other breeds such as Hereford and Jersey.

Taking a late lunch, I managed to catch one of the many rainbow trout inhabiting the river. At least I had some success for the day. I was a long way from camp so I turned my heels and headed for home.

On the way back I had to navigate a gorge. Sidling above it was impossible, so I would have to wade through the water amongst rapids and log jams.

Do you ever come across places in the bush that have an unusual vibe? Well, this gorge had that vibe, a sort of hair-standing-up-on-the-back-of-your-neck intensity I can only describe as an overwhelming sense of balance and spiritual integrity. It felt like what they were trying to capture in *Avatar*, a place where you could feel our oneness with the world. As I was pushing myself through a log jam, much taller than me, I stumbled across a deep hole from which came the annoyed whistle of a male whio. As my eyes adjusted, four yellow eyes squinted out at me from the darkness and there they were, a beautiful breeding pair of ducks in great condition, hiding out where no stoat in its right mind would venture.

Whio like to tuck themselves into the holes of fallen logs or cavities under banks. Finding them in a log jam is not unusual, but finding them on this river was an absolute anomaly. This was only the second pair of whio found in this river, the remainder having died out long before. By clambering up this sketchy section of river and finding these birds, I had effectively doubled the known local whio population.

What is even more weird and exciting is that, as I finally pushed through the log jam, a toutouwai flew down to perch on a twig to see if I had attracted any insects for her to feed on. Toutouwai are our native bush robin, and to my knowledge there had been none seen in this area in recent history. I hunt the area frequently and have certainly never seen or heard any. In the course of five minutes, the remnant relics of the Raukūmara's birdlife had shown itself to me, and went some way to taking my mind off my lack of success.

I guess I will shamefully admit it. On day four it wasn't raining, and I wasn't injured or sick. I just felt like a camp day.

In the course of five minutes, the remnant relics of the Raukūmara's birdlife had shown itself to me, and went some way to taking my mind off my lack of success.

I'd been reading a book, something I never have much time for as a father. After a couple of frustrating days on the hill, tuning in to hear about the life of Genghis Khan sounded appealing.

I swear I had every intention of going for an afternoon hunt but between finishing my book and having a nap I just didn't have time. By 4 p.m. I was going for a swim in the creek. When hunting I usually return home after dark and my evening wash is a quick in and out of the freezing creek water. Having warm rocks to lie on while drying in the sun was an absolute luxury.

It was at this rather inopportune moment that a spiker decided to waltz on into camp. He seemed relatively unperturbed by my presence and just stood and stared. I guess he hadn't seen a human going for a swim before, or maybe he was dazzled by the whiteness of my bare bum. Either way, he hung around. My sneakiness was limited by the sharp rocks digging into the soft soles of my feet. I managed to reach my rifle and was amazed that he was still standing there looking at me. The easy opportunity of a young animal standing on the makeshift helipad had me drawing a bead.

Then I remembered the words of my wife: 'Don't bring home any stanky stag meat.'

She had a point. There were plenty of hinds and yearlings on offer and the spiker was no doubt tastily marinating in his own urine. So down came the rifle and I cooked another feed of Radix as the spiker went about his evening, feeding on the river flats.

Meat Day, when you live and work in the bush, is the day before the chopper arrives. It's the day when it's all hands on deck searching for deer and any form of protein to sustain the family at home. Meat Day is the perfect time to shoot hinds or yearlings, and there's zero risk of meat spoiling as it doesn't have to hang in camp for days on end.

I woke to a stag roaring just above camp, and I wondered if he had any hinds with him. Half asleep, I laced my boots and stashed some muesli bars in my pocket. At 500 metres elevation I was starting to wake up and managed to let out a roar. The stag was close, so I found a high knob with some cover and parked up to wait.

Kererū were feeding on miro berries in the trees around me. The clumsy birds were dropping twigs, snapping branches and making a bit of a racket. While sitting and waiting for a hind, I had many false alarms. A twig would snap, and I would look for the deer that had caused the noise, but it was just another kererū dropping something from above.

Then, suddenly, there she was, feeding her way around the side of a spur 30 metres in front of me. Again the .308 bushpig spoke, and again some fat, tasty steaks and mince were rolling into the creek below.

After a week of immense frustration chasing stags that would not play ball across dry leaf matter that had me walking on eggshells, Meat Day went uncharacteristically smoothly. By lunchtime I had the deer field-dressed and hung in a tree alongside the yearling from earlier in the week. I had admitted defeat for the year on finding 'my stag' but at least I was heading home with meat for the family and news of some rare birdlife on his block for Swanny. It wasn't a total bust.

28. **RAUKŪMARA RED SKINS**

Raukūmara, the home of red deer and wild cattle. The land of pocket-sized pigs with hooks that rival any corn-fed porker. Where giant trout leap from the streams and around every corner is a new slip or river terrace that no man has glassed in the last few months.

There are two ways to access the interior of the remote Raukūmara: by helicopter or by foot. If you choose the sweatier option, you'd better know the local station owner and forestry company well because access is a touchy subject on the best of days. There are next to no public-road access points and you'll need to take out a second mortgage to afford the long helicopter ride. For this reason, Raukūmara is a backcountry hunters' paradise with its easy deer, open rivers and steep hills.

Raukūmara was to be our playground for the next four days. An early-morning start had us pulling into the farmer's driveway for a yarn just as they were cracking eggs into a cast-iron skillet. 'Fill your boots' they reckoned, even offering for us to shoot some yearlings on the way out if we didn't have any luck on the DOC land beyond their boundary. 'Just drop one in to us on your way home.'

With formalities done we headed off for another hour's drive through the station and parked at the top of a steep hill in their back paddock. Our bodies had been softened by summer's festive season and the sun was starting to roll beads of sweat down our foreheads. This mission was just what the doctor ordered to knock our legs into shape prior to autumn's roar trips.

As we stopped for a quick breather fifteen minutes from the truck, Tom pulled out his binos. An understated comment slid from his pursed lips: 'That's a deer. No, that's two deer.'

Eager to see what was on offer, I pulled out my binos and exclaimed, 'There's a mob of six over there.'

TOP Tom with his home-made see-through fly. He's a creative fella, Tom, and one of the world's good buggers.

BOTTOM Unlike Tom, I opted for a hammock and mosquito net set up. Nothing quite beats swinging from the trees and being rocked to sleep by a gentle breeze.

Scott piped up with, 'Yep, and a hind there, too.'

Deer were everywhere. A few folds of the hill later and three young velvet stags jumped out from the scrub where they were feeding and ran off. Overlooking a basin, we saw a mob of eight hinds and fawns saunter off into the scrub as they caught our wind. Today was the first day of the trip and our rifles remained strapped to our packs as we knew full well that the meat would go bad by day four if we were to pull the trigger now.

Making camp that night, the energy was tense. We didn't need reminding how luck can change when hunting, and the old adage 'Don't pass up on day one what you'd shoot on the last day' rattled around in our minds. We all knew things could go horribly pear-shaped and opportunities easily dry up like an old stick. We had seen 21 deer that day and the early sightings did bode well. We were more than excited to see what Raukūmara had in store for us.

Day two had us up later than anticipated and hurrying to check the slips. I'd been given a new watch for Christmas and was struggling to configure the alarm. As we walked the river flats, it was getting well past primetime so Tom and I decided to split up.

There was a productive little side creek downstream that I'd been up once or twice before. It had grassy slip faces scattered with scrub, exactly the type of country deer feel comfortable feeding in. As I stalked my way up, I noticed the distinctive red flash of deer that always seems to be accentuated in the morning light. On further inspection it was indeed a red skin; the deer in this part of Raukūmara are exceptionally red in colour and their hue seems to 'pop' against the colours of the surrounding bush. It was feeding its way off the slip and starting to get too close to the scrub for my liking. Scrambling for a large rock in the riverbed for a rest and not minding getting my bum wet in the creek, I fingered a .308 Whitetail round into the spout. (I run two types of ammo in my .308 bushpig: Whitetail Hornady for longer shots and green-tip Norma rounds for making big holes in animals at close range. I like things to drop where they stand every time.)

I'd lined up a shoulder shot just before the deer slipped into the bush and pulled the trigger. I knew there could have been a few twigs in the way that I hadn't seen but I was fairly sure it was a clean shot. As the deer disappeared into the scrub, I raced up the river and climbed the slip to investigate. There were deer everywhere on that slip, and as I chose my footing wisely, they started to spook and break cover. It was uncanny being surrounded by a mob

TOP Tom and Geoff at the Ruatahunga Hut where I had shot a wild cow a few years earlier.

BOTTOM Tom lining up on a mid-afternoon deer.

of running animals that obviously hadn't been spooked by my shot.

Next minute there was a white Hughes 500 helicopter on top of me, chasing the remainder of the mob. They had the doors off, guns hanging out the window, and I scampered for an open spot in the scrub with my arms flailing to highlight I wasn't a deer. I'm not sure who got the biggest surprise, the chopper pilot or me. Most ground hunters get a bit grumpy with helicopter shooters but I wasn't angry as they were just doing their job, but it was a weird feeling being in their shooting zone.

Bear in mind I know helicopter culling well. I've been the one in the chopper chasing chamois with .243s out the window flaring tussock faces and bluff systems. I know those shooters pull off head shots 95 per cent of the time and identify their targets well. What's more, this part of Raukūmara has a serious deer issue, as we'd seen the day before and I'm fully supportive of helicopters keeping numbers in check. But . . . for a split second I felt like I was the one being chased by the helicopter, until I met the shooter's bulging eyes upon seeing a human in the scrub beneath him.

Most ground hunters get a bit grumpy with helicopter shooters but I wasn't angry as they were just doing their job, but it was a weird feeling being in their shooting zone.

The helicopter flared off and flew another quick circle to make sure I was all good. We gave each other a wave and a thumbs up and they flew off up the valley to continue their work keeping a lid on the deer numbers. Meanwhile I headed off to find my yearling that had conveniently got hung up in a kānuka bush.

With a heavy load I headed back towards the hut and soon bumped into Tom, who was field-dressing his own deer at the bottom of a slip. Having shot a young velvet stag, he was recovering it when the helicopter had buzzed over and upon spotting him had flared off upriver again. We must have dampened the chopper crew's morning but hopefully they were as understanding of us, a crew of meat hunters with families to feed, as we were of them.

Despite the aerial distractions, Tom and I were both over the moon. A couple of deer down was a good way to start the trip.

On returning to camp, we met up with Geoff, who had managed to sneak in on a half-decent stag in the bush. He reckoned the poo from this magnificent beast was the size of horse droppings, its prints the size of cattle hooves, and while it'd kept cruising in front of him, there hadn't been an opportunity for a clean shot. Next thing he knew there was a rather upset chopper buzzing up the valley, zooming this way and that after a bunch of renegade ground hunters cheated him out of a sling-load of venison. The stag Geoff was chasing got proper spooked and wasn't sticking around for anyone.

To add to Geoff's frustrations, the giant rainbow trout he'd tried to hook in the crystal-clear creek that morning had refused his attempts. The trout had followed Geoff's lure on multiple occasions, giving just enough chase to excite the eager hunter, but at the last minute it would look Geoff in the eye and turn tail for the depths of its pool. Geoff was not a happy man when he got back to camp, having been skunked on both counts, but Tom and I were chuffed that we had secured our two deer just in time. I guess that's competing with a helicopter for you.

On day three we shifted camp downstream to a lovely river flat overlooking an incredibly promising grassy slip. We also did a meat load back to the truck. I had preloaded my massive Icey-Tek chilly bin with ice in case we got lucky. The last time I'd carried meat out to the truck in this location was with my then new girlfriend, Roimata. I'd promised her a romantic weekend away in the bush but just two hours in had managed to shoot a wild cattle beast. She and I had lumped the two back legs and back steaks along with all our overnight gear up this massively steep hill, with her crying on and off and me wondering why I do this to people. It took us seven hours and amazingly she didn't break up with me. Thankfully neither Tom, Geoff nor I cried on the way up the hill this time but we lost a fair amount of gravy nonetheless.

Back in the bush, meat chilling on ice, car snacks eaten and soft drinks drunk, it was time to head off for our last evening hunt. I snuck off to a promising little side creek I hadn't ventured up before while Geoff and Tom settled down to watch the slip opposite camp. On the second bend of my creek, I got an opportunity. A hind high up in a scree shoot directly above me was standing broadside, and as I lay back in the riverbed, I knew the shot was steep. Lying on my back and pointing my rifle directly upward while finding a stable rest took some serious yoga movements.

CRACK spoke the rifle and she was sent rolling down, head over heels like a wapiti down a waterfall, to land at my feet in the river. A yearling who wasn't visible prior to my shot broke from cover, followed by the fawn. Try as

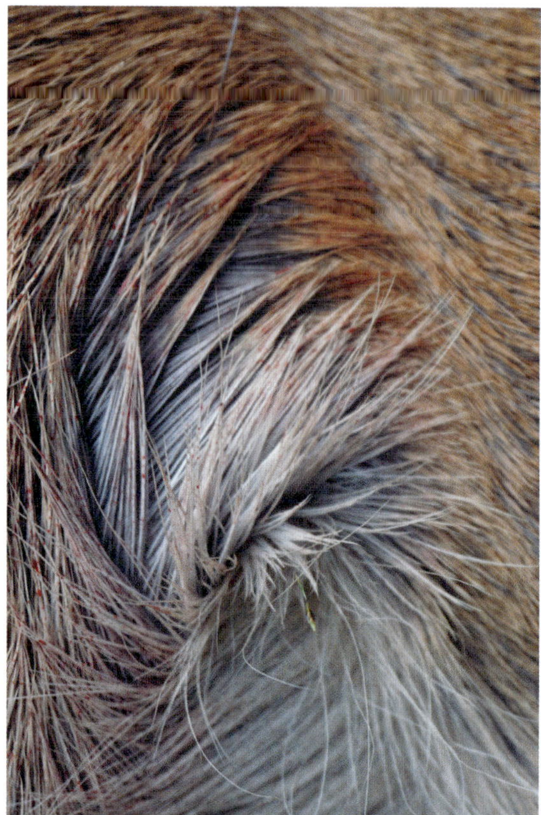

TOP LEFT There was definitely evidence of some good pigs in the area.

TOP RIGHT For some reason I always find the swirls in a deer's hide quite fascinating and end up taking photos of these rather than your classic grip and grin photos. Maybe it's my effort to be respectful or maybe it's just I think they look neat. Either way I have a lot of photos like this in my camera.

BOTTOM A fat young stag. Just one of a whole heap we saw on this trip.

I might, I couldn't get a second shot away at the fawn. It always rests on my conscience when I can't bring them both down, but this is Raukūmara and the deer need culling so hinds are on the menu any time of year.

Geoff also managed to bag his first deer of the trip, a yearling, and was busy hanging meat when I returned to camp. It had been a big day and we all crawled into our respective sleeping places after a wash in the river. Me to my hammock, Tom under his see-through fly, and Geoff burrowed in a grove of low-growing fern.

Day four saw us once again climbing to the top of the hill and jamming the lid down on a bulging chilly bin. We had definitely filled our quota of meat for the trip. Families would be fed, and we would like to think that by taking a few animals out of the Raukūmara, we'd given the chopper a hand with their control efforts. In truth, we had probably been more of a hindrance than a help.

We'd seen 35 deer in four days and walked away with four.

29. LEARNING TO LOVE TARAMEA

As I feel a stabbing pain in my shin I look down knowingly at the little Spaniard hidden inconspicuously amongst the tall tussock. Its sharp, spear-like leaves have once again found its mark just above my protective foam gaiters, drawing beads of blood and no doubt creating an infected abscess if I don't give it a good clean when I get back to camp.

I have to suppress the unmistakable feeling of pissed-off-edness boiling up from my now sore shins. I try to remind myself of the redeeming qualities of the native taramea, of how its taproot is edible and a favourite food of alpine pigs, and how it excretes a sweet-smelling sap that was once a sought-after perfume.

Bending down, I search amongst the taramea's prickly spines for the white gum that is sometimes left on its leaves. I find a few pieces, about the size of wētā eggs, rub them between my fingers and hold the refreshing aroma to my nose. In the old days puhi were sent to the open country to build little fires around taramea. In the early morning they would heat the plants, causing the gum to boil out of the ends of the leaves. The gum was collected in little hue and worn around the neck as a perfumed necklace.

But those days are gone. Taramea may look tough and spiky as an adult, but as a youngster it is soft and tender, just like any child. When ungulate browsers and grazers were introduced to the open country, taramea retreated back into the hills. Much of the flat farmland of Otago and Canterbury was once covered in tussock and sweet-smelling taramea, but cattle and deer soon put an end to that.

Now taramea must hide amongst the tall alpine tussocks, its children sticking close by the base of the protective adults. Taramea must rely on its tough exterior to avoid being eaten by merino, tahr, chamois, pigs and deer. I see similarities between taramea and many of the people of Aotearoa.

Taramea has suffered some pretty damaging multigenerational trauma. Its range has been reduced and replaced by grazing animals.

I can't help thinking that I too would be naturally defensive if I'd been chased to the hills to seek an existence in the harsh and remote mountains. Maybe I'd be a little prickly. Maybe I'd be a little unmotivated to trust or support my fellow mountain dwellers.

In understanding taramea's background and history, it seems unfair to meet its sharp pricks with anger. Instead, I try to meet it with understanding. Fair enough, taramea, you have given so much for the wants and desires of humans. I get why you're defensive of your mountain home. Kia kaha e hoa, let me pick some of your sweet-smelling scent to take home. To re-establish our connection. To let my kids experience all the positives that you bring. Maybe then they will share your stories and maybe once people know your generosity rather than just your prickly side they will bring you back to the productive, flat lands now occupied by cattle in the valleys below.

> I see similarities between taramea and many of the people of Aotearoa. Taramea has suffered some pretty damaging multigenerational trauma. Its range has been reduced and replaced by grazing animals.

I can't help but think that surely in our farming practice we can fence little corners of our paddocks and stock them with tussock, tāwiniwini and taramea. Surely we can learn to share these productive flat lands with its traditional inhabitants, creating space for them to be present in the landscape. After all, who doesn't love the sweet smell of taramea on a cold morning?

Kā mihi to Tamai Sinclair, my father-in-law, for the many hours my wife Roimata spent climbing the mountains of Te Waipounamu as a child. Thank you for sharing stories of taramea with her, with my children and with me. Thank you for helping us to understand this prickly and much disliked plant, and to see past its spines to find its generosity and connection to us as people. It's these multigenerational wanders that retain our connection with place and plant, that retain our place in our ecosystems.

This poem is based on the true story of Levi Heaps, who, after six days of hard hunting in The Remarkables, decided on a tent day. After venturing into the tussock to relieve himself he spotted a good-looking ten-point stag that was skinny and obviously going backwards. Knowing the head wasn't going to improve with age, he opted to pull the trigger. And yes it's true, he did forget the bog roll and he did end up wiping his tender bits with a less-than-soft alpine rock.

FLAT CAMP JACK

Let me tell you a story of Flat Camp Jack,
When his mates went hunting, Flat Camp Jack stayed at camp,

After a week of hunting Flat Camp Jack had a nap,
He stacked piles of z's as he lay on his back,

When he awoke Jack felt a great pressing urge,
The rumbling and grumbling of a guttural purge,

Sweat poured from Jack's forred as he ran for the scrub,
With his rifle in tow (Jack wasn't a mug),

Much relieved our mate pulled his slacks up from socks,
Then sadly recalled he had no paper, just rocks,

He winced at connection between granite and bum,
And he thought to himself that this wasn't much fun,

Next minute old Jack got one hell of a fright,
Because from behind a close bush a stag bellowed with might,

Jack forgot all the rawness from scraping his crack,
And cupped his hands over mouth to give a roar back,

That stag came in running and to Jack's surprise,
He stopped dead broadside and that's how he died,

Now I have never roared stags in with no pants at all,
But what works for Jack could work for us all,

That evening his mates heard yarns of this caper,
Stories of stags and of rocks for paper,

Jack still tells tales of the stag that hangs on his wall,
And of bagging a cracker because nature called.

30. PERCH AND PIKOPIKO

As the ngahere awakes from winter slumbers, it's the ferns that wake first. First the curly little hair of Papatūānuku, mouku and huruuru whenua send forth their new shoots up out of the warm ground into the coldness of still winter air. A gesture of faith that spring will come again this year.

Sometimes they pop prematurely through their protective brown paper-like film during a warm snap, likely to be eaten by a hungry deer or goat famished from winter's barrenness. Then the ferns' growth slows right down again as winter sets back in. I have a lot of respect for the ferns and their opportunistic manner, eking out a living in the gloomy depths of the undergrowth and happy to take their place perched on a precarious rockface.

Wherever there is opportunity, there are ferns. The collectors of soil. The slower of water across the forest floor. The protector of roots. In a way, ferns are the generous caretakers of the decomposing leaf litter, protecting it from erosion during winter flood events and retaining moisture when summer sun threatens to strip it all away.

To us humans, the ferns are generous in a whole other way. They send forth fresh succulent shoots to be eaten all through spring and summer. Many ferns in Aotearoa are carcinogenic but a few species are palatable enough to entice us to pick them.

It's my belief that the forest is conscious in its act of generosity, in providing food. If people care about the ferns and are invested in their existence, then maybe humans will be an active part of the forest once more? Those who forage are those who care and protect the pikopiko beds. When ferns are cared for they thrive, and when they thrive the entire forest benefits. The soil is rich and moist and large trees are protected from the impacts of erosion and drought.

But we as foragers have a role to play. Many a time a forager has

ABOVE Rehua loves wandering the water's edge, net in hand.

experienced the devastation that occurs when deer or goats have ravaged the pikopiko beds. Unlike the forager who practises restraint by harvesting a little here and a little there, ensuring each plant is getting away ample shoots to grow bigger and more voluptuous each season, our friends the ungulates chew through everything they can get their mouths around.

Pikopiko eaters make the best hunters, too. If you know where and when to find pikopiko, the deer won't be far away. The eater of pikopiko knows which sunny faces are home to succulent fern shoots and at what time of year they flourish. They know that a complete meal consists of both meat and vegetables, and that we need to support the bush to be able to provide both. If there are too many deer, there will be no pikopiko. If there is an abundance of pikopiko, the deer will be fat.

To me, that's what it means to be a hunter. We must understand both the deer and the ecosystems they live in.

At least that's how I learnt to be a hunter. We'd hunt down pikopiko beds (mouku being more delicious to deer than huruhuru whenua) and in doing so find deer. More often than not we'd come home with a fat animal for the table and a satchel full of the tight, curly fronds of Papatūānuku to accompany them.

My wife Roimata is Ngāi Tahu and we try to get the kids to Te Waipounamu a few times a year. One of our favourite spots is Lake Kaniere, not least because of its plentiful pikopiko beds.

Each year we make the pilgrimage south to Roimata's whenua, to catch up with family and reconnect the kids with that part of their heritage. It was here one Christmas that my sister-in-law and her boyfriend went 'trout fishing' down at the lake, but instead of catching trout they caught a strange green fish with red fins. We were all baffled as to what it might be, and none of us paid it much attention. It wasn't until the next trip that we found out it was a 'tarakihi of the lake', which they reckon is apparently a 'pest species'.

But one thing's for certain, European perch are the most delicious gamefish that I'd never heard of.

Most places I go, I try to pack a fishing line, and with Roimata keen for Rehua and I to vacate the house for a while, off to the lake we strolled in search of trout, armed with telescopic spinning rods, a landing net, and a variety of spinners, crank and soft baits.

Rehua always likes to have karakia before undertaking any important mahi, so he went about asking Maru, god of fresh water, lakes

TOP LEFT AND RIGHT Roimata, Te Kōtuku and Rehua at Ngāti Waewae Arahura Marae. We make an effort to head south as a whānau at least once a year to ground our kids in their Ngāi Tahu identity.

BOTTOM Fresh pikopiko is a delicacy we love to partake in as a whānau.

and streams, if he would provide young Rehua with an ika to take home to his māmā so she could cook it for dinner. He reminded Maru that it would be preferable if he saw fit to provide 'lots' of ika, because Rehua and his māmā had a hankering for ika that wasn't easily sated. (Please note that Rehua's karakia did not mention anything about providing kai for his pāpā whatsoever!)

Maru being Maru and Rehua's karakia being rather vague as to what type of ika he required, before long we were hooked up to one of those unknown green fish with red fins. It struck decisively with a rather aggressive whack for a small fish and then proceeded to keel over, give up the ghost and let us reel it in with no fight at all.

Not knowing who this creature was, I proceeded to land it in the net and throw it back. Much to young Rehua's disgust!

He chastised me in true three-year-old fashion, 'Pāpā, why you throw mine ika back? That MINE ika, I goin' eat it.' To be fair the little tacker had a point; if you catch a fish you should probably eat it. A quick Google search produced an article written by Peter Langlands about perch in New Zealand.

It turns out that perch are a highly regarded table fish with a firm white flesh and an incredibly sweet taste. They are definitely comparable to tāmure or tarakihi in flavour and texture, although not as big. They are often regarded as a 'pest fish' due to their virility when it comes to breeding, as well as their aggressive predatory nature, so we set our intentions on catching a brace of these perch as quickly as we could. There would be no more throw-backs.

Ten metres down the lakeshore we again got a scarily large smack on our lure. This time I handed the rod to Rehua, and like he'd been doing it all his life, he cranked in the fish and successfully landed it.

This was the first fish Rehua landed by himself without the net and I was over the moon. I was all high-fives and knuckles but he brushed me off as if it was just another day on the job and went looking for the next fish.

The seriousness with which this kid takes providing kai for his whānau is second to none. I can't help but think that fishing is less about enjoyment and more about food for Rehua. Hunting is the same; on turkey shoots he wants me to shoot the turkeys, then he insists on dragging them to the truck, then he wants to go straight home where he will present HIS turkeys to his māmā and insist she cooks them right there on the spot for him.

This afternoon's fishing was no exception. He insisted on carrying the fish home on a stick over his shoulder and presented them to his māmā like a little caveman and said, 'Mine fish, you cook for dinner!'

With an invitation like that, how could his mother refuse? So Rehua and I set about cleaning and filleting the fish. We donated the frames to the backyard weka population, for which they were rather grateful. The pair of weka living in the scrub in the backyard were raising a gaggle of young whippersnappers of their own and I'm guessing they could do with all the help they could get.

With the fish safely deposited in the fridge to chill, it was time for a whole whānau adventure so we headed to the bush. Rehua, his mother, his baby sister and me. In his karakia this time, Rehua asked for 'lots' of pikopiko, and sure enough before long he was shoulders deep in a mouku patch, filling his pōtae with fresh, tasty fronds.

> The seriousness with which this kid takes providing kai for his whānau is second to none. I can't help but think that fishing is less about enjoyment and more about food for Rehua.

While Rehua knows not to harvest too many fronds from each plant, he is less considerate about the number of fronds he harvests from the wider forest ecosystem itself. When told by his mother that he probably had more than enough for his dinner, he looked up with a fiery challenge in his eyes, and clearly stated, 'No, Māmā, I need lots!' I'd like to think that young Rehua was considering the fact that we may receive unexpected visitors for dinner, or that he was planning on dropping a parcel of pikopiko off to the neighbours, but I somewhat suspect this young Ngāti provider shares many of the attributes of a Labrador. He is very food-oriented and although we feed him rather regularly, he eats like he doesn't know where his next meal is coming from.

With bulging pōtae of pikopiko and perch in the fridge, we headed for home where butter and garlic would bind these local delicacies together in a rather palatable plate of sustenance.

Over the next week we were to have many such plates of perch, and found it much to our liking. If you'd like to pursue this underutilised game fish, here are a couple of pointers:

TOP Perch can grow quite large and are an absolutely delicious table fish. Definitely underrated in my opinion.

BOTTOM Fishing is definitely about kai for Rehua.

- Perch respond to a wide range of fishing techniques. You can use soft baits to good effect as well as spinners, crank baits, or edibles such as worms or maggots. Any lure with a red colour works well.
- Perch inhabit a variety of slow-moving rivers and lakes across the South Island and areas of the North Island. I suggest only eating perch from relatively clean waterways as they have a high tolerance for scungy waters and who knows what pollutants you could be eating in the more urban waterways.
- Young perch seem to school around structures and lake edges, while older perch seem to be more solitary.
- Being a fish that likes structures and weed beds, we found the most annoying element of perch fishing was getting lures snagged in structures and weed beds. I've read that it's best to have hooks protruding upward in soft baits to alleviate this problem.
- Perch have rather soft, thin mouths and frequently 'spit' a hook. I suggest using a hook structure that is sharp and barbed. Treble hooks are a good idea, and once a fish strikes, keep your line tight to avoid hooks backing their way out.
- To fish for perch you need a current Fish & Game licence, but there is no daily limit so they are an excellent way to feed the family and a satisfying fish for young anglers.

No West Coast adventure is complete in our whānau without the compulsory pounamu-hunting mission. Not many people are allowed to look for pounamu on the Arahura or Taramakau rivers, but my wife's whānau are shareholders of Mawhera Incorporation and hold whakapapa to Ngāti Waewae so they're some of the lucky ones who can.

Our pounamu searches typically look a little something like this. Over a few cuppas and a long breakfast, ideas about the day's pounamu search will be bandied around in conversation. The location will be decided on through a soft consensus. Kids will be bundled into cars, food packed in bags and changes of clothes too. Sunscreen and insect repellent are a must.

Then, bouncing our way down dirt roads, we pull up outside a side creek that ducks through a farmer's fence. Down the creek we wander, a three-generational gaggle of searchers. Rehua will stop us, saying he needs karakia with his taniwha Poutini, which is fair enough we all reckon, a little sheepish that a three-year old is more switched on to tikanga than any of us.

Then on we march: Rehua and I to throw stones, Te Kōtuku to bounce along in the frontpack, and Roimata and her father Tamai to search in earnest. Truth be told I'm crap at finding pounamu and I reckon it's because I don't whakapapa Ngāi Tahu. I've found the odd little piece, some pretty touchstones but nothing particularly useful. Roimata and Tamai, on the other hand, hardly ever walk away from a trip to Kaniere without finding something large, green and beautiful.

I have stepped right over big pieces of stunning pounamu and Roimata walking behind me picks it up, baffled that I hadn't seen it. They reckon pounamu finds you though, you don't find pounamu, and I'm content with that. I reckon my kids will have that pounamu gene because the only time I found a really pretty piece is the same week I found out Roi was hapū with Rehua, and that seems to make sense.

31. REHUA'S FIRST ROAR

As that big, old donkey of a stag crept up on us, I knew Rehua was going to have an excellent first roar.

Being a three-year-old, Rehua had told me in no uncertain terms, 'Pāpā, this year I'm going to shoot a big stag!'

Well crap, I thought. As a dad I knew he wasn't ready. But a quick translation of three-year-old language told me that what he was really trying to say is that he wanted to come roar hunting with me this year.

No worries son, I can swing that.

But there was one condition. I wanted to make sure this young fella learnt about these animals before we shot one. I needed him to know about how they operate, how we hunt them, and since roar hunting is the pinnacle of hunting enjoyment for me, I needed him to understand the whole culture around how we roar hunt before he got to taste success.

In March we decided on a two-day trip to a mate's hut on the back of his farm. There were plenty of deer about, scrubby gullies, forest boundaries on two sides, but most importantly the terrain was manageable for little legs. What could go wrong?

After a long commute to our block by quad bike we found ourselves on an evening amble along the farm boundary, letting out the occasional unanswered moan. It wasn't until the birds had started to sing their goodnight songs and the sun batted its eyes dozily towards the pink and orange light of the clouds that it finally happened — BROOOOAAAARGH! We'd received a solid response to our roar from a spur far down in the valley below.

Rehua exclaimed with a strained voice, 'Pāpā, that's not a cow.'

'No Rehua, that's not a cow.'

'Pāpā, that's not a sheep.'

'No Rehua, that's not a sheep.'

Finally he asks, 'Pāpā, is that a deer?'

'Yes fella, that's a stag alright and judging by how pissed off he sounds he might just come and check us out.'

Rehua's eyes lit up, slightly nervous, slightly cheeky, and a whole bunch excited.

'Pāpā, I'm going to sneak under it and pat its belly.'

'Firstly son, that's a pretty random thought, but I reckon he will run away before you get that close to him. Stags are usually pretty scared of people.'

It was at this moment that I realised this was the right type of roar mission for our three-year-old. Rehua didn't really want to shoot a stag at all. He wanted to be a hunter. He wanted to spend time hunting. He wanted to bring meat home to his māmā. But he had no real interest in actually shooting a deer. He just wanted to sneak up on it and pat its belly.

I was real happy with my decision to leave the gun at home in this moment, opting instead for the camera and roaring horn. If the stag came in, Rehua would get to see it, interact with it and most importantly realise it was scared of him when it ran away. He was still a little scared of big animals like deer, cattle and horses, and fair enough too, he was three. The beauty of not bringing the rifle was that we could do all the hunting we liked and not have to deal with the killing and butchering side just yet.

'That time will come soon enough, little Hiawatha,' I reckoned.

I caught movement from the corner of my eye. Sure enough, a stonkingly big brown frame slunk its way towards us through the trees. It moved silently; it was clear that I needed to point it out to Rehua so he didn't miss it. I wanted him to see how quiet stags could be and how they use the landscape to sneak around. The young hunter stood up to get a better view over the long grass and as the stag poked its way around a fallen tree not ten metres from us it stopped in its tracks, looked up and stared. He was huge, a big wide twelve-pointer with really well-developed tops.

Rehua quickly hid between my legs and stared back. The stag just watched us, frozen, for what felt like eternity but was probably just seconds. At least it was long enough for me to snap a couple of average photos. Realising that we weren't in fact another stag, he decided to turn tail and exit for more trustworthy surroundings.

The barrage of questions that flowed forth from a quivering and very excited Rehua was unstoppable.

He wanted to know why it was sneaking up on us, why its antlers had

TOP LEFT AND RIGHT Picnics and huts are key reasons why Rehua enjoys coming on adventures. We always make sure we have time for lots of games and down time.

BOTTOM For his first roar we hunted with a camera and his toy rifle.

so many points, why it ran away from us, how did I learn to speak deer, could he learn to speak deer, does a stag have a penis, why didn't it have any friends with it, were cows and stags friends, why did their antlers fall off after the roar . . . The questions kept on coming. His questions were genuine and well thought through and I slowly answered each one in as much detail as my limited knowledge allowed.

I explained how that particular deer was an old stag and probably just past his prime. How his antlers were hard down on his head, which meant his skull had grown as big as it could possibly grow. That in years to come we would search for a stag like this one once Rehua had learned to talk deer and understood the 'way of the walk' in more detail when it came to hunting. That one day he may be able to harvest the meat from such a stag to feed his family and hang the antlers on the wall.

The 'way of the walk' is Rehua's term for differentiating between people who know something and those that don't. If someone doesn't know that tōtara fruit are edible, Rehua will creep up quietly beside me and comment, 'Pāpā, they don't know the way of the walk'. As a young bushman in a generation of gamers, a boy that walks between the many facets of his whakapapa and needs to navigate the collective culture of our nation, this is how he differentiates between those who know our way of being in the world and those that have a different way of orienting themselves.

A little in awe and a little exhausted, Rehua was content with his experience. He was happy to have not shot the stag. As we sat there sharing a meal under the trees in the fading light, I had to admit to myself that I was a little less happy about letting that stag go; he was a solid animal and I would have been proud to take him home as a trophy. But those were the choices I had made. I was about as stoked as I could be to introduce my boy to roar hunting in this way, and I could only hope that letting a monster like that walk gave me some brownie points in the stag department for later on.

A short walk to the hut and a climb into a warm sleeping bag had Rehua grappling with one more big question. Knowing the 'way of the walk' required him to bring food home to his māmā after a trip into the bush. Young Rehua was perplexed; letting the stag go meant that he had no meat to take home.

Just as sleep was about to take him, he thought of it. We had stopped to eat tōtara fruit earlier in the day. He muttered something as his eyes flapped closed. If he took tōtara fruit home, Māmā would see that he still knew the 'way of the walk'. So that's what we did.

TOP We can spend hours prying these juicy red fruit from between spiky leaves. All hunting or trapping gets put on hold when we stumble across a fruiting tōtara tree.

BOTTOM Tōtara fruit is one of our absolute favourite bush lollies.

32. TE UREWERA MIST

The snap and pop of dry houhere logs bounced off the old cast-iron fireplace. It wasn't cold but the hunters were tired and the warmth of fire, balanced perfectly with a cold beer left in a manmade pool in the stream, soothed weary bones on a spring evening in Te Urewera. A joint of lamb sizzled in the camp oven, slow-roasted to crispy perfection. The roast rested on a bed of slightly blackened spuds and carrots that had started to char on one side.

The hut was a red-painted, weatherboard number, an old shearers' quarters at the back of a station where Te Urewera and Raukūmara flirt with each other across the Waioeka River. The hunters were out at the crack of dawn, up before light when the relentless chorus of birdsong woke them. In the gloom they could see mist rolling up the valley, spurred on by the southerly breeze.

Mist is a given in Te Urewera, it's just a question of the density. There's rain mist, where it's thick enough to soak you to the core, but warm; sleet mist, which is bone-chillingly cold; and today it was rolling mist. Rolling mist is our favourite kind of mist. It's soft and comes in sheets, spreading and breaking apart on the landscape. It's gentle enough to penetrate through the outer leaves of the trees and seeps into the space below, turning everything around us to a hazy grey like an out-of-focus photo.

As hunters we don't mind the mist. It hides us from the deer. But it also hides the deer from us. We carefully inspect all dark shapes in the landscape, searching for a giveaway flicker of movement.

The mist is a soft blanket; water particles suspended in air capturing and muffling smell and sound. In this way, mist is our friend. In truth we often hunt with our noses in the bush. Even without a dog, we smell deer before we see them. But, in mist, the hunt plays into our eyesight, a human's

ABOVE Tom's a really great hunter. Calm, calculated and good fun to be around. Life's too short for dodgy hunting mates.

strongest sense. We can get close, real close, and the fact that the water in the air slows down the spread of scent means the deer is at a disadvantage. This is why we enjoy Te Urewera.

Early-morning walks in a quiet grey world. A world where time slows down, you are hydrated through your skin by the water in the air, and everything has a sense of calm.

A beautiful way to start the day.

As far as hunters go, this shoot it was Tom, George and me. A couple of mates out for a weekend shoot in the conservation project we volunteer on.

Tom is a good mate, a fella I've done plenty of time in the scrub with. Big hands, the type that reach out, grab and shake you just about all the way up to the elbow. Curly, dark hair and a nose that makes you wonder if he's Māori, but his appearance and manner make you wonder if he's a Coasty. He's neither! But there's something going on there. He definitely has the warmth, humour and easy-going nature of someone from our part of the world. Not bad for a Hamilton lad.

Tom sells fuel for a living to farmers and contractors. He spends a lot of time driving up rural back roads having cups of tea and, being a genuine, disarming fella, people end up just wanting to do him a favour. I guess qualities like that do a lot for you in the sales caper. Folks tend to light up when they see the Northfuels ute bouncing up their drive. Yep, Tom's just a real good bugger and a relaxing kind of chap to be around.

Then there's Dangerman, a nickname he caught as a young mulleted surf grom from Wainui Beach. Real name George Zame. An apprentice plumber by trade. National longboard surfing champion a few years back and an absolute charger in the surf.

Turns out George has another side to him, a quiet, humble, backcountry type of critter. A fly fisherman, a trapper and now, since the powers that be saw fit to give him his firearms licence, a fully-fledged deer slayer. A couple of years back we managed to get Danger his first deer in this exact patch of bush. He'd been hunting a lot with mates since, but last week he bought his first rifle, a Tikka .308, and it seemed only fitting to return to the Eastern Whio Link project to blood it in.

Then there's me, Sam the Trap Man, your friendly bushman.

The day before had been a cracker. Tom and I were up early, and stalked into a few handy bush clearings we knew about. You can normally rely on a couple of reds to be cropping the short winter grass. The wind was a little all

TOP We try to spot deer across the valley, finding gaps amongst the rolling banks of mist.

BOTTOM I have always liked the golden glow of evening rays on tawa leaves.

over the snow and spring growth had just started to kick in, spreading the feed options for hungry deer.

As we stalked through a small side creek we were busted by a fallow doe and a raggedy wee buck. I peeked out from around a tree to see the doe eyeballing me. Tom had the rifle, and from where he was, he couldn't see them. A moment later they spooked and our first opportunity was missed.

Pushing through ponga groves and houhere thickets, we crested the ridge. Out came the spotting scope and a total of seventeen deer were seen scattered across various slips and clearings. Now that's what we were talking about. We had options. Even in this swirly wind, something was surely going down this morning.

As I mucked around trying to get footage with the phone scope and checking out our options as far as yearlings and hinds went, Tom found himself a couple of closer candidates with the binos. The wind was horrible and the deer were only 150 metres away, so using a houhere tree for cover Tom descended the hill in front of us to a decent shooting spot amidst a tangle of bracken.

Boom! The hind who had been looking at us dropped. Her yearling broke for cover and shot through a mob of ten black-and-ginger pigs scarpering across the clearing where the hind lay ready for Tom to do the honours. Talk about game rich. If you can't shoot deer on the Eastern Whio Link, there's something wrong.

On the climb back up the hill we managed to bump a mob of six reds, not ten metres from Tom's shooting position, and another ten in the ponga face. We had our meat for the morning though and adding more weight to our load wasn't our idea of a relaxing morning hunt. There was still plenty of the weekend left and our breakfast, bunks and books were calling.

After Saturday-morning football, a game George's team lost, a silver station wagon skidded its way up beside the hut. A very excited Dangerman emerged, and after a short session sighting in his new boomstick, we hit the hill.

As evening's calm spread its way up the valley, the deer started to emerge. We stalked down a side basin high up in the catchment and inspected the smatterings of cover for white bums, brown bodies and movement. Before long we managed to pop our heads out onto a clear vantage point and spot both reds and fallow feeding amongst the scrub under a tall canopy of tōtara.

Danger snuck in with all the grace of a gangly heron about to strike at

TOP Sometimes I just like to sit and watch the sun disappear beyond the horizon and wait for the creatures of the night to emerge before walking back to the hut.

BOTTOM The ridges of the Waioeka rolling on and merging into Te Urewera.

a fish. Up came the .308 and just about deafened the entire valley. If it hadn't hit a deer, something was sure to have died of fright. It definitely made my ears sing and we all agreed a suppressor was probably a good investment on his next payday.

But there on the ground lay a beautifully fat yearling. The .308 had done its job securing meat for the freezer and had embarked on a career as Danger's bullet slinger. We headed back to camp with one deer, poking our heads into various nooks and crannies for a nosey but either the .308 had scared them all away or there wasn't much else about. Not to worry though, there was a lamb roast waiting for us back at camp and we were definitely looking forward to a fire and a cup of tea.

The heat of a fire, a full puku of warm meat and a disarming good brew has a way of putting a man to slumber and well before 9 p.m. we were headed for the bunks with the promise of an early-morning stalk.

It had rained in the night but by 6 a.m. it backed off to a soft drizzle that morphed into a rolling mist as the morning progressed. It was our last chance for some action with Tom needing to head for Hamilton by lunchtime. In the way of last hunts, there's always a little bit of added pressure to deliver on day one's hopes and dreams of what the trip might be.

I'm not sure about you but on the drive into a weekend away, I'm like a fella with an undrawn Lotto ticket in my wallet. I can't help but let my mind wander through the possibilities of what could happen, how many deer could be shot and what awesome yet unlikely adventures might unfold. It's like my mind is writing a Barry Crump novel, and no matter how awesome the trip is, it's a hard job living up to my imagination.

But on that last hunt, there's still the potential of endless possibility. Still the opportunity for epic and outrageous success. Maybe that elusive fourteen-point stag could walk out. You just never know. But with it comes just a little pressure and the desire to increase the quantity of meat heading home to the freezer.

Tom was in front; we'd opted for the same ponga faces as the day before. A small mob of reds caught our wind at a distance and Tom had no time for a shot. Then Danger went in front, and as the mist pushed through ponga fronds and hazed the view in front of us to a questionable distance, there was a CRACK and Danger had a yearling stag on the deck.

'Not a bad start, fella. Tom and I might push on if you want to gut this one and hunt in the other direction? We'll catch up with you later.'

TOP George with a fat yearling.

BOTTOM Two Waioeka deer, alert to our presence but confused as to what direction we were actually in.

So leaving Danger behind, Tom and I climbed the hill to where he'd shot his deer the day before. With mist covering our descent, we managed to slip through the scrubby face unnoticed and not too far from yesterday's gut pile we parked up to glass the slips on the opposite face. We picked up two reds at 250 metres, a little beyond comfort for us North Island bushmen. Then two more at 200 metres and a fallow feeding in the scrub below them.

Tom, being a much better shot than I am, settled in at 200 metres with his 6.5 Creedmoor. Boom, boom and a kick from a red hind. Seventeen more reds emerged from the scrubby face around her and hurtled their way downhill and into the cover of the creek while the fallow just continued to feed undisturbed.

We decided to drop elevation to check on the hind we thought we'd hit, but as we did so the fallow emerged in a much-too-tempting clearing, this time with a mate, and just stood there feeding. Always one to oblige, Tom once again made himself comfortable behind the bipod and cracked two shots off in their direction, dropping both of them. While he skinned the pretty wee fallow, I searched for the red, but try as I might, with no blood trail and after looking at the video footage I was 90 per cent certain the shot had gone low, which would explain the kick in the air and the lack of any blood.

So far we had two fallow and a red for the morning and there sat a steep hill between us and the hut. Talk about sweat as we climbed. I was sure glad we didn't have an extra animal or two on board.

At the top of the hill we met Danger, and on the way back picked up his deer. We headed for the hut, a quick butchery session, and loaded chilly bins into trucks for the potholed drive home. Some folk reckon it's hard hunting in the Waioeka but there are good numbers in pockets. Where there's feed there are plenty, and on most volunteer trips on the Eastern Whio Link project the crew walks away with a few deer. The trout fishing is incredible too and we just like the fact that, as hunters and fishers, we can look after the bush that looks after us.

TOP Where the Koranga and the Kahunui meet, the Waioeka begins. These three rivers are the heart of the Eastern Whio Link project.

BOTTOM Tom with a fat deer for the freezer.

33. A REMARKABLE ROAR

Like a painting from a European hunting lodge, he stood there in the early-morning sun. The stillness of the crisp morning air was broken periodically by his exhausted yet gut-wrenching moans. The warmth of his breath billowed out in wet clouds as he pushed forth his challenge towards the small number of satellite stags that circled his harem of hinds.

The scene before us is exactly what we had ventured to Otago for. Open tussock, steep hills and big stags. Since opening the door of the truck, we hadn't been disappointed. In the first 24 hours we'd seen more than ten stags, all out in the open and all roaring hard. Most lacked the credentials we'd come to chase but things were promising. This was already the most action any of us had seen in the last few years of roar hunting.

We'd made the effort to travel south for the 2022 roar on what we thought was a good date, but we also had enough experience to know that it was a gamble. This time the gamble had paid off. We had struck this incredible block in the midst of the roar, and it was going to be a trip to remember.

This was our crew: Jimmy Edward aka Jimmy Jangs is a bit of a legend in my book. He has an incredibly selfless and positive outlook on life and a penchant for climbing steep hills on hot days to have a look at what's in the valley beyond.

Jimmy and I grew up in the same village, Haumoana, on the East Coast of the North Island. Back in the day I used to borrow his driver's licence as a fake I.D. despite the height difference and eye colour, which gave me access to all kinds of mischief.

Nowadays Jimmy is a builder in Queenstown. He's the one who invited us two North Island boys down on the trip. Being the good bugger that he is, it's no wonder he has such great hunting access.

Levi Heaps is a sheep and beef farmer in Hawke's Bay. He lives in

ABOVE Levi Heaps with his remarkable red. An oddly even 12-pointer.

Haumoana and his life reads like a Barry Crump novel. This guy has done just about everything except shoot a good red stag, hence being keen as beans on this trip. He's had loads of opportunities to shoot stags on farms but he's always refrained from pulling the trigger, believing that for him it's not really a trophy if you can drive to within 500 metres of it.

And then there's me. An unfit dad bod who's used to taking close shots in tight bush with a cut-down .308 bushpig. My fitness peaked in Fiordland many years ago when packs, mountains and incredible hunts were a weekly occurrence. But now they're a distant memory, a collection of stories I cherish and remember of a time when I was unstoppable. But this week I was being thrown in the deep end with two fit, childless hunting machines. It was going to be tough, it was going to be sore, but the rewards were there if I could wrangle mind over body.

And with two nervous protest spews out of my system we were in the mountains and ready to go.

But this week I was being thrown in the deep end with two fit, childless hunting machines. It was going to be tough, it was going to be sore, but the rewards were there if I could wrangle mind over body.

We had woken on day two perched on a river flat about the size of a thumbnail, with two tents pitched just about on top of each other. It was dark, but the shimmer of ice on our tents confirmed that it had in fact been as cold as us North Islanders felt it was last night. The stags had been going to town all night but in the quiet chill of the morning they had finally shut up shop. They were happy enough to let the valley sleep in for a while, so we donned frozen boots and started to climb.

Jimmy, the fittest of us three, chose a high sidle out of the creek and up along the tussock faces of the valley. He'd been here before and knew that it was named Staircase Creek for a reason. It was really a series of small gorges and waterfalls making the usual up-the-creek approach near impossible.

As we climbed the wet tussock, we were grateful for the advice to bring poles with us. We were all top-heavy with packs maxing out the scales at 35 kilograms, so the slippery tussock would have been treacherous without the stability of poles.

With the first rays of sunlight breaking over the rocky skyline peaks,

TOP As Levi lined up for his shot he had sun clearing into his eyes.

BOTTOM Like a book of *Where's Wally*, we would just sit and wait scanning the tussock with our binoculars until the shapes of deer separated themselves from their same coloured landscapes.

the first roars of the morning reached our ears. We had learned to bridle our excitement the day before as what we had thought were big, deep, baritone roars in fact belonged to young eight-pointers.

There were two stags roaring on the opposite face. Our Swarovski glass cut through the morning rays to show us a large nine-point and a smaller six-point stag making their way downhill towards the valley floor. They were roaring at a third stag situated in a large boulder field further up the valley from where we sat.

Our expectations weren't exactly sky high. As we attached the phone scope, an incredible invention that makes assessing deer a much more interactive and social event for the whole crew, we swung the spotting scope towards the boulder field and there in the screen stood an absolute mind-boggler.

The three of us just sat in silence, stunned, as we watched him lean his mighty rack back, straighten his throat and challenge the two younger stags. Moments later the roar reached us, sending shivers down our spines. Yep, this was indeed a ripper. It was clear that this stag was a step above anything we'd seen so far on the trip. Levi broke the silence. Sounding like an excited ten-year-old boy given five bucks at the local dairy, he muttered, 'Can I shoot that?'

Jimmy and I looked at each other and just shrugged as Levi quickly gathered what he needed for a stalk.

The plan was that we would drop down a slight wrinkle in the landscape to the valley floor. We'd have to slide on our butts or crawl to keep out of sight. With so many stags in the valley and who knows how many hinds, the chances of getting busted were high. From the valley floor we could use the creek itself as cover and hopefully edge our way up the side of a short spur into shooting position on the big stag. Jimmy would stay behind and film.

It was going to be tricky, as the two smaller stags were heading for exactly the same spot in the creek as we were. We'd hopefully be able to let them pass us by unnoticed. The sun would be directly in our eyes when Levi took the shot and that's never easy. But the opportunity was there, and we were all in.

Our descent to the valley floor happened fast. We slid easily on the wet tussock and were dropping our packs in the creek.

As we snuck along the creek using banks as cover, we edged forward. Our efforts were obviously not as sneaky as we'd thought, as with a grunt and a bark,

TOP A big old 10-pointer roaring himself silly after we spooked his hinds.

BOTTOM When we found the straggly mobs of merino sheep we usually found deer. It didn't take long for us to figure out that it was a lot easier to identify the areas of good tucker by spotting white sheep rather than brown deer in the tussock.

we managed to spook the nine-pointer and he hightailed it for safer ground. The nine was right in view of our big stag and he shut up shop, not roaring anymore. Things weren't looking good for us, and with tails between our legs and a sinking feeling in our stomachs, we knew we'd stuffed it.

But then the big fella roared, from the same place as before in his boulder field.

With binos desperately searching the country before us, we struggled against the sun to locate him. We spotted a hind, then another, and after what seemed like eternity the stag stepped into view. He was long, he was wide, and with an abundance of well-pronounced tips scraping his rump we knew he was a shooter.

> The three of us just sat in silence, stunned, as we watched him lean his mighty rack back, straighten his throat and challenge the two younger stags. Moments later the roar reached us, sending shivers down our spines. Yep, this was indeed a ripper.

Levi settled on a rock and made certain of his shot. It felt good. It sounded good. But with the crack of the rifle and the sun in our eyes neither of us saw him drop. We gave him ten nervously measured minutes before climbing to search for him in the tussock. It's amazing how the brown of a downed deer can blend in with the tawny tussock. It took ages and our anxiety was peaking the whole time. Eventually we found him rolled into a crevice. We were overjoyed.

Things don't always go to plan, but this time we had pulled it off. A cracker stag, a beautifully heavy and an even twelve in the main valley just above the creek where the hunting traffic was sure to be the highest. We'd had just about everything to our disadvantage: the wind, the sun, spooked animals and very little cover, but Levi had managed to pull it off. An absolute stag of a lifetime and it was only day two of a seven-day hunt.

With grins on our faces, Jimmy and I couldn't help but wonder what was in store for us now Levi was tagged out. Could we find two more rippers in this large expanse of tussock or would we miss out like the many trips we'd each made before?

That afternoon we stumbled onto a large marshy flat on the valley floor where two streams collided. Our weary bodies didn't take long to pitch

TOP The landscapes of the Remarkable Range are truly, well . . . remarkable.

BOTTOM Tāwiniwini or snow berries are one of my favourite alpine snacks. A burst of freshness in an often dull backcountry diet.

tents and set about brewing up the evening meal. Jimmy Jangs, ever the opportunistic optimist, heard a faint roar and pulled out the glassing gear to reveal what looked like a half-decent ten- or twelve-pointer halfway up the valley wall above us.

Spurring our tired legs into action, he and I set off while Levi sat back at camp tidying up his deer head. We climbed for a solid twenty minutes but although we got close to the stag, who turned out to be a really solid ten with three on each top, we never did get close enough for a shot. With head torches shining, we half slid and half fell down the tussock-clad faces in the dark back to camp.

Day three was set to be a goodie. We planned to climb high up the face we had scaled the evening before. That way we could hopefully catch up with the ten-pointer from the night before. Then our mission was to sidle our way into a hanging head basin that held some interesting-looking lakes, as surely there'd be deer hanging out in this sheltered, lush grass bowl.

We had each written down our intentions for the trip prior to coming. Levi was happy with a solid ten and he had far exceeded expectations on day two. I was after a twelve, but would take a ten if it had three solid points on each top. Jimmy was going to save himself for something different. He really wanted to take a fourteen and was happy to wait, maybe not this year, maybe not ever, but that's what he wanted.

So there it was. We climbed high but found no stag. We sidled towards the head basin and heard plenty of roars from an eight in a rock garden on the opposite face. Although he was holding hinds he definitely wasn't what we were after, so we carried on. We saw merino sheep, which was a good sign, then a mob of spikers and hinds feeding beside one of the lakes, and far up in the crags at the head of the valley we spotted a whānau of chamois. Now that was a discussion we hadn't had. Sitting down over a snack and a brew we laid our cards on the table about how we felt about chamois.

Levi had shot a decent one, Jimmy had too, but I wasn't that keen on shooting a goat. Not sure why, but I'd never understood the appeal of chamois. I could almost grapple with the idea of hunting the majestic Hairy Maclary tahr, but chamois just didn't excite me. After an extended glassing and video session, it was decided. None of the chamois were better than the two the lads had at home, and I wasn't keen to pull the trigger on them today either.

So we headed off a fraction disappointed about not seeing any decent

TOP When we spotted a stag through the binoculars Jimmy would then settle down with the spotting scope to see how big he was. It's difficult to assess from a distance the number of points a stag has without a spotting scope.

BOTTOM During the roar, late season tāwiniwini fruit can be found hiding in shaded cracks and crevices.

stags in the head basin, but still blown away by the incredible scenery and excellent run of weather we were having.

We'd decided to venture down through the rock garden where we'd seen that eight-pointer earlier, and lo and behold we saw a stag. Not a donkey but a fairly respectable ten-pointer. The problem was that it was dead, splayed out on the boulders with no obvious gunshot wounds. This would explain why that scrappy eight-pointer was holding so many girls. Maybe the ten had been shot, maybe he'd been killed by another stag, or maybe he'd just fallen and died. Whatever the cause, it was a real shame that he had exited the gene pool as he was only a couple of years away from being a real stunning head.

It had started to get cold, and the clouds pushing up the valley were starting to look ominous. The whole vibe of the place just changed mid-afternoon to a dark, damp, frigid winter landscape. Still beautiful but a little more hostile. It made you feel small in comparison.

Exhausted, we looked through the glass of the spotting scope, each of us secretly hoping it wasn't anything worth chasing, as a quiet wander back to camp would feel real good right now.

Then a roar came from above us, deep and guttural, from the tussocky faces we'd sidled through earlier that morning. Exhausted, we looked through the glass of the spotting scope, each of us secretly hoping it wasn't anything worth chasing, as a quiet wander back to camp would feel real good right now. However, the ten from the evening before had once again worked his way down from wherever he'd been hiding and into our valley for the evening.

Jimmy, being the eternally motivated human that he is, rallied the troops and we climbed half-heartedly to a tangle of rocks from where we could glass. Surprisingly, the stag had worked his way towards us, close enough for a shot. Well, that's what Levi and Jimmy reckoned anyway. At 500 metres there's no way this North Island hunter was about to pull the trigger. Give me 100 metres any day, 150 metres at a stretch, but 500 metres — that was way beyond my capability. I passed up the shot.

Jimmy, who had a lot more experience at that range, wasn't about to pull trigger either as he was waiting for his fourteen-pointer. A plan was made for me to stalk in solo, using the natural wrinkles of the tussock country to conceal me. As I moved forward I couldn't hear or see anything of the stag,

TOP The big head basins held plenty of young stags but we were searching for something bigger.

BOTTOM Every few hundred metres we would let out a roar to try and locate a stag worth looking at.

his roars muffled by the wet folds of tussock. I could keep track of how far I had come using my GPS and cresting a spur: it felt like I must be right on top of him.

Then I saw an antler rocking back and forth in the tussock and his head emerged. I mentally checked in with myself: 'No moving head shots. Wait for the body.' His neck came into view but then a hind barked, the tussock erupted with running deer, and the big ten disappeared once more. It was last light, and try as I might to get a visual on where he had run to, I found nothing. Once again we descended to the valley floor below with head torches burning and a sense of deflation in our hearts.

That evening was freezing; I slept in my puffer jacket, woollen thermals and two pairs of socks inside a sleeping bag. I hadn't felt this cold since working as an under-resourced trapper in Fiordland many years ago. We woke to day four with snow on the hills and a crisp breeze in the air.

As Jimmy and I went for water, we found out why the head valley had been disappointingly lacking in mature animals and the last couple of days had been difficult for hunting. We were definitely covering the distance and seeing deer, but there was another camp only a hundred metres from ours. A recent hunting party had obviously been flown in to this exact spot and left behind discarded food, rubbish and several red stag and chamois head skins. That may have had something to do with our struggle to find a mature animal in the upper valley.

With that news we decided to break camp and head back down to where Levi had shot his stag a few days prior. For days we had climbed into the snowline, to 2000 metres, and glassed. We'd seen an abundance of sixes, eights and tens all holding hinds and we even lowered aspirations of twelves to chase a couple of the larger tens.

It felt good to have a clean break from the last two days. We could leave it behind and look into some new country. Jimmy and I had resigned ourselves to the possibility that we may not score this trip, but new country and new opportunities never hurt anyone.

We ambled along, Levi in front with his huge rack swaying from side to side and Jimmy and I following, making up funny songs and snacking on summer's leftover snowberries nestled in shady spots. We found an adequate camp at the entrance to a valley not far from Levi's stag.

Before we even pitched the tents we heard a roar. We must have disturbed a small mob of hinds that started disappearing over a nearby hill with a scruffy

TOP Jimmy and Levi sitting and watching a small mob of chamois. They had both shot decent examples of these petite mountain goats and I had no real interest so we let them be as they frolicked about their craggy homes.

BOTTOM Being able to attach your phone to your spotting scope is such a great innovation as far as being able to capture memories in video and photo to take home with us.

stag following them. But what happened next is quite comical. Not 50 metres away, a yearling popped out onto a clear space amongst the tussock and Jimmy makes a call that he wouldn't mind some camp meat. He pulls out his rifle, takes a rest on his pack, and BOOMFA! He drops the yearling.

Sure of his shot, Jimmy heads up hill to retrieve his meat with nothing but a knife. But he has kneecapped the poor thing. Next we hear a yell and see this poor young deer jumping with its back legs and hurtling itself into the air and down the hill. With each jump it sprawls itself forward, unable to catch itself on its broken front legs. It tumbles its way towards the bottom with Jimmy, knife drawn, bounding after it like a demented pirate.

Levi and I were in hysterics. There was something about the absolute terribleness of the scene, the horror of the deer's predicament, what Jimmy must have been feeling after stuffing up such an easy shot, and the futility of his chase which had Levi and I buckled over in fits of uncontrollable laughter.

We tried to yell at Jimmy to put the knife away, as we were mindful of Murphy's Law that anything that can go wrong will go wrong. Jimmy running down an uneven rock and tussock face, knife at full draw; it could go even worse for Jimmy than for the deer if he misplaced a step. No one wants to be skewered by their own hunting knife, that's for sure.

In the end Jimmy finally caught up with this jack-in-the-box deer in the stream bed and subdued the bedraggled creature. If you've ever cut a deer's throat in a creek, you'll know what happened next. Jimmy had quite a biblical moment where he turned the river red for near on 100 metres downstream. It was a sobering end to a somewhat ill-fated shot.

There are a couple of things to take away from this little yarn:

1. Always take your rifle with you when retrieving a downed animal. Who knows, you might even get a shot at a second animal.
2. Keep your knife sheathed until you need it. Jimmy's chase could have ended a whole lot differently.
3. Sometimes the easy shots are the hardest shots to make. I have definitely missed my share.

As snow clung to the walls of the valley, we searched fruitlessly for the willpower to extract tired legs from warm, comfortable sleeping bags. We were five days in and with each passing day our spirits had dampened. The

TOP AND BOTTOM As three lads all with a connection to the coastal village of Haumoana we hadn't really thought we would find ourselves together in this remote and beautiful landscape.

cumulative exhaustion of traversing such massive country had started to take its toll on our bodies. We had woken during the night with cramps, our backs ached with the weight of heavy packs, and our skin chafed where pack straps had rubbed our shoulders raw.

After Levi's early success we'd thought that the entire block would be full of giant stags roaring their heads off. But we had hit a slump, and so far we were yet to find another big boy.

At 9 a.m. we finally managed to pry ourselves from the sleep sack. Jimmy boiled a brew and his usual positive banter kicked into gear. For me it was a case of getting as much tucker in my system as possible before we set off for the day. Being a skinny bugger, I'm useless if I don't have enough food.

We had seen what we thought could be a mature stag high up in a head basin the day before, but at over a kilometre even our Swarovski glass wasn't able to make out his credentials. We had spent half the day gaining the elevation necessary to get a better look at him but when we got there he and his hinds had evaporated into thin air.

Today Jimmy and I were heading back in a last-ditch effort on the last day to find a decent stag. Levi was going to stick around camp, as an old foot injury was giving him grief and a rest day was in order.

As we kicked frozen boots through wet tussock and heaved ourselves upward using walking poles for support, we slowly gained elevation. The morning sun was gentle and warm on our windburned faces. After a time, the high tussock gave way to shale and alpine plants and it was here that we stopped, taking shelter behind large rocky outcrops to glass. Again, our searching came up short and it wasn't until 2 p.m. that we finally saw our first deer for the day.

We had discovered a strategy earlier in the trip: if you can find the merino sheep in this environment then chances are you'll find deer close by. Thankfully we'd managed to spot a mob of around 30 of the roll-skinned rock-eaters feeding amongst the shale cliffs. This was promising so we settled down to a cheese, salami and crackers picnic as we investigated the country in more detail.

Before long we laid eyes on a hind, then another, and further across the face a few more. We were looking at a group of seven animals: spikers, hinds and yearlings, with a six-point stag asserting dominance. We searched the surrounding country for a more mature animal but try as we might he could not be located.

ABOVE Each detail of Levi's stag was brimming with character. The curly forelocks, the gnarled beading, the perfect evenness of the tines. It was a unique head in that it was missing bey tines, but the incredibly strong crowns more than made up for it. A stag of a lifetime.

With the day waning and the added pressure of knowing this was our last day of hunting, we pushed on. But alas the rest of the afternoon offered much the same as the morning, a severe lack of deer.

Feeling broken and knowing this was the end of our hunting trip, Jimmy and I retreated back down the valley, taking a mid-face sidle in case we'd missed something hiding in the folds of the creek bed below. And sure enough, to our surprise we had the camera out, sneaking in on a trio of feeding deer. A hind, a spiker and a yearling. Not that exciting but a few close-up photos are better than nothing. We snuck within twenty metres and took some great shots. Then came a roar from the other side of the valley.

Jimmy pulled the Swarovskis from their holster like he was in a Clint Eastwood film and in disbelief we saw, standing in the middle of a nearby hanging valley, our stag from yesterday. He had travelled quite some distance from where we'd seen him the day before and was holding his hinds in a spot that was actually surprisingly accessible to us before the imminent last light of the evening.

Knowing I'd messed up a couple of stalks earlier in the trip and being relatively inexperienced in open tussock hunting, I handed the reins over to Jimmy, who was more than happy to guide me in.

We slid down the now-dry tussock on our arses once again, using the wrinkles of the landscape to disguise us as we descended to the creek below. In full cover of the cold alpine stream, we took a minute to fill drink bottles and catch our breaths. We talked strategy, made sure we were on the same page, and came up with a plan.

Then up we went, exhausted from many days on the hill yet urging our legs onward. We were past the point of excitement. Like a problem gambler we'd thrown the dice many times on this trip and lost out on all but one occasion, so a nagging thought in my brain told me not to get my hopes up. There was this dread that once again something would step in the way of success and we would still be walking away empty-handed.

And sure enough, as we dipped behind the shadow of the granite shute he stopped roaring. For what seemed like forever, as we climbed we had no visual and no roaring to affirm that this stag hadn't spotted us. We had learned the hard way that while the younger stags in this catchment were curious and unperturbed by the presence of people, the older stags were incredibly flighty.

Emerging into the afternoon sun once more, we saw him, no more than

TOP The moments after pulling the trigger on a majestic animal are bittersweet. I just sat there exhausted after six days of hard hunting as a wave of emotions rattled through me.

BOTTOM We had been incredibly lucky with the weather. It had barely even rained. There was a fresh dump of snow one evening but the rest of the trip had been blue skies and sunshine.

a hundred metres below us. Open tussock, a splattering of alpine shrubs and rock formations, and the stag standing broadside with his hinds. This was a shot I could make, that any North Island hunter could make, and as he leaned his head back to roar his dominance I knew he was a shooter. Three on each top, that's all I saw as I settled into a rest. But tussock filled my scope, I had a hiccup loading the rifle, and somehow at 100 metres the first shot missed!

> Like a problem gambler we'd thrown the dice many times on this trip and lost out on all but one occasion, so a nagging thought in my brain told me not to get my hopes up.

Thankfully the follow-up shot was true and Jimmy and I just looked at each other in disbelief that it had all come together. So many near misses, so many things that went wrong and could have gone wrong, but we had a stag on the deck. It was emotional, not sad, just overwhelming with exhaustion and knowing that this stag was a long time coming. He was an even twelve with a broken bay tine, a true trophy in my books.

With my second kid on the way, chances were that these South Island roar trips would be off the table for me over the next few years. I'd been chasing backcountry stags in the roar for a while and until now I hadn't seen something I wanted to pull the trigger on. It had finally happened and I could step into temporary retirement with a cracker red stag on the wall.

I was pretty stoked with my stag. He was an absolute ripper and a wall hanger to be proud of but there was still a niggle in the back of my brain that it wasn't quite as big as the one hanging above the porch at my grandfather's. As I lay in the dark, surrounded by the smells of the tussock and the tang of seven days' sweat, I laughed at myself. Maybe I was turning into a trophy hunter after all. The insatiable appetite for a bigger stag had snuck in and bitten me. I wasn't at all comfortable with the idea, but I still had a scratch that needed itching and the feeling that could only be filled by a truly magnificent wild stag of epic proportions. But that is another tale and a story to be told at another time.

ABOVE After searching all these years I had found a really decent stag. He was no record breaker and definitely no match for Poppa's 17-pointer but my 12 with a broken tine was the trophy I had been searching for. An absolute beauty in my books and represented many years of hard hunting.

© Strike Photography

ACKNOWLEDGEMENTS

I would like to acknowledge the many bushmen that have walked the hills before me. Those that through generations have accumulated a knowledge of our place in the world. Thank you for sharing your mātauranga and bush knowledge with our generation.

I would like to thank those that see the potential in slightly awkward youngsters and tuck them under their wing, offering an opportunity to work hard and figure out which path is right for them. Even if it's just one trip, a couple of weeks' work or an experience they otherwise wouldn't get. I'd like to thank those who opened doors for me as a teenager and early in my career. I was really lucky to have great mentors and amazing parents and grandparents.

To Darren Peters, Paddy Stewart, Lindsay Wilson, Dan Baigent, Hemi Barsdell, Keith, Max Smart, Debashis Dutta and many others.

I would like to thank my better half Roimata for understanding the way I live and my need to be in our wild places. Thanks for trusting us to raise our kids in the bush and for letting me bundle them into helicopters, toss them down cliffs and introduce them to all the wonderful kai in the ngahere.

To my friends who are mentioned in the book and the many more who have shared adventures with me along the way, thank you.

Also a special thank you to my publisher, Tess, and editor, Tracey, for their tolerance in teaching me how to write a book. It's not something I had anticipated doing at this stage of my life but here it is. Thanks to you both.

Huge thanks as well to Leo, my project editor, Megan the designer, and Brennan, who shot the cover, for getting this book made and making it look so good. A huge thank you to Debra Quaadgras, my editor at NZ Outdoor magazine, for her support and encouragement in my writing journey. You really got me into sharing my adventures on paper and allowed me to grow as a writer.

Lastly, I would like to acknowledge the amazing Steiner school system that was willing to see me for who I was and allowed me to find a path through education that ensured I thrived.

REO MĀORI

Many Māori words have more than one meaning. The list below gives the meaning in the context of how the word has been used in this book.

atua	god
awa	river
hākari	feast or a big spread of food often to celebrate or mark an occasion
hapū	pregnant
Haumia-tiketike	god of all fruiting things in the forest, of bush food and bountifulness in the ngahere
hīnaki	eel trap
hinu	fat, the type of fat that runs down your beard and keeps you warm in winter. Often we speak of fat with reverence in the bush: fat birds, fat eels, fat deer, pigs or trout. Everything fat is a good thing in the bush. A sign of abundance.
hoa	friend
horopito	pepper tree. The tree we use to wash our hands with, the tree we use to flavour meat and the tree we use to kill bacteria.
houhere	lacebark
hue	gourd
hui	'hui' usually means a gathering, or a meeting. But when we talk about harvesting tītī, hui is a bundle of harvested birds: five tītī tied by their necks to the end of a string and at the other end of that string is tied another evenly balanced bundle of birds. In this way

	birds come together on a string to form a hui. If only all meetings were so evenly balanced.
huruhuru whenua	a layer of ferns that are likened to the hairs of Papatūānuku. These are often very palatable to both deer and people and help retain the moisture in the soil as well as protect the soil from erosion. Sometimes called uruuruwhenua.
ika	fish
kā mihi	Ngāi Tahu dialect for ngā mihi (thank you)
kahikatea	a tree gifted to Tāne from Rehua to feed the manu (birds) of the forest. It acts as the liver of the forest, cleaning the water that runs through the earth. In addition it is very generous with its tasty fruit, known as koroī. The English name for kahikatea is white pine — a little boring if you ask me.
kaitiaki	guardian
kākano	seed
karakia	a prayer, a turning of your thoughts to the spiritual world or those that contribute to the being of something
kareao	supplejack. A twisted-up vine that has a knack for tripping you up and being very difficult to walk through. Also a very tasty substitute for asparagus and a staple vegetable for bushmen.
kārearea	New Zealand falcon. A beautiful creature with a knack for plucking cicadas out of the air mid-flight and nesting high up in dead trees.
kete	basket
kia kaha e hoa	be strong, friend
kiaka	a small, struggling tītī chick. Perhaps it hasn't been fed well enough, or could possibly be sick and isn't going to make it to fledging. It will pass its nutrients back to Papatūānuku, serving a really important role in transfering the goodness of the ocean into the soils so plants can grow strong.

kiekie	an epiphyte that has the most delicious-tasting petals and fruit. It's also helpful at binding things, and building crayfish pots and hīnaki. Its leaves are used for tukutuku panels.
kōhia	our lovely native passionfruit, with a sweet pungent flavour when fully ripe. The birds, possums and rats love it too.
kōnini	possibly the tastiest fruit in the entire bush. It grows on the kōtukutuku tree and is a prized delicacy.
koroī	fruit of the kahikatea
kōwaowao	our bush lettuce, a staple part of the backcountry diet of Aotearoa. It tastes like macadamia nuts, and when you have been in the hills for a few days, it's a welcome source of vegetables.
mahinga kai	the process of gathering, tending or preparing food
māhoe	one of our fire trees in the bush. You can use it to make fire using the friction method, but most of us now carry a BIC lighter. Māhoe does however still provide us with dry standing kindling and firewood even in torential storms, and is a host tree for many tasty edible mushrooms.
mana	power (including spiritual power), charisma, authority, influence. When you revere or admire someone, or hold them in high esteem, you are acknowledging their mana.
mana whenua	people who have mana over the land in any particular area
manu	bird, and other winged creatures including bats, butterflies and cicadas
maomao	blue maomao, a bright blue fish
Maru	god of the streams, lakes and rivers
mataora	facial tattoo
mātauranga	knowledge. In the context of this book, more particularly bush knowledge.
maunga	mountain

mingimingi	a tightly woven, scraggly bush that provides the most incredibly sweet fruit as well as an excellent hiding place for lizards, wētā and small birds
mokomoko	lizard, usually referring to a gecko
mokopuna	grandchildren
mouku	one of several tasty ferns that grow in the huruhuru layer. Its delicate new shoots are known as pikopiko and are a very welcome vegetable snack in the bush. Its English name is hen and chicken fern.
ngahere	the bush
ngārara	insect
pāhau	beard
Papatūānuku	our mother. The atua (god) of whenua (land). The mother of many of the other gods including Tāne and Haumie. Wife to Rangi the sky father.
pepetuna	pūriri moth larvae
pīkau	a small kete (basket) or bag worn as a backpack. Traditionally woven from flax, but in the context of the bush many bushmen have pīkau made from a hessian sack or flour bag with a length of rope as the pack straps.
pikopiko	delicate new fronds of Aotearoa's tasty edible ferns
piripiri	a rather annoying plant whose seedheads tend to stick to everything — socks, hair, pants — and it's near impossible to get out. It does however make a good brew of tea and is comparable to Dilmah.
pīwakawaka	fantail, also known as tīwaiwaka
ponga	tree fern
pōpokotea	a small forest bird that flits through the trees in a pack, hunting insects. It has a white head and therefore has the prosaic English name 'whitehead'.
pōtae	hat
poto	short or stumpy, akin to the build of a garden gnome

pōua	a Ngāi Tahu word for 'grandfather'
puhi	a young woman who has been untainted by the world's desires
puku	stomach
rākau	a tree or stick
Rakiura	Stewart Island
rangatira	chief, leader
Rangi	The atua (god) of the sky. Our father and husband to Papatūānuku. We all descend from this union.
raupō	a plant that grows in the swamp. It can be used to make flour for bread and other things.
reo, te reo Māori	language, the Māori language
rewawera	a beautiful tree with stunning red flamboyant flowers. Its nectar can soothe sore throats and its bark can help heal cuts without infection or scarring. Its timber is soft yet has a beautiful dark streak through it.
ruru	morepork
taiao, te taiao	the earth, the environment
tamariki	children
tāmure	snapper
tāne	man
Tāne	god of the forest
taonga	treasure
taramea	a spiky plant that once inhabited many barren areas but now has retreated to the tussocky alpine regions due to its palatability to stock, deer and pigs. It is known as 'Spaniard' and is the bain of alpine hunters.
tarata	a tree with a refreshing, strong lemon smell and taste to its sap and flowers
Tāwhirimātea	god of the wind and weather. Known in the bush to throw the odd temper tantrum, but it's all part of the balance of things in the end.

tātarāmoa	a brambling vine that is humorously known as 'wait-a-minute vine' or 'bush lawyer' because its hooks have a habit of grabbing on to your clothing and stopping you in your tracks. Tātarāmoa leaves can also be used in a tea to help you sleep well and have therefore been used by bushmen to help them sleep in huts full of snorers or on uneven or cold ground.
tāua	a Ngāi Tahu word for 'grandmother'
tawa	a tall cousin of the olive. Famous for its slightly turpentine-flavoured fruits whose rich, creamy kernels are much like roasted almonds when prepared correctly.
tāwaka	a delicious mushroom that can be found growing on dead wood and is a favourite summer food in the bush
tāwiniwini	a dainty little alpine plant. It makes an excellent home for wētā and produces a juicy white berry reminiscent of a watered-down blueberry.
tīeke	a rather boisterous and high-energy forest bird with orange wattles and orange and black feathers. Said to have laughed at Māui when he requested water after slowing down the sun.
Te Waipounamu	South Island of Aotearoa. Not the most southern island of course as there is also Rakiura (Stewart Island) and other smaller islands.
tī kōuka	cabbage tree, a staple food source in Aotearoa. We can often see the markings of old trails as people have planted tī kōuka along the way as they travelled.
tikanga	the agreed way in which things are expected to be done
tīpuna	ancestors
titipounamu	a small forest bird — actually the smallest bird in Aotearoa
tītoki	a large tree with a trunk that has many woven cavities or 'fairy houses' as Rehua likes to call them. Its fruit looks like a red raspberry and has a large black seed that was traditionally highly valued for oil.

tītī	muttonbird
tohu	a sign. Tohu can literally mean a road sign, or more commonly in the bush we look for the tohu that the forest gives us to affirm our actions. Birds give us signs, the way trees grow give us signs, and the land shows us what's going on. That's the mark of a bushman; we read the environments around us and listen to what they are telling us. To disregard tohu is to walk out of step with our ecosystems.
toutouwai	our native robin, a rather social little creature that can be forgiven for thinking bootlaces are earthworms when they are hungry. They can be rather friendly and will peck sandflies from your legs if given a chance.
tuna	eels, the big, beautiful caretakers of our rivers and streams. Our native eels are the ultimate top-of-the-food-chain fish and are exceptionally long-lived.
tutu	a gangly shrub that is famous for being poisonous, but has many redeeming medicinal qualities if you get to know it. Sometimes we affectionately refer to someone who fidgets or is a little nosey as a tutu or haututu.
wahine	woman
waiata	song
wētā	a flightless cricket-like creature of which there are many species that have evolved to inhabit just about every ecosystem in Aotearoa
whakapapa	geneaology
whānau	family
wharenui	meeting house
whenua	land
whio	blue duck. A comical creature of backcountry waterways

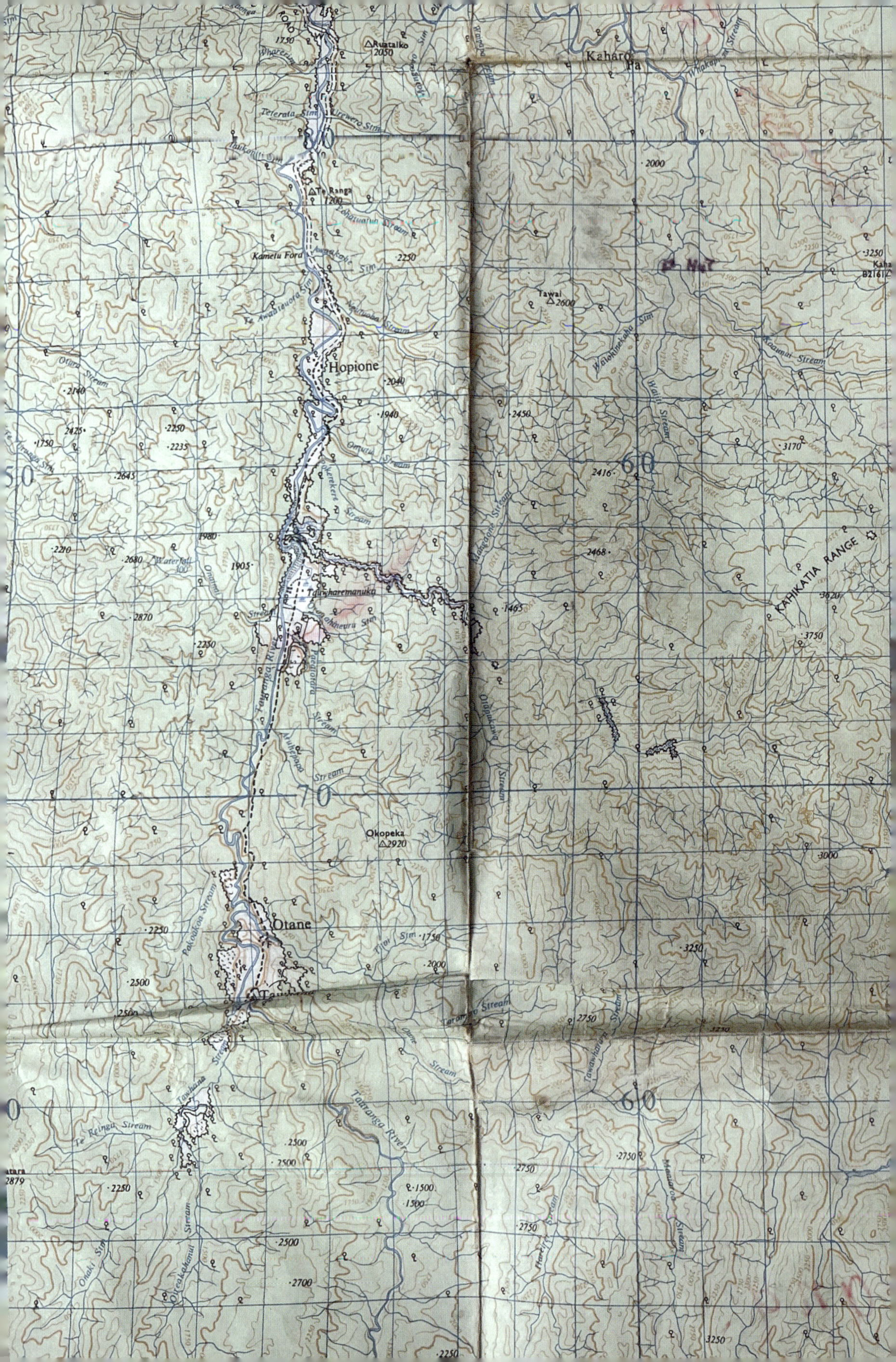

Ruataiko
2050
Kaharo
Te Ranga
Kamelu Ford
Hopione
Tawai
2600
KAHIKATIA RANGE
Tauwharemanuka
Okopeka
2920
Otane
Tauranga River
Te Reinga Stream
Waterfall